T0355450

Illuminating the Mind

BUDDHIST PHILOSOPHY FOR PHILOSOPHERS

Jan Westerhoff, University of Oxford, *Series Editor*

Illuminating the Mind: An Introduction to Buddhist Epistemology
Jonathan Stoltz

Buddhist Ethics: A Philosophical Exploration
Jay L. Garfield

Illuminating the Mind

An Introduction to Buddhist Epistemology

JONATHAN STOLTZ

OXFORD
UNIVERSITY PRESS

OXFORD
UNIVERSITY PRESS

Oxford University Press is a department of the University of Oxford. It furthers the University's objective of excellence in research, scholarship, and education by publishing worldwide. Oxford is a registered trade mark of Oxford University Press in the UK and certain other countries.

Published in the United States of America by Oxford University Press
198 Madison Avenue, New York, NY 10016, United States of America.

© Oxford University Press 2021

All rights reserved. No part of this publication may be reproduced, stored in a retrieval system, or transmitted, in any form or by any means, without the prior permission in writing of Oxford University Press, or as expressly permitted by law, by license, or under terms agreed with the appropriate reproduction rights organization. Inquiries concerning reproduction outside the scope of the above should be sent to the Rights Department, Oxford University Press, at the address above.

You must not circulate this work in any other form
and you must impose this same condition on any acquirer.

Library of Congress Cataloging-in-Publication Data
Names: Stoltz, Jonathan, author.
Title: Illuminating the mind : an introduction to Buddhist epistemology /
Jonathan Stoltz.
Description: New York : Oxford University Press, 2021. |
Series: Buddhist
phil for philosophers series | Includes bibliographical references and index.
Identifiers: LCCN 2020046592 (print) | LCCN 2020046593 (ebook) |
ISBN 9780190907532 (hardback) | ISBN 9780190907549 (paperback) |
ISBN 9780190907563 (epub)
Subjects: LCSH: Knowledge, Theory of (Buddhism) | Knowledge, Theory of—India. |
Knowledge, Theory of—China—Tibet Autonomous Region. |
Intellect—Religious aspects—Buddhism.
Classification: LCC BQ4440 .S86 2021 (print) | LCC BQ4440 (ebook) |
DDC 181/.043—dc23
LC record available at https://lccn.loc.gov/2020046592
LC ebook record available at https://lccn.loc.gov/2020046593

DOI: 10.1093/oso/9780190907532.001.0001

Contents

Preface

It is not uncommon for me to be asked—either by my students or by nonacademic acquaintances—who my philosophical heroes are. As common as the question is, I invariably struggle to give a satisfactory response. Regardless of the philosopher, my first impulse is to find fault with his or her views. It could very well be that this struggle stems from my belief that it is far easier in philosophy to be wrong than it is to be right. This hesitation with respect to identifying my philosophical heroes should not be taken as evidence that I do not appreciate the works of earlier philosophers. Even among the accounts of those philosophers with whom I am inclined to disagree vigorously, there are many cases in which I am nothing short of in awe of the authors' argumentative acumen and philosophical creativity.

My first deep exposure to what is now commonly called "analytic philosophy" came as an undergraduate student, from reading numerous articles on the philosophy of logic and mathematics by (among others) W. V. Quine and Hilary Putnam. I did not necessarily agree with the conclusions that Quine and Putnam reached, but I was captivated by their approach to philosophy and the style of their writing. I could say the same in reference to philosophers like David Lewis and Timothy Williamson, whose writing I was first exposed to in graduate school. I am far from persuaded that they get the right answers in their respective writings, but the rigor of their philosophical analyses has long struck me as truly remarkable. In short, what I've learned to appreciate most in philosophy is not the writing by thinkers whose views I take to be correct, but the writing that I take to be the most argumentatively rigorous and creative.

At the top of my list of philosophers whose writing impresses me the most is the late nineteenth- and early twentieth-century German logician, Gottlob Frege. His style of writing epitomizes the argumentative rigor that I take to be central to analytic philosophy. Yet there is much to disagree with in Frege's writing. Take, for instance, the opening two sentences of his truly excellent work *The Foundations of Arithmetic*:[1]

> After deserting for a time the old Euclidean standards of rigour, mathematics is now returning to them, and even making efforts to go beyond them. In arithmetic, if only because many of its methods and concepts originated in India, it has been the tradition to reason less strictly than in geometry, which was in the main developed by the Greeks.

Even when I first read this passage, I could see that Frege was revealing his ignorance of Indian intellectual history. It is true that many arithmetic concepts originated in India, and also true that the axiomatic proof system of geometry was popularized in ancient Greece. But Frege was also insinuating—though, admittedly, not directly stating—that the methods of reasoning in (ancient?) India are not as rigorous as those in Greece. It is this presumption that, even as a twenty-two-year-old graduate student, I knew to be mistaken.

During my years as a graduate student pursuing a PhD in philosophy, and while immersed in the analytic tradition of philosophy, I was simultaneously exploring the Indian tradition of philosophy—and, in particular, the Indian and Tibetan Buddhist traditions of logic and epistemology. Historical Indian treatises on logic and epistemology are undoubtedly more tersely written and more stylistically rigid than are writings in the Greek tradition of philosophy, but Indian philosophy is no less argumentative in tone or content than Western philosophy, and it certainly grapples just as intensely with many of the same questions. In this respect, it is beyond question that the Indian intellectual tradition and its thinkers reason no less rigorously than do European philosophers.

One of my overarching goals as a philosopher working in the area of Buddhist philosophy has always been to *show* readers that the themes addressed (and arguments made) by Buddhist philosophers are just as relevant and incisive as are the themes (and arguments) put forward by philosophers in the Western tradition of philosophy. I use the word *show* in the preceding sentence because I do not believe it to be necessary to *argue that*, let alone *prove that*, the writing by Buddhist philosophers contains insightful arguments on themes that are relevant to contemporary philosophy. In this regard, I adopt a perspective slightly different from that held by the late University of Oxford philosopher B. K. Matilal. As Matilal noted in his excellent book on Indian philosophy, *Perception*:[2]

> I have sometimes faced, rightly I believe, the criticism that there is a little "leaning over backwards" in my writings to show the analytic nature of Indian philosophy. I accept the criticism and can only say that this gesture is needed to correct persisting misconceptions, and sometimes remove ignorance.

In my view, there is no need to lean over backwards in order to demonstrate the analytic tendencies of Indian philosophy or Buddhist philosophy. I *do* want readers to see that Buddhist epistemology shares much in common with contemporary analytic epistemology, including a reliance on sharply argumentative reasoning. But I do not believe that one must lean over backwards in order to show this.

In this book I will be providing readers with an introduction to Buddhist epistemology—an introduction that is foremost written for those who have some familiarity with "Western philosophy," including epistemology, but little or no knowledge of Buddhist philosophical thought. While the topics in this book should be of interest to, and accessible to, persons with backgrounds and/or interests in Indian philosophy and Buddhist intellectual thought, the book presupposes no background knowledge of Indian Buddhism, let alone Buddhist epistemology. Given these two points, in calling this *An Introduction to Buddhist Epistemology*, the term "Introduction" is applied more directly to the *Buddhist* part of "Buddhist epistemology" than it is to the *epistemology* side of the topic.

Because the central aim of this book is to make the themes and arguments of Buddhist epistemology accessible to philosophers and students of philosophy who have little or no familiarity with Buddhist philosophical thought, I have deliberately chosen to structure this book around a series of prominent themes in the field of contemporary epistemology. In other words, I have pursued a "topical approach" to writing about Buddhist epistemology. This topical approach stands in contrast to the perhaps more common "historical approach" to writing about a given philosophical tradition. Authors who adopt a historical approach generally structure their books in a more or less chronological order and tend to focus individual chapters on the contributions of specific philosophers or time periods.

It is my firm belief that the most fruitful way by which to communicate the power and relevance of Buddhist epistemology to those whose primary training and background is in the European and Anglo-American traditions of philosophy is by adopting a topical approach. I want to show readers that, for example, just as contemporary analytic epistemologists are concerned with issues like the problem of skepticism, the status of testimonial knowledge, and disputes about epistemic luck, so, too, were Buddhist epistemologists worried about these same matters.

Be that as it may, arranging this book into chapters devoted to specific epistemological themes is not a wholly unproblematic endeavor. There can be reasonable concerns about pursuing a topical approach—an approach that pulls Buddhist philosophical arguments and debates out of their textual and historical contexts and then repackages those arguments into neatly formed chapters dedicated to specific themes. I believe those concerns to be well-founded, and I acknowledge that a deeper understanding of Buddhist epistemology can be achieved by being attentive to the development of philosophical theories within their historical context. Such a historical treatment of Buddhist epistemology, including an examination of the gradual changes to philosophers' views over time, would be well worth the reader's time once a foundational understanding of Buddhist epistemology has been secured. But as an introductory work on Buddhist epistemology, and one whose primary audience is persons trained in the Western tradition of philosophy, I believe that a topical approach provides the most fruitful point of entry to the Buddhist tradition of epistemology.

Of course, even if one is accepting of a topical approach to Buddhist epistemology, there can be disagreements about what the most relevant topics are to be covered. As can be seen from the chapter titles in this volume, I have focused on a set of themes that I take to be central to both Anglo-American epistemology and Buddhist epistemology. While I believe that this is right and proper, it would also have been possible to provide a topical approach to Buddhist epistemology that zooms in on a very different set of philosophical themes. Within classical texts on Buddhist epistemology, the authors develop a range of philosophical views, not only on matters pertinent to epistemology but also on issues of ontology, logic, and language. Insofar as this is the case, it is not uncommon to see some modern scholars of Buddhist philosophy focus largely or entirely on these latter topics when writing about the Buddhist tradition of epistemology.[3] This approach may be rooted in the view that "Buddhist epistemology" refers to a specific historical school of thought—one that is linked to a specific group of texts and a commentarial tradition, sometimes now referred to as *Pramāṇavāda*—wherein any and all philosophical questions taken up in those texts are accepted as a part of "Buddhist epistemology."

To cite a more specific example of this phenomenon, in various writings about the Buddhist tradition of epistemology one can find scholars focusing on the Buddhist theory of *exclusion* (*apoha*), which is a prominent topic in Buddhist philosophy—one relevant to core questions about the nature of language and its connection to reality. But though the topic of *exclusion* is an incredibly important one in Buddhist philosophy, and though the topic is indeed developed by classical Buddhist epistemologists, it is not, at its core, an epistemological thesis. The Buddhist theory of exclusion is something that would most properly be addressed in an introductory book on Buddhist philosophy of language or philosophy of mind.[4] The point that I am making about the Buddhist theory of exclusion is just one example among many that could be cited.

I believe that we should understand the scope of "Buddhist epistemology" differently. On the view presented in this book, Buddhist epistemology is an area of philosophical investigation that is demarcated by a range of themes intimately connected to questions about the nature and scope of knowledge. It is true that these themes are foremost addressed in *Pramāṇavāda* texts, but it is not the case that all topics addressed in those texts are inherently epistemological. An author's theory of, for instance, perceptual knowledge may very well be impacted by that author's ontological commitments, but it is important to distinguish these ontological concerns from those that are more properly epistemological. In this book, I have tried to distill the most important epistemological themes from the Buddhist tradition of epistemology, and I have been careful not to let these epistemological topics get overwhelmed by the surrounding questions of metaphysics, language, and mind.

Above all else, this book seeks to introduce Western-trained philosophers to the field of Buddhist philosophy. I hope that the chapters that follow succeed in giving philosophers and students of philosophy a deeper understanding and appreciation of Buddhist contributions to the field of epistemology, and that this understanding is accompanied by a recognition that Buddhist epistemology is neither philosophically vapid nor inscrutable to those who have been trained exclusively in the Western tradition of philosophy. If these hopes go unrealized, the fault is entirely my own and not due to any failure of the Buddhist philosophers discussed herein.

There are far too many people for me to thank than can be acknowledged here. Because Buddhist epistemology is, as readers will soon see, an investigation into the *instruments* or *sources* of knowledge, it would be appropriate for me to acknowledge the people who played instrumental roles in my journey within the fields of philosophy and Buddhist studies. First, I'd like to thank my undergraduate advisor, Jeffrey Turner, who introduced me to the field of philosophy. I'd also like to thank my doctoral advisor, James Cargile, who pushed me for years to be a more critical thinker (as well as a better teacher). Thanks also go to Hubert Decleer and Andy Quintman, who were the directors of the Tibetan Studies study abroad program that introduced me to the field of Buddhist studies and, indirectly, to Buddhist logic and epistemology. Additional thanks should go to David Germano and others affiliated with the University of Virginia and its Center for South Asian Studies, who were willing to "invest" in me during my years as a graduate student through the support of multiple U.S. Department of Education FLAS fellowships. Were it not for that early financial support, my study of Tibetan language and of Buddhist epistemology texts could never have happened. Most importantly, I'd like to thank my wife and best friend, Sarah, for everything that she has done.

Illuminating the Mind

1
Preliminaries

According to traditional Buddhist teachings, a root cause of suffering is *ignorance* (*avidyā*);[1] and the core goal of Buddhism is the elimination of suffering. It is, therefore, imperative to combat ignorance. *Knowledge* is the antidote to ignorance.[2]

When confronted with a choice between knowledge and ignorance, most people would choose the former; we do, after all, value knowledge. And yet it must be recognized that knowledge is not easily obtained. Attaining knowledge requires, in many cases, the collection of *evidence*, or of *good reasons*, or of *justification*; and these can be incredibly difficult to acquire. It is much easier simply to glide through one's life without worrying about annoying things like evidence and justification. At the same time, it is said that *knowledge is power* and, owing to a belief in that edict, societies have pushed for the education of their children and the education of their workforce. The acquisition of knowledge can be costly and time consuming, but the reward for being a knowledgeable person is among the most prized in contemporary society.

With what confidence, however, can I assert the various claims in the preceding paragraph? I claim that knowledge is valued, that knowledge often requires evidence or reasons, that knowledge is power, and that knowledge comes from education. But how can I make these claims? Do I need to know what knowledge is before I can know whether knowledge is valued? Do I need to know what knowledge is before I can know whether knowledge can be attained through education? In everyday life, assertions of knowledge flow relatively freely. Informed assertions about *the nature of knowledge*, however, are more delicate and call for deeper philosophical exploration.

The study of knowledge, its nature, and its scope has long been at the heart of European philosophy. Twenty-four hundred years ago, Plato grappled with the questions of how knowledge is obtained and how it is different from mere true opinion. He also explored the relationship between knowledge and teaching/learning. One way to interpret Plato's broad message in the *Meno*, which is among his most important dialogues on the topic of knowledge, is

Illuminating the Mind. Jonathan Stoltz, Oxford University Press (2021). © Oxford University Press.
DOI: 10.1093/oso/9780190907532.003.0001

as a proclamation that knowledge does not come from teaching. Teaching, at best, can only give rise to true opinion. The acquisition of knowledge, according to Plato, requires the "tying down" of our opinions by giving "an account of the reasons why."[3] This process of tying down, or *justifying*, our beliefs does not, on Plato's account, come directly from others. Instead, justification is a process that he believes must take place inside oneself. In this respect, teaching cannot transmit knowledge from a teacher to her students. It can only transmit true beliefs that, when reflectively engaged by those students, can be tied down and thus transformed into knowledge.

The theory of knowledge in ancient India has no less central a place within that culture's tradition of philosophy than it does in the ancient Greek tradition. Philosophers in ancient India were deeply concerned with questions concerning how knowledge is obtained—that is, what the principal sources of knowledge are—and the conditions under which a person's beliefs and experiences can be said to yield knowledge. Within the Indian tradition, it was widely acknowledged that the acquisition of knowledge can serve to *dispel ignorance*, and Indian philosophers likewise recognized that organized reflection on the nature of knowledge serves to *illuminate the mind*.

Buddhist philosophers in the first millennium of the Common Era, steeped as they were within the larger Indian tradition of philosophical discourse, explored questions of knowledge with the same intensity and sophistication as did their non-Buddhist counterparts in India. Philosophical reflections on knowledge were undoubtedly carried out by a great many Buddhist scholars throughout the first thousand years of Buddhist writings in India. But it is finally in the lifetime of the sixth-century Buddhist thinker Dignāga that we can safely identify a sustained and systematic exploration of the theoretical underpinnings of knowledge, and thus the beginning of a field of study fittingly called *Buddhist Epistemology*.

The aims of this opening chapter are threefold. One purpose is to provide a brief overview of what is meant in this book by "the Buddhist tradition of epistemology" and of how I shall be interpreting the relevant scope of that tradition. In so doing, the reader will also gain a better sense of the relationship between Buddhist epistemology and the broader Indian tradition of philosophy. A second goal is to introduce readers to some of the most fundamental terms and concepts that are deployed in writings on Buddhist epistemology and to call attention to the similarities and differences between the relevant Sanskrit terms and those that are employed within contemporary Anglo-American accounts of the theory of knowledge.[4] The third aim, one that pervades the entirety of the chapter but which is not as directly articulated as are the first two goals, is to begin the project of putting the subject of Buddhist epistemology in conversation with some of the core themes and ideas associated with the contemporary analytic tradition of epistemology as it is pursued in much of Europe and English-speaking parts of the world. This conversation will take place throughout the book, but this chapter begins that process by highlighting some of the most foundational terms and concepts that will undergird the themes and puzzles addressed over the remainder of the book.

1.1. Two Histories

1.1.1. Buddhist Epistemology

This book offers an introduction to and exploration of Buddhist epistemology. There is, to be clear, no single set of mutually compatible claims that makes up the totality of Buddhist epistemological speculation. Instead, Buddhist epistemology, like its contemporary Anglo-American counterpart, consists of a number of competing theses and interpretations, internal debates and factions. Some foundational claims are, as readers will see, widely agreed upon and have remained integral to Buddhist epistemology for a millennium or longer. Other ideas and theories about the nature of knowledge were developed only later in the Buddhist epistemological tradition and/or were contested by various factions within that tradition. For example, views that were accepted by Buddhist epistemologists in the seventh century may not have been adopted by writers in the ninth century. Distinctions that were operative (and terminologies that flourished) in the eleventh century may have been nonexistent within earlier strands of Buddhist epistemological discourse. We should, therefore, not assume that there is any single set of claims that can definitively be called "the Buddhist account" of the theory of knowledge.

Even more pertinently, ostensibly incompatible epistemological theses are sometimes found not just among different Buddhist philosophers but also within the set of claims put forward by a single philosopher. In particular, many contemporary scholars of Buddhist philosophy are now convinced that the claims and arguments that are put forward by individual Buddhist epistemologists can reflect multiple—and seemingly incompatible—metaphysical accounts of the nature of reality; and these differing metaphysical assumptions can have an impact on how certain epistemological theses are to be understood. As will be seen more clearly in chapter 3, while Buddhist epistemologists frequently endorse, or at least presuppose, a version of *external realism*, those same philosophers occasionally shift to an idealist framework when addressing certain epistemological puzzles. This shift from one metaphysical framework to another has been described as capturing Buddhist philosophers' proclivity for "ascending scales of analysis."[5] Given that a single thinker's epistemological theory may, in one context, require an external realist interpretation of objects and, in other contexts, an idealist interpretation, this makes it difficult to speak, unequivocally, of that philosopher's theory of, for example, the nature of perceptual knowledge.

Keeping these initial points in mind, this book proceeds under a rough classificatory rubric in which Buddhist epistemological writings are grouped into four time periods (see Table 1.1). The most important period is that which runs from the time of Dignāga (c. 480–540 CE) in the first half of the sixth century through the time of his most famous "commentator," Dharmakīrti (c. 550–650 CE), who flourished likely around the first half of the seventh century. I shall often refer to this as the period of "classical Buddhist epistemology" and at other times as "Dharmakīrtian epistemology." It constitutes the most significant time period within the Buddhist epistemological tradition, and the writings by Dignāga and Dharmakīrti are the ones that are most central to Buddhist epistemological discourse.

Buddhist discussions of knowledge before the time of Dignāga shall be termed "pre-Dignāgan Buddhist epistemology" and constitute the earliest period of Buddhist reflections on knowledge. This period includes Buddhist teachings on knowledge and ignorance that were composed in the centuries immediately following the life of the historical Buddha, and it extends into the first five centuries of the Common Era. Included in the pre-Dignāgan period are the treatises expressing skepticism of the whole project of epistemology that were composed by Nāgārjuna in the early centuries of the Common Era, as well as the substantive claims about knowledge contained within texts written by the philosopher Vasubandhu in the fourth or fifth century.

The period of Buddhist epistemological theorizing in India after the time of Dharmakīrti shall be referred to as "post-Dharmakīrtian Indian Buddhist epistemology." This time period, spanning from the seventh century to the

Table 1.1

Philosopher	Approximate Dates
Pre-Dignāgan Period	
Nāgārjuna	Second or third century
Vasubandhu	Fourth or fifth century
Classical Period	
Dignāga	480–540
Dharmakīrti	550–650
Post-Dharmakīrtian Period	
Devendrabuddhi	630–690
Śākyabuddhi	660–720
Vinītadeva	710–770
Śāntarakṣita	725–788
Kamalaśīla	740–795
Dharmottara	740–800
Prajñākaragupta	750–810
Jinendrabuddhi	Eighth or ninth century
Śaṅkaranandana	940–1020
Ratnakīrti	990–1050
Mokṣākaragupta	Eleventh or twelfth century
Early Tibetan Period	
Ngog Lotsawa	1059–1109
Chaba Chokyi Senge	1109–1169
Sakya Paṇḍita	1182–1251

twelfth century, includes many figures, and it reflects a range of developments on (and modifications of) the theories that had been put forward by Dignāga and (especially) Dharmakīrti. The most fruitful segment of time in this period appears to have been the eighth century, during which time numerous (still extant) epistemological works were composed. Among the most important Buddhist figures writing about epistemology in the eighth century were Vinītadeva, Śāntarakṣita, Kamalaśīla, and Dharmottara.

The fourth and final period of Buddhist epistemology discussed in this book is the tradition of "early Tibetan epistemology" that developed in central Tibet from the eleventh to thirteenth centuries.[6] Though this period is in many respects an extension of the post-Dharmakīrtian period of Buddhist epistemology, it will be classified separately owing to the fact that once this Tibetan tradition of epistemology took hold, many of the most important arguments that were debated by Tibetan epistemologists had only tenuous ties to the earlier Indian tradition of epistemology. Despite the fact that Tibetan epistemology was based on Dignāga's and (especially) Dharmakīrti's foundational texts, that tradition's distance from its Indian predecessors allowed for the flourishing of a great many philosophical and terminological developments that departed—sometimes rather sharply—from the range of views attested within Indian Buddhist epistemological texts.

To be clear, in each of the four periods noted earlier, texts on Buddhist epistemology did not arise within a cultural or intellectual vacuum. The Buddhist tradition of philosophical scholarship in India was situated within the larger Indian tradition of philosophical speculation, and the key philosophers within the Buddhist epistemological tradition were, in nearly all cases, both aware of and influenced by the debates, theories, and terminological conventions that permeated Indian philosophical discourse. Among the most important non-Buddhist "schools" of Indian philosophy that impacted thinkers like Dignāga and Dharmakīrti were the Nyāya School of reasoning and the Mīmāṃsā School of hermeneutics. Also influencing Dignāga were the works of Indian grammarians such as the circa fifth-century scholar Bhartṛhari.[7] As will be seen later in this chapter and in various places in later chapters, it is not possible to make sense of, let alone appreciate the significance of, a great number of key concepts and claims in Buddhist epistemology without framing those claims within the broader Indian context out of which they arose.

Dignāga and Dharmakīrti are, as has been stated earlier, the two most significant and foundational thinkers within the Buddhist tradition of epistemology. Dignāga's *Compendium of Knowledge* (*Pramāṇasamuccaya*)—and his auto-commentary on that root text—is so important that it is spoken of as the "*sūtra*" of Buddhist epistemology. Ostensibly, this text by Dignāga synthesizes the scattered claims about knowledge that he had made in various earlier works. Dharmakīrti, writing several generations after Dignāga, is famed for his seven texts on epistemology that comment on and clarify (or expand upon) the claims made in Dignāga's works. Of those seven texts, his two longest treatises, the *Commentary on [Dignāga's Compendium of] Knowledge* (*Pramāṇavārttika*) and the *Ascertainment of Knowledge* (*Pramāṇaviniścaya*), are of such importance that they should be regarded not just as the most important texts on Indian Buddhist epistemology but as among the most important works on epistemology in the history of philosophy. In the centuries that followed Dharmakīrti's life, these texts would be the subject of numerous commentaries by subsequent Buddhist philosophers—a tradition of commentarial literature that has continued into modern times within Tibetan Buddhist monastic institutions.

1.1.2. Analytic Epistemology

As an introduction to Buddhist epistemology, one primary goal of this book is to elucidate Buddhist accounts of knowledge in such a way that those accounts are accessible to students and scholars of Anglo-American philosophy who have little or no familiarity with Indian philosophical thought. The central themes within the Buddhist tradition of epistemology will be brought into a fruitful dialogue with contemporary themes in epistemology as those themes are taken up within universities across Europe, North America, and much of the rest of the world. In particular, the predominant scholastic approach toward the theory of knowledge over the past half century is that which may be called *analytic epistemology*.

Just as the Buddhist epistemological tradition that springs from the works of Dignāga and Dharmakīrti has its roots in earlier Indian philosophical thought, so, too, the contemporary analytic tradition of epistemology that is now predominant in academic departments of philosophy has its roots in earlier philosophical traditions in Europe. The origins of analytic epistemology go back to ancient Greece and pass through much of Europe, but this tradition of epistemology finds its contemporary trajectory guided by developments taking place largely within British and American universities such as Oxford, Harvard, Princeton, Brown, and Pittsburgh in the middle part of the twentieth century. Key figures in this tradition of epistemology include philosophers such as A. J. Ayer, W. V. Quine, Wilfrid Sellars, and Roderick Chisholm. These philosophers, together with their direct and indirect students, refined a series of pressing problems in the field of epistemology and cultivated a well-respected method of philosophical analysis for addressing those problems.

Following the publication of Edmund Gettier's three-page-long 1963 essay, "Is Justified True Belief Knowledge?" the trajectory of analytic epistemology was altered so as to accommodate a new series of debates concerning the nature and analysis of knowledge. Some philosophers see the post-Gettier period of analytic epistemology as the golden age of epistemology, whereas others regard this period as one of misguided intellectual pretension. What is undeniable is that the study of epistemology has been dramatically changed by Gettier's 1963 article. The epistemological questions that are emphasized, the ways in which those questions are framed, and the ways in which those questions are answered have been indelibly altered by Gettier.[8]

Though Buddhist epistemology and analytic epistemology are situated within larger philosophical traditions that are temporally and geographically remote from one another, it is possible to put these two traditions in conversation with each other. Many of the most significant epistemological themes are shared between these two traditions, and some of the biggest problems in analytic epistemology were likewise puzzled over by Buddhist epistemologists. This book aims to give a voice to Buddhist epistemological thought so that it can be better appreciated by those whose familiarity with the theory of knowledge is currently limited to contemporary analytic epistemology and its Western predecessors.

1.2. Core Terms and Concepts

Giving a voice to Buddhist epistemology, and putting it into conversation with contemporary analytic epistemology, is an exercise fraught with challenges. After all, the central questions of epistemology as it has developed in the Western tradition are grounded in historical exchanges and chains of disputation that have proceeded over many hundreds of years in European (and later in American and Australasian) countries. Ruminations on the theory of knowledge in the Indian Buddhist tradition are not merely temporally and spatially remote from those in the Western tradition, however. They are also linguistically distant, for Buddhist epistemological works were traditionally composed in Sanskrit. Sanskrit is indeed part of the Indo-European family of languages, and there are linguistic links between, for example, the English word "know," the Greek (to Latin) root "*gno-*", and the Sanskrit root "*jñā-*". Nevertheless, the distinctive semantic roles played by terms having these roots in the Anglo-American tradition of epistemology developed largely independently from the roles played by the comparable terms in the Indian tradition. As a result of these distinct cultural and philosophical developments, it is far from easy to identify philosophically adequate equivalencies for the key epistemological terms found in the Anglo-American and Indian traditions.

The Anglo-American tradition of epistemology that springs from figures like Plato and Aristotle emphasizes a *reason-based* conception of knowledge. As mentioned earlier, Plato conceives of knowledge as being associated with the tying down of beliefs or opinions by giving an account of the reasons why something is true. For Aristotle, this reason-based understanding of knowledge gets blended with his theory of logical argumentation and the idea of demonstrative reasoning. Beliefs can be said to be "tied down" to the extent that they can be situated as conclusions of demonstrative proofs. This general approach toward knowledge has been passed down over the centuries and forms the basis for the twentieth-century idea that knowledge is inextricably linked to providing evidential support or justification.

In particular, the notion of *justification* grew to take on an especially weighty role within the twentieth-century analytic tradition of epistemology. As one prominent epistemologist wrote in 1985, "The concept of epistemic justification is clearly the central concept in the whole theory of knowledge, and this book is largely devoted to exploring in detail certain of its facets and ramifications."[9] I have my doubts about the truth of this claim, let alone its obviousness, but perhaps that is because I am inclined to adopt a broader perspective of "the whole theory of knowledge" than does the author cited. Ironically, since the time that the aforementioned book was published, debates within analytic epistemology have shifted quite a bit, and a sizable number of philosophers now reject the assumption that justification needs to play, or even should play, such an integral role. In its place have come other important concepts such as *warrant* and *reliability*.[10]

I raise these points because, as will be argued in much more detail in the next chapter, there does not appear to be any single term in Sanskrit, nor any single concept in Indian or Buddhist epistemology, that is the exact equivalent to that of *justification*. Knowledge, as described by Buddhist epistemologists, may very well require more than a mere true belief, but what is required is not formulated in terms of something comparable to justification. This does not mean, of course, that the Buddhist tradition of epistemology is conceptually impoverished. Instead, if anything, it suggests that analytic epistemology's emphasis on developing a theory of justification is a narrowly constrained approach to characterizing knowledge. As has been stated by Jonardon Ganeri in a recent work on Indian epistemology, "It would thus be wrong to translate *pramā* as *knowledge*, and then to wonder what counts as justification in the Sanskrit model. The answer is that nothing does, because justification is a parochial feature of a way of thinking rooted in English lexical quirks."[11]

Ganeri's point is an important one, but we need to be careful not to take his thesis too far. After all, the Anglo-American emphasis on providing something like *evidence* or *reasons* in support of one's beliefs does have very close parallels within the Indian tradition. To the extent that epistemological theorizing is linked with argumentative reasoning, Indian philosophers—both Buddhist and non-Buddhist—are keen to emphasize the importance of grounding inferences (and arguments) in evidence or reasons. Buddhist epistemologists are likewise committed to the idea that successful inferential reasoning depends on an appeal to some sort of logical reason or piece of evidence. In this regard, Buddhist accounts of inferential knowledge have strong affinities to the reason-based conception of knowledge found in Western epistemology. This appeal to evidence in inferential reasoning will be addressed at length in chapter 4.

Ordinarily, when analytic epistemologists speak of justification and reason-based epistemology, it is tied to the view that the items needing justification—the very things that need to be supported with reasons—are mental states of *belief*. Though there are certainly well-entrenched *logical* applications of the terms "justification" and "reason," ones that apply to statements or propositions, what is typically at stake in discussions of epistemological justification are not mind independent entities like statements or proposition, but rather the mental states of a given individual—for example, person S's *belief* that *p*. Some of the beliefs that humans hold have well-reasoned support and others may not have such support, but it is generally granted that knowledge depends on the possession of beliefs—beliefs that are supported with reasons or justification.

In the Indian context, the relevant counterpart to "belief" is the Sanskrit term *jñāna*. A *jñāna* is an episode or event of mentation—and, more specifically, an episode of *cognition*. Though the term *jñāna* has the same etymological roots as the English word "know," and though cognates of the word *jñāna* are used in languages such as Hindi, Bengali, and the like to express verbs colloquially approximating the English verb "to know," the term *jñāna*, as it is applied in classical Indian and Buddhist epistemology, has a much broader semantic scope, one that does not imply the possession of knowledge. Rather, the term *jñāna* designates any generic cognitive episode—one that could be correct (or accurate) or one that could be incorrect (or inaccurate). For example, when a person visually perceives a vase, she has a *cognition* (*jñāna*) that apprehends a vase. So, too, were that person to have a hallucinatory experience as of a vase, she would be having a cognition that apprehends a vase. Note, in addition, the fact that while every cognition/*jñāna* is a cognition *of* something, its object or content may very well be nonpropositional. In the earlier example, the person has a cognition *of* a vase, not the cognition *that* there is a vase.

Without question, the Sanskrit term *jñāna*—which I shall typically translate as "cognition" or "cognitive episode"—is one of the most important notions in all of Indian and Buddhist epistemology. As just stated, it plays a role roughly analogous to that occupied by belief in the contemporary analytic tradition of epistemology. *Jñāna* is not, however, the single most important concept in Indian epistemology. This is because *jñāna* has a semantic scope broader than that of "knowledge." There is a specific subset of cognitive episodes that comprises all instances of knowledge, and those are the ones classified as *pramā*. The instruments responsible for generating these instances of knowledge are called *pramāṇa*, and it is this latter term that is, far and away, the most significant one in all of Indian (and Buddhist) epistemology.

1.3. *Pramāṇa*

1.3.1. The Origins of *Pramāṇa* Theory

The most fundamental concept in all of Indian epistemology, both for Buddhists and non-Buddhists, is the concept of *pramāṇa*. Epistemology as a field of philosophical study is, for Indian philosophers, primarily an investigation into and elucidation of the nature of *pramāṇas*. Stated most straightforwardly, a *pramāṇa* is a *means* or *instrument* by which a subject attains knowledge.[12] More technically, a *pramāṇa* is held to be the instrument via which a cognitive agent achieves *pramā*—where *pramā* is an episode of knowledge. Just as a person might eat food *with a spoon*, or clean one's teeth *with a toothbrush*, or cut down a tree *with an axe*, so, too, whenever a person knows something, he or she does so through some instrument. A *pramāṇa* is the instrument used for attaining an instance of knowledge.

The claim that a *pramāṇa* is an instrument used for the attainment of knowledge is tied to the Indian tradition's broad predilection for a causal theory of cognition (and knowledge). This causal account will be discussed more fully in later chapters, but it is important to drive home the initial point that, in the Indian tradition of epistemology, knowledge is represented as a kind of event that occurs at a moment in time, and a *pramāṇa* is the dominant causal element that brings about, and culminates in, an episode of knowledge.

Linguistically, the term for an instance of knowledge, *pramā*, consists of the root *mā*, meaning "to measure," and the prefix *pra-*, which expresses a kind of superiority or excellence. In this way, a *pramā* can be seen as a "measurement par excellence," and thus a *pramāṇa* is the means or instrument for making such a measurement. Inasmuch as measurement is, loosely speaking, an activity of weighing or judging something, we can think of a *pramā*, more intuitively, as a kind of excellent (epistemic) judgment, and likewise understand a *pramāṇa* as a tool or instrument by which these excellent judgments are made.

As this book proceeds, only rarely will this idea of a *pramāṇa* as a tool for measurement be of critical concern. One such place, however, is in the discussion of skepticism found in chapter 7. There, the focus is on how one can establish *pramāṇas* as instruments for achieving knowledge. Skeptical criticisms are raised about the whole project of measurement. We can, for example, use a ruler so as to determine the length of a piece of wood. But how do we measure a ruler? What device can we use to determine how long a ruler is? This is a question of meta-measurement. The parallel question can be raised in terms of *pramāṇas* as instruments for knowledge. A *pramāṇa* can be used to "measure" some object or state of affairs. But how can we measure or establish a *pramāṇa*? Similar to Ludwig Wittgenstein's reflections on the measurement of the standard meter in Paris, the Buddhist philosopher Nāgārjuna presses the issue of how—or with what instrument—a *pramāṇa* can be established.[13]

There is yet another, and slightly different, way of construing what is meant by a *pramāṇa*. In its most literal sense it is an instrument by which one achieves *pramā*, or an episode of knowledge. But, by extension, we can think of *pramāṇas* as *sources of knowledge*. It is not very common within twentieth- or twenty-first-century analytic epistemology to talk of "instruments of knowledge." Yet the idea that there are a small number of fundamental sources of knowledge is widespread within the analytic tradition of philosophy. For example, the pioneering twentieth-century epistemologist Roderick Chisholm, in his important work, *Theory of Knowledge*, frames many of his views around the assumption that there are various "sources" of knowledge. As he asserts:[14]

> Thus, it is traditional in Western philosophy to say that there are four such sources:
> 1. "external perception"
> 2. memory
> 3. "self-awareness" ("reflection," or "inner consciousness")
> 4. reason

The exact breakdown that Chisholm provides is philosophically debatable, but he is no doubt right that this reference to various sources of knowledge is a familiar one within Western philosophy. The appeal to *pramāṇas* in traditional Indian philosophy plays a very similar role. Though, literally, a *pramāṇa* is an instrument for achieving knowledge, we can additionally think of these instruments as picking out individual sources of knowledge.

A large quantity of argumentation in Indian epistemological texts centers on disagreements about what these sources of knowledge are. Different philosophical schools uphold different sets of *pramāṇas* as legitimate. All Indian schools of thought accept *perception* (*pratyakṣa*) as a source of knowledge. And, except for the Cārvāka School of materialism, all Indian philosophical systems accept *inferential reasoning* (*anumāna*) as a source of knowledge as well. As will be described much more fully in chapter 2 and following, it is these two items, perception and inferential reasoning, that are accepted as the only legitimate sources of knowledge in the Buddhist tradition of epistemology that derives from Dignāga. Other traditions in India argue in support of additional sources, however. To give but one example, the Nyāya School accepts four sources of knowledge—the aforementioned perception and inference, together with *analogy* (*upamāna*) and *testimony* (*śabda*).

In summary, the concept of a *pramāṇa*, in the Indian tradition of philosophy, represents a source of knowledge or an instrument for attaining knowledge or an instrument by which one accurately measures reality. These three ways by which to speak of *pramāṇas* are essentially equivalent, but they differently emphasize the role or roles that *pramāṇas* play in the cognitive lives of human beings.

1.3.2. Buddhism and *Pramāṇa*

Buddhist epistemologists in India consent to this broad way of approaching the study of knowledge. Just like other Indian philosophers, they accept the idea that theoretical investigations of knowledge should be focused on exploring the concept of a *pramāṇa*. Yet in the tradition of Buddhist epistemology that derives from Dignāga and Dharmakīrti, the exact role played by the term *pramāṇa* gets fundamentally changed. The traditional Indian account, described earlier, treats a *pramāṇa* as the instrument that brings about an episode of knowledge, where the episode of knowledge consists in a cognition that is the result (*phala*) of a causal process brought about by the *pramāṇa*. In the tradition of Dignāga and Dharmakīrti, however, it is argued that the *pramāṇa* is no different from the cognition that is its result (the *pramāṇaphala*). In other words, the cognition itself—an episode of knowledge—is considered a *pramāṇa*.

This entails a conceptual shift in Buddhist epistemology where the central focus moves from the instruments of knowledge (*pramāṇas* qua instruments) to the cognitive episodes of knowledge themselves (*pramāṇas* qua cognitions). The traditional sense of *pramāṇa* as a means of knowledge is not lost and forgotten by Buddhist epistemologists, but the way in which they typically make sense of epistemological questions is changed. So, for example, instead of thinking of perception and inferential reasoning as two distinct *sources* of knowledge, Buddhists are more inclined to conceive of these *pramāṇas* as two different *types* of cognition—the two types of cognition that comprise episodes of knowledge.

When understood in this way, a *pramāṇa* is a specific subtype of cognition (*jñāna*). It is a subtype of cognition that meets the conditions necessary for knowledge. (Much more will be said about these conditions in the next chapter.) Buddhist epistemologists then contend that there are two subclasses within the class of *pramāṇas*: perceptual cognitions and inferential cognitions. In light of this Buddhist understanding of a *pramāṇa* as a subtype of cognition, the term *pramāṇa* has frequently been translated into English as "valid cognition." This translation has the virtue of calling attention to the fact that *pramāṇa* are not instances of *belief*, but rather *cognitions*. However, the expression "valid cognition" is an artificial verbiage that was created by Indologists, and one that signifies little to those situated within the Anglo-American tradition of philosophy. There is, after all, no clear meaning associated with calling a cognition "valid" within English language philosophy. It can even incite confusion among Western trained philosophers, given how the term "valid" is commonly used in contexts of deductive logic.

My own preference is to translate *pramāṇa*—within the Buddhist context—as "episode of knowledge," or "knowledge episode," or even simply as "knowledge." In doing so, I am following the precedent set by the former University of Oxford philosopher B. K. Matilal, who utilized similar language in many of his writings on Indian epistemology.[15] One must, of course, be very cautious in adopting such a translation. To speak of a *pramāṇa* as "an episode of knowledge," much less as "knowledge," is to call upon an English term—namely, "knowledge"—that carries a full set of connotations within contemporary analytic philosophy. I certainly do not mean to imply that the terms *pramāṇa* and *knowledge* are semantically equivalent. As readers will see in chapter 2, the standard Buddhist understanding of *pramāṇa* has a semantic scope and usage that is subtly but importantly different from that of how knowledge is paradigmatically treated in contemporary analytic epistemology.

Though much more will be said as this book proceeds about the central differences between the Buddhist's "*pramāṇa*" and analytic epistemology's "knowledge," I will briefly call the reader's attention to two significant dissimilarities, both of which will be addressed more fully in the pages that follow. First, in contemporary analytic epistemology, much of the focus is on identifying the conditions under which it can be said that 'S knows that *p*,' where *p* represents some proposition that is known. This promotes an interpretation wherein knowledge is viewed as a kind of two-place *relation* between a person/subject and a proposition—for example, K(S, *p*). Even in cases of perceptual knowledge, it has become common to describe such knowledge as involving a person perceptually knowing that *p*, for some proposition *p*. Discussions of *nonpropositional knowledge* in analytic epistemology have been shoved off into the far corners of the epistemological universe of discourse. In the Buddhist tradition of philosophy, by contrast, the most paradigmatic cases of knowledge are nonpropositional. What is known is an *object*, where this object could be a real, particular thing, or it could be an aggregate of an object and a quality/property. For example, on the Buddhist account, perception might give a person knowledge of *the moon* itself.[16]

A second key difference, even more important than that involving the object of knowledge, has to do with the underlying form of mentation that is operable in instances of knowledge. Nearly all analytic epistemologists now assume that knowledge has *belief* as one of its necessary conditions. Standardly, however, beliefs are construed as *dispositional states* of an individual. A person can believe a proposition—for example, that 2 + 2 = 4—continuously from, let's say, age four until age eighty-five. Even when a person is asleep, she can be regarded as holding the belief that 2 + 2 = 4. Matters are rather different in the Buddhist, and broader Indian, tradition of epistemology. As will be detailed more fully later, the cognitions that are at the heart of Buddhist epistemological theorizing are fleeting episodes. These cognitions arise through some causal process, occur at a single moment, and then pass out of existence. As such, what are at issue in the Buddhist (and broader Indian) tradition of epistemology are *episodes* of knowledge, not dispositional states of knowing.

Nevertheless, I believe there are benefits associated with referring to *pramāṇas* as "episodes of knowledge"—benefits that far outweigh any potential misunderstandings that could arise from how knowledge is standardly treated in contemporary analytic epistemology. In particular, it is important for readers to be consciously aware of the fact that the propositional and dispositional portrayal of knowledge in the analytic tradition is actually a highly idiosyncratic way of representing knowledge. Thus, to translate the term *pramāṇa* as "episode of knowledge" or even as "knowledge" serves to remind readers of just how idiosyncratic the contemporary analytic conception of knowledge has become, and to make it known that knowledge can extend beyond the standard propositional cases that have become the bread and butter of twentieth- and twenty-first-century epistemological theorizing.

Returning once again to the concept of *pramāṇa*, there is one final way that Buddhist epistemologists deploy the term that it is worth mentioning. In the salutation at the beginning of his key text, the *Compendium of Knowledge*, Dignāga refers to the Buddha as "one who has become a *pramāṇa*" (*pramāṇabhūta*). This reference will be addressed more fully in chapter 5 when discussing the idea of knowledge via testimony. What needs to be called attention to at present, however, is the simple idea that a person, or perhaps the words of a person, could be considered a *pramāṇa*. In other words, the term *pramāṇa* can be interpreted to mean something like "authority." Calling the Buddha "one who has become a *pramāṇa*" can be likened to saying that the Buddha is someone whose proclamations are epistemically authoritative.[17]

It has become relatively common over the past twenty-five years or so for Buddhist studies scholars to translate the term *pramāṇa* as "authority" within the context of attributions of *pramāṇa*-hood to the Buddha (and sometimes even to other religious teachers). There is, after all, a close connection between representing a *pramāṇa* as an authority and representing it as a source of knowledge. Just as the Buddha, or the words of the Buddha, might be regarded by religious adherents to be an authority on certain religious (or metaphysical) matters, so, too, we can think of the Buddha and his teachings as a source of knowledge for ordinary humans.

However, a small tension may be noted with respect to translating *pramāṇa* as "authority." The Buddha is not, strictly speaking, a cognitive episode, and thus he is not a *pramāṇa* in the aforementioned sense of being an episode of knowledge. As such, a number of (classical and contemporary) scholars argue that we should see Dignāga's claim that the Buddha has "become a *pramāṇa*" as being a metaphorical extension of the term *pramāṇa*. For even if, in its traditional sense, a *pramāṇa* can refer to a source of knowledge, the Buddha is not, strictly speaking, one of the sources of knowledge that are recognized by Buddhist epistemologists.

We have, altogether then, a variety of different ways in which to make sense of this fundamental notion of a *pramāṇa*. Even while granting that most of these senses may be mutually compatible, the term *pramāṇa* could express:

a. an instrument of knowledge,
b. an instrument of measurement par excellence,
c. a source of knowledge,
d. an episode of knowledge, or
e. an epistemic authority.

The most operative meaning of the term within the tradition of Buddhist epistemology that flows from Dignāga and Dharmakīrti is that of an *episode of knowledge*. Nevertheless, it is important for readers to keep track of these other senses of the term and to recognize that the Buddhist interpretation of *pramāṇas* as episodes of knowledge is itself a modification of the earlier, more standard, Indian sense of the term as an instrument for attaining knowledge. Though this book will most frequently translate the term *pramāṇa* as "episode of knowledge," in some cases the word will be left untranslated—in part so as to call the reader's attention to the broader set of connotations that could be associated with the term.

1.4. The Episodic Nature of Cognition/Knowledge

There is one final matter that needs to be addressed more fully before diving into the main content of this book in the chapters that follow, and that is about the *episodic* nature of *jñāna* (cognition) and *pramāṇa* (knowledge). As has been mentioned earlier, in the Buddhist epistemological tradition, attributions of knowledge are linked to occurrences of mental events or episodes. Just as in contemporary analytic epistemology holding a belief is ordinarily regarded to be a necessary condition for knowledge, so, too, in the Buddhist epistemological tradition it is a cognition or *jñāna* that is deemed the necessary mental component for knowledge. But whereas beliefs are typically conceived of as dispositional states that persist over long stretches of time, *jñānas* do not persist unchanged over time. Cognitions in the Indian epistemological tradition are momentary mental episodes. Each cognitive episode arises at one particular moment in time as a result of certain causal conditions, serves as a causal factor for a subsequent cognitive episode, and then passes out of existence.

So, for example, suppose that a person looks toward the top of a mountain and observes smoke on a mountain pass. In such a situation, the person has, let us assume, a perceptual cognition of smoke. Expressed differently, let us suppose that the person has a veridical perceptual experience. This experience may very well give rise to a subsequent, reflective judgment—the judgment that there is smoke on the mountain pass—but the perceptual cognition itself is, according to Buddhist philosophers, a momentary episode. And it is this momentary perceptual cognition that is the mental basis for knowledge in Buddhist epistemology. Now, even in analytic epistemology, where knowledge is paradigmatically conceived of as propositional, there is a clear route to interpreting momentary perceptual experiences like observing smoke on the mountain pass as instances of (perceptual) knowledge. Doing so may require granting that raw sensations can amount to knowledge, but such an attribution is not overly remarkable.

What is much more remarkable about the Buddhist tradition of epistemology is that this episodic understanding of cognition and knowledge is extended to rational, inferential cases as well. Let us assume that the aforementioned perceptual experience of smoke on the mountain pass is succeeded by the judgment *that* there is smoke on the mountain pass. As we will see in future chapters, this judgment, in contrast to the initial perceptual experience, is deemed by Buddhist epistemologists to be endowed with conceptual content. But this subsequent judgment is, as with the initial perceptual experience, a momentary cognition (*jñāna*). So, too, were a person to draw an inference from this observation of smoke—say, the inferential judgment that there is *fire* on the mountain pass—this inferential cognition would likewise be a momentary mental episode.

This episodic portrayal of cognition may seem odd to analytic philosophers, but it is right at home in the Buddhist tradition of philosophy. Buddhist philosophers long before the time of Dignāga and Dharmakīrti were inclined toward a reductive metaphysics. There was a prominent belief that commonsense objects are actually composites of spatio-temporal parts. In particular, the Buddhist theory of momentariness held that real objects do not persist over time, but instead have only a fleeting existence. Likewise, Buddhist philosophers were long committed to reductionist views of personhood that rejected the existence of unchanging essences of persons. A person is, instead, just a conventional designation attributed to what is actually five heaps of material and mental components that are changing moment by moment. Given this ancient Buddhist understanding of persons, the idea that one's mental basis for knowledge is something momentary or episodic is a rather comfortable position to adopt.[18]

Of course, this all stands in contrast to how beliefs are typically construed in contemporary analytic philosophy. Perceptual experiences may very well give rise to (perceptual) beliefs, but these beliefs, even though caused by evanescent experiences, are nevertheless deemed to be persisting mental states. A person's belief that there is smoke on the mountain pass can be caused by a fleeting perceptual experience, but the resulting belief is not fleeting or episodic at all. The person could be in the state of believing that there is smoke on the mountain pass for minutes or hours if not longer. Admittedly, beliefs about the existence of smoke on a mountain pass may very well be more temporary than many "abstract" beliefs, such as the belief that fires are hot or the belief that $2 + 2 = 4$. Yet the standard model of belief in analytic epistemology is still one involving a persisting mental state.

Given that each *jñāna* is conceived of as a momentary episode of cognition, and given that a *pramāṇa* is a specific kind of *jñāna*, *pramāṇas* are likewise to be understood episodically. As has been mentioned earlier, for Buddhist epistemologists, a *pramāṇa* is an *episode* of knowledge. But since beliefs are generally taken to be the mental bases for knowledge within analytic epistemology, and beliefs are persisting states, that carries the implication that knowledge is not standardly treated as episodic in contemporary analytic epistemology.

Be that as it may, we should not let the Buddhist tradition's appeal to episodic cognitions, and their lack of devotion to persisting mental states such as belief, lead us to conclude that attributions of knowledge cannot be made within the Buddhist epistemological tradition. As will be argued more forcefully in chapter 2, the investigations into *pramāṇas* that are found in the writings of figures like Dignāga and Dharmakīrti certainly do constitute rigorous theories of knowledge. The fact that *pramāṇas* are taken to be episodic rather than static is less an indication that the Buddhist tradition does not offer an account of knowledge than it is an indication of how narrowly constrained standard descriptions of knowledge are in contemporary analytic philosophy.

Despite the important differences between episodic cognitions in the Buddhist epistemological tradition and dispositional beliefs in contemporary analytic epistemology, in various parts of this book, and especially when discussing inferential knowledge, I shall, for the sake of simplicity, refer to certain cognitive judgments with standard language of "believing that *p*" for some proposition *p*. These inferential cognitions are not equivalent to beliefs, but they play roles that parallel those played by beliefs in the analytic tradition.

1.5. Main Themes of the Book

The nine remaining chapters of this book explore a range of themes that are integral to Buddhist epistemology, and the chapters are organized thematically rather than historically. Each individual chapter focuses on a specific topic in epistemology and the key problems associated with that topic in the Buddhist tradition. The next six chapters are organized around themes that are central to and explicitly discussed in Buddhist presentations of the theory of knowledge: knowledge, perception, inference, testimony, ignorance, and skepticism. The final three chapters—on sensitivity and safety (chapter 8), internalism and externalism (chapter 9), and experimental and cross-cultural epistemology (chapter 10)—explore themes that are of keen interest to contemporary epistemologists, and for which historical Buddhist epistemological writings can be fruitfully put in conversation with contemporary debates on these matters.

Chapter 2 sets the stage for the remainder of the book by focusing on the key question of what is meant by an episode of knowledge in the Buddhist tradition of epistemology. It examines the possible necessary conditions for knowledge as well as the philosophical implications of regarding those conditions as being essential to the concept of knowledge. Chapters 3 and 4 explicate the two sources of knowledge that are accepted by classical Buddhist epistemologists, perception and inferential cognition. Those chapters will demarcate the scopes of those two forms of knowledge and explore some of the key philosophical concerns about those two kinds of cognitive episodes.

Chapter 5 takes up one further *potential* source of knowledge—knowledge by testimony—and looks at how testimony is understood within the Buddhist epistemological tradition, given that tradition's core assertion that perception and inference are the only two authentic sources of knowledge. Chapters 6 and 7 cover topics falling outside the domain of knowledge. First, there is an examination of instances of cognition that do not impart knowledge—episodes of ignorant cognition. That chapter details a series of cognitive episodes that, for one reason or another, fall short of what is required for knowledge, even though in many such cases a person may have a correct or accurate cognition. Next, chapter 7 takes up the question of whether knowledge is ever possible in the first place. It explores skeptical criticisms that some Buddhist philosophers put forward concerning the whole project of *pramāṇa*-based epistemology.

Those six chapters on core themes in Buddhist epistemology are supplemented by three final chapters that are designed to be more philosophically exploratory. In those last three chapters the goal is not so much to introduce readers to the Buddhist theory of knowledge, but rather to call attention to how the accounts developed by Buddhist epistemologists can be put into fruitful dialogue with contemporary epistemology on a number of present-day disputes in the field. As such, those final three chapters take on a more argumentative tone and are pitched at a somewhat higher philosophical level than are the first seven chapters of the book.

Chapter 8 takes up a series of questions surrounding the concepts of sensitivity and safety as those items relate to both contemporary analytic epistemology and the Buddhist epistemological tradition. It also explores how the idea of perceptual discrimination figures into some Buddhist accounts of knowledge. Chapter 9 addresses the ongoing debate between internalism and externalism in contemporary epistemology, and grapples with the question of how we should understand Buddhist accounts of knowledge in relation to that debate. Chapter 10 dives into ongoing debates about the value of experimental epistemology and the role that Indian and Buddhist epistemology can play in these debates. This exploration of Buddhist epistemology's place in discussions of experimental philosophy will lead into a subsequent assessment of the value of taking seriously a cross-cultural dimension within contemporary treatments of the theory of knowledge.

Further Reading

For a clearly written introduction to epistemology in the Indian tradition, see Ganeri, J. (2018). Epistemology from a Sanskritic point of view. In S. Stich, M. Mizumoto, & E. McCready (Eds.), *Epistemology for the rest of the world* (pp. 12–21). New York: Oxford University Press.

For a fuller treatment of the (non-Buddhist) tradition of epistemology in India, see Phillips, S. (2011). *Epistemology in classical India: The knowledge sources of the Nyāya school*. New York: Routledge.

For an extensive treatment of (Buddhist and non-Buddhist) epistemology in India, and its relationship to various concerns in "Western" philosophy, see Matilal, B. K. (1986). *Perception: An essay on classical Indian theories of knowledge*. Oxford: Clarendon Press.

2
Knowledge

As was made clear in the preceding chapter, for Buddhist epistemologists the term *pramāṇa* refers not just to instruments of knowledge but also to those cognitions that constitute episodes of knowledge. This chapter explores the defining characteristics of those cognitions that are *pramāṇas*. Given that we are dealing with an *episodic* conception of knowledge, it should not be surprising if the conditions necessary for an episode of knowledge are different from those articulated within contemporary analytic formulations of knowledge. However, if *pramāṇas* are really episodes of *knowledge*, we should expect the defining features of these episodes to be relatively similar to those encountered in analytic philosophy; otherwise it would call into question the very idea that Buddhist philosophers actually provide a theory of knowledge. For example, were it to turn out that Buddhist accounts of *pramāṇa* allow that cognitions ascertaining patently false states of affairs can still have the status of *pramāṇa*, that would call into question the claim that *pramāṇas* are genuinely episodes of knowledge.

The first half of this chapter will walk through the foundational definitions of the term *pramāṇa* that are offered by the Buddhist philosopher Dharmakīrti in or around the first half of the seventh century. After elaborating on those definitions and how they were interpreted by later Buddhist commentators, the second half of the chapter will take a step back from the Dharmakīrtian account of knowledge and examine the similarities and differences between this classical Buddhist formulation of knowledge episodes and the most common portrayals of knowledge in contemporary analytic epistemology.

2.1. Defining Knowledge?

Contemporary philosophical investigations of knowledge generally seek to determine the set of conditions that are individually necessary and jointly sufficient for the possession of knowledge. Likewise, we might ask: What are

Illuminating the Mind. Jonathan Stoltz, Oxford University Press (2021). © Oxford University Press.
DOI: 10.1093/oso/9780190907532.003.0002

the defining features of knowledge episodes in the classical Buddhist tradition of epistemology?

For a variety of reasons, answering this question is not as easy or straightforward as one might hope. First of all, just as in the Western tradition of epistemology, it would be fair to expect individual philosophers in the Buddhist tradition to defend different and mutually incompatible definitions of knowledge. In this way, there may be no such thing as *the* defining conditions for an episode of knowledge in Buddhist epistemology. Yet, in point of fact, there does turn out to be widespread agreement about the general parameters of knowledge episodes in the Buddhist epistemological tradition, and there is a general agreement that Dharmakīrti's definitions found in his *Commentary on [Dignāga's Compendium of] Knowledge* are to be accepted as correct.[1]

There is, however, the potential for an even more fundamental difficulty in speaking of the defining conditions of knowledge in the Buddhist context. This is because the definitions that were first laid out by Dharmakīrti in his *Commentary* may not have been intended as definitive, overarching characterizations of the term *pramāṇa* at all. While contemporary philosophers generally take it for granted that any adequate epistemological theory will contain a universally applicable set of defining conditions for knowledge, it is not at all clear that Dharmakīrti held such a view. Dharmakīrti's predecessor, Dignāga, writing in the early sixth century, does not appear to provide any explicit definition of the term *pramāṇa* at all. Instead, Dignāga argues that there are just two types of knowledge episodes—perception and inference—and then focuses on identifying adequate defining conditions for each of those two *pramāṇas*. It may have been that Dignāga expected all the epistemological weight to be borne by his two *specific* characterizations of perception and inference, and that there was no role to be played by a *general* definition of the overarching notion of a *pramāṇa*.

In his commentary on Dignāga's *Compendium of Knowledge*, Dharmakīrti is credited with providing (not just one but) two definitions for the term *pramāṇa*. At first glance, this may seem rather odd. If Dignāga provides no general definition of knowledge episodes in his *Compendium*, why would Dharmakīrti introduce new definitions in his commentary on Dignāga's treatise? It is not entirely clear, however, how authoritative Dharmakīrti's purported definitions of the term *pramāṇa* were intended to be. It is quite possible that his definitions carried only little explanatory weight within Dharmakīrti's own epistemological thinking, and that, just as with Dignāga, the majority of the weight was to fall on his elucidations of perception and inference. But even if that's the case, it is undeniably true that, in the centuries after Dharmakīrti's texts were written, later Buddhist epistemologists placed more and more emphasis on articulating and defending a precise, overarching definition for the term *pramāṇa*. In fact, by the time we reach the twelfth century, Buddhist epistemological treatises in Tibet not only contain long sections on the definition of *pramāṇa*—sections in which they first discuss and refute others' proposed definitions and interpretations of the term *pramāṇa* and then defend their own preferred definition—they also include detailed, systematic theories of the nature of definitions in general.[2]

Given that Dignāga provided no formal definition of the term *pramāṇa*, and yet later Tibetan epistemologists devoted many, many pages to that term's definition, we need to see what happened in the period between these extremes; and, in particular, we need to look at Dharmakīrti's account of knowledge episodes, as well as how his views were interpreted by his successors in India. It is not so easy to pin down Dharmakīrti's account, however. As mentioned earlier, it is traditionally maintained that Dharmakīrti puts forward *two* separate definitions of knowledge episodes; and this leads later Buddhist writers to engage in interpretive gymnastics that are aimed at clarifying the relationship between those two purported definitions. Are the two definitions meant to be equivalent? Are they meant to complement each other, with each of the two definitions providing necessary (but not sufficient) conditions for episodes of knowledge? Are the two definitions designed for two separate audiences? On the other end of the spectrum, some modern scholars have bitten the bullet and argued that Dharmakīrti, just like his predecessor Dignāga, does not provide any formal, overarching definition of *pramāṇa* at all, and that the two purported definitions that Dharmakīrti is credited with were never intended to be construed as general definitions at all.[3]

This uncertainty with respect to Dharmakīrti's intentions has to do largely with the argumentative context in which he offers his two characterizations of knowledge episodes. The formulations that are typically cited as Dharmakīrti's definitions of *pramāṇa* are found at the beginning of the second chapter of his *Commentary on [Dignāga's Compendium of] Knowledge*, a chapter that is ostensibly aimed at establishing the authoritativeness of the Buddha—that is, establishing that the Buddha can be seen as a source of knowledge, or as a *pramāṇa*. Given this context, there is room to argue that the characterizations of knowledge episodes provided in that chapter are not intended as official definitions, but only as informal characterizations serving to establish the authoritativeness of the Buddha and his teachings. In particular, it is possible that Dharmakīrti was just making use of already common, albeit informal, understandings of knowledge in the broader Indian tradition.[4]

There is, however, one major challenge to arguing that Dharmakīrti did not put forward any formal definition(s) of *pramāṇa*. The problem is that, regardless of how historically well-founded and hermeneutically persuasive those arguments may be, many Indian (and later Tibetan) Buddhist epistemologists writing after Dharmakīrti certainly *did* take his two formulations to be official (and authoritative) definitions of knowledge episodes. Let us, therefore, examine in detail Dharmakīrti's two purported definitions, as well as later Buddhist thinkers' clarifications of those definitions.

2.2. Revealing the Unknown

Most of this chapter will be focused on and structured around Dharmakīrti's *first* definition of knowledge episodes. Before addressing that first definition, however, I shall begin with a brief discussion of what is considered Dharmakīrti's second or "alternate" definition. We will return to his first definition of the term *pramāṇa* in section 3.

After having briefly discussed some implications of his first characterization of knowledge episodes (to be described later), Dharmakīrti provides the following definition: "Or, [a *pramāṇa* is] the revealing of a state of affairs that is not [already] known."[5] In other words, an episode of knowledge is a cognition that reveals something not already known.

The reference to "revealing a state of affairs"—or of "revealing an object," as it could be translated—points to two key features of episodes of knowledge. First, episodes of knowledge disclose or reveal things as they actually are. In Buddhist epistemological texts, objects of knowledge are not ordinarily expressed propositionally, but we can still think of this as capturing a kind of 'truth constraint' on knowledge episodes. Dharmakīrti's language strongly suggests that to reveal a state of affairs is to present or disclose things as they actually exist. Truth or factual existence is deemed a necessary condition for knowledge episodes.[6] Dharmakīrti does not, to be clear, explicitly speak of truth as a condition for knowledge. It would not be until sometime later that Buddhist epistemologists explicitly invoke the notion of truth as a component of knowledge episodes.[7] Yet, even in Dharmakīrti's presentation, it is made clear that episodes of knowledge must be correct cognitions. For example, a visual cognition of a cow could not qualify as an episode of knowledge unless it reveals an actual cow. In this way, his understanding of knowledge is one that carries with it a restriction that contemporary philosophers would regard as a kind of 'truth constraint.'

The second key implication of Dharmakīrti's definition is tied to the verb that he uses in his formulation. Episodes of knowledge *reveal* (or "make clear"; Skt: *prakāśa*) a state of affairs. Knowledge is a cognitive event that *discloses* something that was not previously known. Once an object or state of affairs has been revealed or disclosed to a person, it may be cognized again, but provided that the subsequent cognition reveals nothing new, it is not, according to Dharmakīrti, an episode of knowledge. For instance, upon looking off into a field, I may visually apprehend a red barn. That visual cognition, if accurate, may be an instance of knowledge. But Dharmakīrti and other Buddhist epistemologists contend that, in an important sense, it is only the first moment of conscious awareness of the red barn that is a *pramāṇa*, for only the first moment of sight reveals an unknown object. Immediately after having this visual perception I may, with my eyes now attending to the road, *recall* the visual experience of a red barn that I have just had. This recollection may very well apprehend reality correctly, but it is not considered an episode of knowledge since it does not provide any new information. In time, as the Buddhist epistemological tradition further developed, this feature became codified much more explicitly as a kind of 'novelty constraint' on knowledge episodes.

At first glance, this 'novelty constraint' on knowledge might strike many readers as rather odd. The idea that just the first moment of cognition is an instance of knowledge has little resonance with how knowledge is understood in contemporary analytic epistemology. We must bear in mind, however, that in the Indian tradition of epistemology what are at issue are not dispositional states of a person but are instead momentary episodes of cognitive awareness. The first moment of awareness in which I visually apprehend a red barn may very well constitute an episode of knowledge, but the subsequent episodes of recollection will not, for they don't genuinely *disclose* anything at all—the red barn has already been disclosed.

One explanation for why Dharmakīrti supports the view that knowledge episodes must reveal something not previously known is so as to make it clear to his readers that, with respect to perception, it is the initial raw, sensory awareness that is the *pramāṇa*, and not the subsequent conceptual cognition that arises from that sensory awareness. When I perceive a red barn, Buddhist thinkers like Dignāga and Dharmakīrti would maintain that it is the visual sensory cognition of the red barn that constitutes the episode of knowledge. Immediately after having this visual sensation, I may very well form the conceptual judgment that there is a red barn in the field. But on Dharmakīrti's view this conceptual judgment is not a *pramāṇa*; it is not a source of knowledge. Only the initial perceptual (and nonconceptual) cognition is deemed to be a source of knowledge. The 'novelty constraint' on episodes of knowledge thus serves as a way to drive home the point that only the initial, nonconceptual visual awareness, and not the subsequent conceptual judgment, is a *pramāṇa*. This is a topic that will be discussed more fully in chapter 3.

As I've described matters thus far, Dharmakīrti's second definition points toward two necessary conditions for episodes of knowledge—truth and novelty. This might suggest that, for Dharmakīrti, knowledge is to be characterized as a cognition that is true and provides novel information. Whether these conditions are meant to be jointly sufficient for knowledge, however, cannot be definitively determined from what has been said so far. Let us, therefore, move on to discussing Dharmakīrti's initial characterization of *pramāṇa* that comes four verses earlier than that which has just been covered.

2.3. Nondeceptive Cognition

Dharmakīrti's first characterization of *pramāṇa*, an episode of knowledge, is that it is "a nondeceptive cognition."[8] To define episodes of knowledge in terms of the "nondeceptiveness" of cognition, however, adds little immediate clarity, for the expression "nondeceptive" (*avisaṃvādi*) is just as much a technical term in Buddhist epistemology as is *pramāṇa*. Dharmakīrti immediately informs his readers that a cognition's nondeceptiveness consists in there being "the capacity to perform a function." This capacity to carry out a function (or "to accomplish an objective"; Skt: *arthakriyā*) is standardly taken by Buddhist epistemologists to be a property exclusively possessed by *real* entities. Real things are claimed to have causal or functional powers, unlike unreal abstract or conceptual entities which lack such powers. As Dharmakīrti's disciple Devendrabuddhi notes in this context, the capacity to carry out a function includes such things as a fire's ability to burn and cook things.[9] Insofar as a real fire can accomplish these functional purposes, it is said to have the capacity to perform a function. Unreal entities, such as the generic idea of fire or the concept of water, do not have these sorts of causal powers. The idea of a fire cannot cook food and the concept of water cannot quench one's thirst.

This hints at a peculiarity in Dharmakīrti's first definition of an episode of knowledge. When he proclaims that episodes of knowledge are "nondeceptive cognitions," the most straightforward reading is that 'nondeceptiveness' is a property that applies to *cognitions*—that is, that some cognitions have the property of being 'deceptive' and others have the property of being 'nondeceptive.' However, the property of 'having the capacity to perform a function' is a property possessed by certain *objects* of cognition, and it is not a property of cognitions themselves.[10] In this way, there is an apparent mismatch between what nondeceptiveness attaches to (episodes of cognition) and how the nondeceptiveness of a cognition is explained (by way of a quality of its object).

Dharmakīrti's assertion here is standardly understood to indicate that a cognition's nondeceptiveness consists in the fact that the cognition engages a real, causally effective object. For example, when I perceive a fire, my cognition is nondeceptive because it engages a real fire—a fire having the capacity to burn things. A deceptive cognition, by contrast, would be one that entertains an object lacking these causal capacities. Were I to have a hallucinatory experience as of a fire, the "object" entertained would not be something possessing the capacity to burn or cook things. Understood in this way, the category of nondeceptive cognitions should include within it all *veridical perceptual experiences* (as that notion is commonly understood in contemporary philosophy), for veridical perceptual experiences are ones that engage real, causally effective objects.

What is less obvious is how Dharmakīrti's first definition of *pramāṇa* is to be extended to nonperceptual cases. Suppose a person comes to know that clay pots are impermanent things—that is, that clay pots have only a momentary existence and do not persist unchanged over time. This is, according to Buddhist philosophers, something that ordinary humans can gain knowledge of, but only through inferential reasoning. What does it mean to say that gaining knowledge of the impermanence of clay pots is a matter of a person's cognition being nondeceptive? As will be explained more fully in chapter 4, coming to know that clay pots are impermanent requires applications of conceptual reasoning—reasoning that appeals to general, conceptual entities, such as the idea or concept of a clay pot. But on Buddhist accounts these conceptual entities are *not* real—for example, the idea of a clay pot doesn't have functional capacities like the capacity to hold water. How then can Dharmakīrti and other Buddhist epistemologists defend the definition of knowledge as "nondeceptive cognition" in cases of inferential reasoning? Dharmakīrti clearly does believe that inferential reasoning can provide knowledge, but explaining how this is consistent with his definition of a knowledge episode is not so straightforward.

The status of inferential knowledge will be detailed more fully in chapter 4, but here is a very brief synopsis of how "nondeceptiveness" can be extended to inferential, conceptual cognitions. First, Buddhist epistemologists draw a distinction between "deceptive" cognitions and "erroneous" (*bhrānta*) cognitions. Conceptual cognitions, such as the cognition that clay pots are impermanent, are deemed erroneous. This is because they directly apprehend unreal, general entities (such as the generic idea of a clay pot). But, according to Dharmakīrti and other Buddhist epistemologists, ordinary humans conflate these general entities with real, particular objects (such as a real, individual clay pot). This conflation of conceptual, general entities with real, particular entities is, according to Buddhist tradition, pervasive in conceptual cognition, and it is thus taken as grounds for concluding that all conceptual cognitions are erroneous. Be that as it may, some of these erroneous conceptual cognitions are still "nondeceptive" in the sense of engaging things as they actually are. For even if the inferential judgment that clay pots are impermanent conflates the general idea of a clay pot with a real, "concrete" clay pot, the fact of the matter is that real clay pots are indeed impermanent, and so the cognition is one whose intended objects are causally effective.

2.3.1. Interpreting Dharmakīrti

In the generations after Dharmakīrti, Buddhist epistemologists do not set out to prove or refute Dharmakīrti's definitions of *pramāṇa*, nor do they explicitly aim to redefine what it means to be an episode of knowledge. Their project is, rather, one primarily of exegesis. That is, later Buddhist epistemologists aim to elucidate Dharmakīrti's definition(s). Insofar as this is the case, the first task for these epistemologists is to make sense of the two, ostensibly different, definitions that Dharmakīrti has provided of the term *pramāṇa*. They need to explain the relationship between calling a *pramāṇa* a "nondeceptive cognition" and calling it a cognition that "reveals a state of affairs not already known."

The earliest, extant commentary on Dharmakīrti's *Commentary on [Dignāga's Compendium of] Knowledge* is that by the late seventh-century epistemologist Devendrabuddhi. He discusses both of Dharmakīrti's two definitions but does not explicitly address how the two definitions relate to each other. Devendrabuddhi gives examples in which it is made clear that episodes of knowledge are cognitions that satisfy *both* definitions—and that such cognitions are *pramāṇas* by virtue of the fact that they satisfy both definitions.[11] About a century later, the Buddhist philosopher Prajñākaragupta defends what appears to be an importantly different interpretation of Dharmakīrti. He argues that the two definitions capture two different senses of knowledge. There is conventional knowledge (or knowledge of conventional reality) and there is ultimate knowledge (or knowledge of ultimate reality). On Prajñākaragupta's view, Dharmakīrti's first definition applies to conventional reality, and the second definition applies to ultimate reality.

The late eighth-century Buddhist epistemologist Dharmottara defends a different understanding of Dharmakīrti's definitions. Instead of the two definitions being independent of each other, Dharmottara contends that there is really only one definition of *pramāṇa*; and it is a cognition that is nondeceptive. Dharmakīrti's "second definition" merely spells out, in different words, information that is logically entailed by the nondeceptiveness of cognition. In this way, Dharmottara's view is that having a nondeceptive cognition is both necessary and sufficient for knowledge. This understanding is not necessarily incompatible with Devendrabuddhi's earlier account—after all, they would agree that, for any cognition that is an episode of knowledge, it will have both (a) the property of being nondeceptive and (b) the property of revealing a state of affairs not previously known. The difference is that Dharmottara, unlike Devendrabuddhi, provides an explanation of the relationship between these two respective definitional criteria.

2.3.2. Epistemic Pragmatism?

There is much more that could be said concerning the hermeneutical details of Dharmakīrti's two characterizations of knowledge episodes. What we need to do now, however, is take a step back and make some broader philosophical observations in light of these definitions of *pramāṇa*. To be honest, being told that an episode of knowledge is a nondeceptive cognition, or even that it is a cognition that reveals a state of affairs not already known, is not entirely helpful information. Neither of Dharmakīrti's definitions, for example, serves as a particularly helpful guide for determining whether, in a given scenario, a person's cognition is or is not a *pramāṇa*.

Some Buddhist studies scholars have argued that Dharmakīrti's first definition of knowledge episodes reflects his support for a *pragmatic* conception of knowledge.[12] In particular, what has earlier been translated as "performing a function" (*arthakriyā*) can be charitably interpreted to mean something along the lines of "fulfilling a (human) purpose."[13] On this reading, a nondeceptive cognition is one that is pragmatically successful, inasmuch as it leads to the fulfillment of one's objectives. For example, the inferential judgment that there is a fire on the mountain pass is a nondeceptive cognition to the extent that such a judgment is one that would lead to practical success—such as a person's ability to receive warmth from a fire upon traveling to the mountain pass.

This claim that Dharmakīrti's first characterization of knowledge episodes reflects a pragmatic conception of knowledge is not without historical support in the Indian Buddhist tradition. One of Dharmakīrti's key commentators, the eighth-century philosopher Dharmottara, does understand the appeal to nondeceptiveness to have a clear pragmatic dimension. On Dharmottara's view, a cognition is nondeceptive provided that it allows us to obtain the object specified by the cognition. As such, a nondeceptive cognition puts one in contact with a real object, not just in the sense that the person (mentally) apprehends a real object, but in the more practical sense that the person is *induced to obtain* a real object. Such a reading is in line with the earlier stated idea that an inferential judgment that there is a fire on the mountain pass is nondeceptive insofar as it could induce a person to obtain a fire.

2.3.3. Epistemic Luck?

This pragmatic understanding of knowledge episodes is not without difficulties, however. If nondeceptiveness is *merely* a matter of achieving pragmatic success—of obtaining one's intended object—then it sure looks like this understanding of knowledge will not serve to rule out cases of *epistemic luck*.

Cognitions that are accurate by mere chance would seem to satisfy this pragmatic conception of knowledge. For example, suppose that a person looks off toward a distant mountain pass and catches a glimpse of something rising into the air. What is rising into the air is actually a large swarm of flies, but the person mistakenly believes it to be smoke. As a result of believing that there is smoke on the mountain pass, the person deduces that there is a fire on the mountain pass as well. And let us suppose that, just by happenstance, there actually is a fire burning on the mountain pass.

The person's cognition that there is a fire on the mountain pass is correct, and so that cognition is one that would allow him to obtain his intended object, a fire. But surely it would be odd to say that the person's cognition that there is a fire on the mountain pass should count as an instance of knowledge. After all, the only reason why the person formed that judgment was because he mistakenly believed that there was smoke there (though it was actually just a swarm of flies). The resulting cognition was correct only due to luck. Is it really the case that Dharmottara, much less Dharmakīrti, intended pragmatic success to be *sufficient* for knowledge?

There are solid grounds for concluding that Dharmottara did not believe that (merely having) a correct cognition was sufficient for knowledge. In particular, Dharmottara himself offers the very example, described earlier, of deducing fire's existence from an incorrect belief that there is smoke, and Dharmottara contends that this is *not* an episode of knowledge at all. (He claims that this judgment should be regarded as an instance of cognitive doubt.) So Dharmottara surely believed that mere pragmatic success—in terms of obtaining a true object—even when combined with novelty, is not enough for knowledge. What else is required?

2.3.4. Truth-Tracking

Some quality over and above truth (or the correctness of cognition) appears to be needed in order for this Dharmakīrtian account of knowledge episodes to prevent cases of cognitive luck from counting as knowledge. Whether Dharmakīrti himself consciously recognized the nondeceptiveness of cognition to consist of more than just engaging real objects—that is, as more than having a correct or true cognition—is not 100 percent clear. What is clear is that, as the centuries went by, those Buddhist epistemologists who accepted Dharmakīrti's definitions of *pramāṇa* did interpret his definition in such a way as to make it clear that nondeceptiveness requires not just the actual truth or correctness of one's cognition, but instead requires that there is something along the lines of a *law-like guarantee* of the cognition's truth or correctness.

On this very matter, Buddhist studies scholar Georges Dreyfus has described the Dharmakīrtian account of knowledge as requiring not just truth but what he calls "normative truth."[14] Another scholar attempts to capture this law-like guarantee of truth or correctness by translating the key notion of "nondeceptive cognition" (*avisaṃvādi jñānam*) as "reliable cognition."[15] There is some merit to both of these formulations. A more appropriate way to express this point, however, is to say that on the Buddhist account a cognition's nondeceptiveness consists not simply in it accurately engaging real things but also in the cognition's correctness being grounded in its ability to *invariably track the truth.*

More will be said about this truth-tracking requirement for episodes of knowledge later in this chapter, and then again in more detail in chapter 8 (when the thesis of sensitivity is discussed in greater detail) and also in chapter 9 (when discussing the topic of epistemic externalism). Before moving on to other issues, however, and just to give a flavor of what is to come, let me briefly spell out how this truth-tracking interpretation of Dharmakīrti's "nondeceptive cognition" plays out in later Buddhist accounts of knowledge in twelfth-century Tibet. Many twelfth-century Tibetan epistemologists contend that to have an episode of knowledge requires one's cognition to have the correct "mode of apprehension," where the correct mode of apprehension is one that ensures that a person's cognition is *sensitive to the truth* (or sensitive to the existence of its object). In particular, having the right mode of apprehension is explained in terms of the counterfactual conditional, "If the object hadn't existed, there wouldn't have been the cognition [(as) of that object]."[16]

This closely resembles the sensitivity requirement on knowledge that is commonly discussed in analytic epistemology. Just as we might say that knowledge requires not merely having a true belief, but having a belief that is sensitive to the truth—sensitive in the sense that, if the claim were not true, the person wouldn't have believed it—so, too, Tibetan Buddhist epistemologists in the twelfth century understood knowledge episodes to require not just having a correct cognition but also having a cognition that is counterfactually sensitive to the object or state of affairs that is cognized. In this way, and thinking back to the earlier example from Dharmottara about a person who judges, correctly as chance would have it, that there is a fire on the mountain pass as a result of mistaking a swarm of flies for a funnel of smoke, twelfth-century Tibetan Buddhist epistemologists have a clear route to explaining why the judgment is not an instance of knowledge. Yes, the person forms a correct belief—there is indeed a fire on the mountain pass—but the judgment is not an instance of knowledge because it is not sensitive to the truth. This is because even if there had been no fire on the mountain pass, the person still would have believed that there was a fire, since the judgment was derived from the misapprehension of the swarm of bugs as being smoke. By failing this test of sensitivity, it is recognized that the cognition, though true, doesn't genuinely track the truth. As these Tibetan epistemologists put the point, the cognition does not have the right "mode of apprehension." On this reading, the nondeceptiveness of cognition requires not just that the cognition is correct or true, but instead that the cognition invariably tracks the truth.

The view just presented is, to be clear, not explicit in Dharmakīrti's writing. It is only over the course of multiple commentarial elaborations in the centuries following Dharmakīrti that this truth-tracking account becomes fully evident. It is not at all obvious whether Dharmakīrti himself intended the nondeceptiveness of cognition to imply a law-like tracking of the truth. What is much clearer is that Dharmakīrti did *not* intend for accidentally true cognitions to qualify as episodes of knowledge. That this is so comes not from examining his definitions of *pramāṇa*, but instead from looking at his definitions of—and more detailed elucidations of—perception and inference, the only two types of knowledge episodes that Dharmakīrti countenances. As readers will see in chapters 3 and 4, both perceptual and inferential cognitions are ones that provide a law-like guarantee of truth/correctness.

In light of what has been said earlier, it can be hypothesized that, following the model of his predecessor Dignāga, Dharmakīrti expected his definitions of *perception* and *inference* to carry the largest epistemological burden—including the work of excluding accidentally true cognitions from the realm of knowledge—and that he placed little explanatory weight on his general definition of *pramāṇa* as "nondeceptive cognition." As time went on, however, later Buddhist epistemologists placed a greater and greater explanatory burden on Dharmakīrti's definition of *pramāṇa*, and thus found it necessary to read into and attach to that definition a law-like guarantee of the cognition's truth.

Given all of the aforementioned information, we can summarize the standard post-Dharmakīrtian Buddhist account of knowledge episodes in the following way:

An episode of knowledge, that is, a *pramāṇa*, is

(1) a cognition that
(2) tracks the truth (or sensitively engages a real object/state of affairs),
(3) with respect to that which is not already known.

Or, even more simply, an episode of knowledge is *a novel, truth-tracking cognition.*

To be clear, the claim is not that Dharmakīrti *defines* episodes of knowledge as novel, truth-tracking cognitions. Instead, the idea is that Dharmakīrti's two definitions get fleshed out by later Buddhist epistemologists in such a way that conditions (1) through (3) can be seen as individually necessary and jointly sufficient for having an episode of knowledge.

2.4. Analytic Theories of Knowledge and "the Standard Analysis"

In order to better understand the implications of Dharmakīrti's definitions of *pramāṇa*, let us now explore how this Buddhist understanding of knowledge episodes relates to contemporary, "Western" accounts of knowledge. Since at least the time of Plato, philosophers have almost universally agreed that knowledge demands more than just having a true opinion. While it is standardly granted that truth or correctness is necessary for knowledge, it is also acknowledged that being correct is not sufficient for knowledge. Plato suggests that what is needed, beyond holding a true opinion, is for that opinion to be "tied down" in a way that permits one to specify the reason(s) why that opinion is true. In short, knowledge is a true opinion that is tied down. Whether or not one accepts Plato's formulation, his approach toward addressing the issue has contributed to a historical emphasis on so-called *analytic theories of knowledge*. Generally speaking, analytic theories aim to understand their topics by breaking down the items in question into their component parts. In this case, an analytic account of knowledge attempts to characterize or "define" knowledge by identifying a set of properties or conditions that are individually necessary and jointly sufficient for having knowledge.

As is exemplified in Plato's assessment, analytic theories of knowledge tend to begin with the assertion that two ingredients are necessary for having knowledge: (A1) being in some mental state such as the state of belief, and (A2) having that mental state, or the contents of that mental state, be true or correct. Yet, as Plato well notes, it seems that any adequate analytic account of knowledge must contain some additional ingredient over and above belief and truth. More formally, a person S has knowledge if and only if:

(A1) S is in the mental state, B,
(A2) B satisfies a truth or correctness condition, T, and
(A3) B meets some additional condition, X.

In this way, knowledge is analyzed as B + T + X. What this final ingredient X amounts to will differ from theory to theory, and it is possible that the condition X might be further analyzable into multiple subconditions, such as X_1 and X_2. Let us call any such formulation of knowledge a *Platonic analysis*. On a Platonic analysis, knowledge is analyzed as a true belief that meets some further condition(s).

Is the Buddhist account of knowledge episodes an example of an analytic theory and/or a Platonic analysis? This question requires a two-part answer. To be sure, Dharmakīrti's description of knowledge as a "nondeceptive cognition" does not explicitly suggest any analytic approach toward knowledge. Yet, as Buddhist epistemological writings matured in the centuries following Dharmakīrti, it becomes clearer and clearer that these later Indian and Tibetan Buddhists did seek to distill a number of necessary and sufficient conditions for having an episode of knowledge. By the time the Buddhist epistemological tradition became entrenched in Tibet in the early part of the second millennium of the Common Era, authors were strongly disposed toward analytic accounts of not just the conditions necessary for an episode of knowledge but also for the component conditions of numerous types of cognitive episodes that fall short of knowledge.[17] So in this sense, yes, the Buddhist account of knowledge that flows from Dharmakīrti is certainly compatible with, and sometimes even explicated as, an analytic treatment of knowledge episodes.

But even on the assumption that Buddhist epistemologists in the centuries following Dharmakīrti could or would endorse an analytic theory of knowledge episodes, this should not be taken to imply that the Buddhist account is a Platonic analysis of knowledge. As described in the preceding section, and as will be discussed more fully later, the Buddhist account of *pramāṇa* that derives from Dharmakīrti is not a Platonic analysis, for it does not include condition (A2) as a separate analytic component of knowledge episodes. To have an episode of knowledge does indeed entail that one's cognition is true/correct, but knowledge is not analyzed as a cognition that is true and which meets some further condition X.

There are a number of additional differences between Buddhist analyses of knowledge and the kinds of analyses that we find in contemporary epistemology. First, in contemporary analytic epistemology, the project of analyzing knowledge is generally focused on specifying the set of conditions that are necessary and sufficient conditions for affirming that 'S knows that *p*.' This project of identifying an adequate set of conditions necessary and sufficient for the truth of 'S knows that *p*' may be a noble one, but it is certainly not the same thing as determining what knowledge is. In particular, contemporary analytic portrayals of knowledge tend to be completely silent about the metaphysical nature of knowledge. Is knowledge a psychological state? Is it a kind of objective, two-place relation between a person and a proposition? Those sorts of questions are not answered, or even intended to be answered, by philosophers whose aim is to identify the necessary and sufficient conditions for the truth of 'S knows that *p*.' Many contemporary analyses of knowledge are *consistent with* the thesis that knowledge is a relation between a person, S, and a proposition, *p*. But even if consistent with such an interpretation of knowledge, these analyses do not require that interpretation, or any other specific interpretation, of what the nature of knowledge is.

There is a second important point to keep in mind about contemporary analytic treatments of knowledge. Given the focus on identifying necessary and sufficient conditions for the truth of 'S knows that *p*,' contemporary analytic accounts often either restrict themselves to investigating instances of *propositional* knowledge or they flat out take for granted that all knowledge is propositional. This restriction of theorizing to just propositional knowledge often goes unnoticed by contemporary philosophers. Yet it is largely out of tune with pre-1963 accounts of knowledge. Bertrand Russell, for example, held that knowledge is of two types: *knowledge of things* and *knowledge of truths*.[18] Propositional knowledge falls into the latter category. The idea that there might also be a "knowledge of things," by contrast, has largely disappeared from contemporary analytic treatments of knowledge, where the focus is on identifying the conditions necessary for the truth of 'S knows that *p*.' But, again, matters are different in the Buddhist epistemological tradition. That tradition treats knowledge of things as the paradigmatic form of knowledge.

Edmund Gettier begins his famous 1963 article "Is Justified True Belief Knowledge?" with the following proposed analysis:[19]

(a) S knows that *p* *IFF* (i) *p* is true,
(ii) S believes that *p*, and
(iii) S is justified in believing *p*.

Let us call this *the standard analysis* of propositional knowledge. The standard analysis, thanks largely to Gettier, is now widely rejected. Yet, as mentioned earlier, the project of identifying a set of necessary and sufficient conditions for 'S knows that *p*' is still central to analytic epistemology, and the standard analysis of knowledge as a justified true belief often serves as the starting point for explorations of knowledge in contemporary philosophy.

Even if Buddhist epistemologists do put forward analytic treatments of knowledge, those accounts are not instances of the standard analysis, since they are not compatible with the broader Platonic analysis of knowledge. For Dharmakīrti and his followers, episodes of knowledge are not true cognitions for which some additional condition holds. Nevertheless, owing to the central place held by the standard analysis in contemporary epistemology, it will prove helpful to examine how this conception of knowledge relates to Dharmakīrti's account of knowledge. To that end, I now want to explore in greater detail how the Dharmakīrtian account of knowledge episodes compares with the standard analytic treatment of knowledge. Given what has been said already, we should expect there to be some large differences. Yet, if it is to be an account of knowledge at all, we should also hope that many core features will be shared in common.[20]

2.4.1. Belief

The mental component at the heart of the Buddhist account of knowledge is that of cognition (*jñāna*). As already noted in the preceding chapter, however, the Indian understanding of cognition differs from analytic epistemology's portrayal of belief in several key respects. First of all, beliefs are held to be *dispositional* states of an individual—states that can persist over long stretches of time. Cognitions in the Indian tradition of epistemology, by contrast, are *occurrent* mental episodes that last only a fleeting moment. A second difference is that beliefs are held to be propositional attitudes, whereas cognitions need not (and often do not) have anything like propositional contents at all. Perceptual cognitions, in particular, are affirmed by Buddhist epistemologists to have individual, real objects as their contents. For example, a person might have a perceptual cognition of the moon or a perceptual cognition of blue.

There is yet a third respect in which the role played by cognition (*jñāna*) in Dharmakīrti's account is different from that played by belief in the standard analysis of knowledge. On the standard analysis, whenever someone knows a proposition *p*, it logically follows that the person holds the belief that *p*. Belief, on this analysis, is held to be a specific kind of mental state, and, in particular, a kind of propositional attitude. Thus, in order for a person to *know that* birds are warm-blooded, it is deemed to be necessary for the person to *believe that* birds are warm-blooded. Yet, while belief is a mental state and belief is necessary for knowledge, it does not thereby follow that knowledge itself is a mental state. In fact, on the standard analysis, knowledge is not affirmed to be a mental state at all. (But again, any time a person has propositional knowledge that *p*, the person is in the mental state of *believing p*.)

On the Buddhist account, by contrast, episodes of knowledge are in fact instances of cognition, and as such episodes of knowledge are themselves mental events. It is easy to gloss over this distinction, but it is an incredibly important point of contrast between the two traditions of epistemology. Again, on Dharmakīrti's account, episodes of knowledge are themselves cognitions—and, specifically, cognitions having the property of being nondeceptive. To see the importance of this point, let us look at the contrast between two basic cases of inference-like belief/cognition.

(Case I) *S* observes smoke rising from a mountain pass, and as such deduces that there is a fire on the mountain pass. In this case, let us assume that *S* thereby *knows* that there is a fire on the mountain pass.

(Case M) *S* misapprehends a plume of dust as smoke, and thus mistakenly takes there to be smoke rising from a mountain pass. As a result, *S* deduces that there is fire on the mountain pass. In this case, we should agree that *S does not know* that there is a fire on the mountain pass.

What should we say of the relation between the beliefs/cognitions that arise in these two cases?

On the standard analytic treatment of belief, we should say that in both Case I and Case M the person forms the same belief, and thus that person *S* is in the *same mental state* of believing that there is a fire on the mountain pass. Yes, it is true that the causal origins of the beliefs differ in the two cases, and it may be granted that the belief is justified in Case I but not justified in Case M, but the resultant mental state is the same in the two cases—they are both instances of *S* believing that there is fire on the mountain pass. And insofar as the resultant mental state is the same in the two cases but the person has knowledge only in the former case and not in the latter, it follows that knowledge is not exclusively determined by the mental state the person is in. In short, on the standard analysis, knowledge is not a mental state.

On the Buddhist account of knowledge that flows from Dharmakīrti, by contrast, the cognitions that are formed in the two cases noted earlier must be different in kind. In Case I, *S*'s cognition is an instance of knowledge, and that cognition is one that engages a real fire on the mountain pass. In Case M, however, person *S* has a cognition that is different in kind from the cognition that arises in Case I. To be clear, Buddhist epistemologists would maintain that both cases are ones where *S* has a cognition *apprehending* fire on the mountain pass (i.e., *S* takes there to be a fire on the mountain pass in both cases). But the cognitive episodes are not the same in all other respects, and are thus deemed to be different in kind. In particular, as noted earlier, Case I involves a cognition that *engages* a real fire on the mountain pass, whereas Case M does not. Because the resultant cognitions are deemed to be different in the two cases, Buddhist epistemologists are in the position to endorse the thesis that episodes of knowledge constitute a special kind of cognition.

More will be said about this topic in chapter 9. In that chapter, the fact that episodes of knowledge constitute a special type of cognition will play an important role in showing why the Buddhist account should be seen as a version of externalism about mental states/episodes. What is important here is just to illuminate the key differences between the mental components of knowing in the Buddhist and analytic traditions of epistemology: belief and cognition. As noted earlier, three main differences need to be kept in mind. The Buddhist epistemologist's cognitions (1) are occurrent episodes, not dispositional states, (2) frequently have nonpropositional contents, and (3) are not merely necessary conditions for having knowledge but the actual mental constituents of knowledge episodes.

2.4.2. Truth

In contemporary analytic epistemology, it is close to universally agreed that knowledge entails truth, in the sense that a person can know that *p* only if *p* is true. Ordinarily, and as indicated in the preceding sentence, contemporary philosophers take truth to be a property or attribute of the proposition that is the content of the knower's belief. Relatedly, truth is commonly held to be a kind of correspondence between a proposition and the world. Taking truth to be a property of propositions is not the only possible interpretation, however. In the Middle Ages, the most common understanding of truth, stemming from figures like Thomas Aquinas, was as a correspondence between the *intellect* and *things*. This is captured in Aquinas's assertion that "*Veritas est adaequatio rei et intellectus*"—truth is the correspondence of things and intellect.[21] On this medieval model, what is true or false is not exactly a proposition but rather a judgment made by the intellect. This distinction between truth as a property of propositions versus truth as a property of judgment/belief is often glossed over in contemporary epistemological debates. Yet it is helpful to keep in mind that it is possible to understand the 'truth constraint' on knowledge in ways other than as a property of propositions.

It has been pointed out earlier that the Dharmakīrtian account places a 'truth constraint' on knowledge. Any and all instances of knowledge are correct/true cognitions. (And again, this is the case even though Buddhist approaches toward knowledge episodes are not necessarily structured around a propositional interpretation.) Yet, as has been described earlier, this truth constraint is not an explicit component in either of Dharmakīrti's two formulations of knowledge episodes. Moreover, it must be made perfectly clear that the standard account of knowledge in the post-Dharmakīrtian Buddhist tradition is *not* one in which knowledge is analyzed as (1) a cognition that (2) is true (or correct) and which (3) meets some further condition or conditions. Rather, an episode of knowledge is just a cognition that is nondeceptive, where nondeceptiveness entails not just truth but an invariable sensitivity to the truth.

There is one factor that complicates how we should understand classical Buddhist epistemologists' assent to a truth constraint on episodes of knowledge. Namely, the accounts of knowledge that are provided by Dharmakīrti and his followers could be mapped onto any number of different metaphysical accounts of the nature of reality. Some Buddhist philosophical texts defend a version of *external realism* about reality. Other Buddhist texts argue in support of an *idealist* conception of reality. Obviously, what the truth constraint on knowledge will look like, and how its satisfaction will be determined, depends on what metaphysical standpoint is adopted. When explicating their theories of knowledge, Dharmakīrti and his followers most often adopt an external realist perspective of reality, one that is frequently characterized as reflective of the *Sautrāntika* system of Buddhist thought.[22] That said, when addressing a narrow range of epistemological issues, Dharmakīrti and his followers shift their ontological perspectives and promote an idealist understanding of reality, one associated with the *Yogācāra* tradition of Buddhist thought.[23]

Insofar as Dharmakīrti, in the vast majority of cases, assumes an external realist perspective when grappling with epistemological problems, I will, throughout this book, largely restrict my discussions to analyses of their theories on the assumption of external realism. So, for example, in the case of perceptual knowledge episodes, the truth constraint is generally explained in terms of perceptual cognitions corresponding to, or being in accord with real, external objects. Dharmottara, for instance, argues that the deceptiveness of various experiences can be explained by virtue of the fact that the corresponding external objects do not exist. In cases of visual illusion, such as when (for a person who's eyesight is bad) there is an appearance as of a double moon, or when (for a person who is standing on moving boat) there is an appearance as of moving trees, Dharmottara affirms that there is a lack of accordance between the cognition and real things in these cases, because "a double moon and moving trees do not exist in external reality."[24] Genuine instances of perceptual knowledge, by contrast, do exhibit this accordance with real, external things.

How this account of correspondence with real things is to be extended to cases of conceptual and inferential episodes of knowledge is a more delicate matter that will not be discussed here. Nevertheless, the idea that all episodes of knowledge, whether perceptual or conceptual, must exhibit a correspondence or accordance between the cognition and the objects known is a central feature of the Buddhist account. In this way, while the Dharmakīrtian account of knowledge is not a Platonic analysis containing an independent truth condition, it does nonetheless bring with it a 'truth constraint' on knowledge.

2.4.3. Justification

The first two elements of the standard analysis of knowledge, belief and truth, are relatively uncontroversial in contemporary epistemology. Determining *what else* is required for propositional knowledge over and above having a true belief is a much more hotly debated matter. The standard analysis affirms that what is required over and above a true belief is that the belief in question be justified. What "justification" means in this context, and what its properties are, is frequently left unspecified. Edmund Gettier, when laying out the standard analysis, identifies two basic features of justified belief, both of which, though they could be questioned, are still largely accepted by philosophers when discussing the notion of justification.[25] The first property of justification is that it is mutually consistent with the falsity of one's belief. That is, it is possible for a belief that *p* to be justified even in a situation where *p* is false.[26] I might, for example, be justified in believing, based on a large body of evidence, that person *A* murdered person *B*, and yet be flat-out wrong. We can call this first property *justification fallibilism*. Second, Gettier assumes that justified belief is something that is passed on by, or transmitted through, known entailments. Simplifying slightly, his assumption is that if I am justified in believing *p*, and I know that *p* entails *q*, then I am justified in believing *q*. Let us call this property the *deductive closure of justification*. (The so-called Gettier problem arises directly from these two assumptions about the nature of justification.[27])

I have already declared in chapter 1 that the Buddhist tradition of epistemology does not make use of a concept equivalent to that of justification, at least not as that concept plays out in Gettier's formulation of the standard analysis. We are now in a position to see why that is the case. It is because the relevant concepts in the Buddhist epistemological tradition are all ones that entail the correctness or truth of a cognition. For example, the core notion of "nondeceptiveness" is one that entails truth or correctness in the sense that whenever a person's cognition of *x* is nondeceptive, it is guaranteed that *x* exists and that the person's cognition is correct. So if one of the essential characteristics of justification is its fallibility, then we cannot understand the nondeceptiveness of cognition as playing a role parallel to the justification of a belief.

The aforementioned point generalizes. Many contemporary philosophers now eschew the idea that knowledge requires the justification of one's beliefs. Philosophers have supplanted the property of justification with other properties that, while different from justification, are supposed to play relevantly similar roles in their analyses of knowledge. Alvin Plantinga, for example, popularized the idea of *warranted* belief. Likewise, Alvin Goldman and others have supported an appeal to the *reliability* of belief. Yet, as long as these notions are consistent with falsity—that is, as long as a warranted belief could be false, or a reliable belief-forming process could yield a false belief in some instance—we have good reason to conclude that those notions do not capture the same sense as that associated with Dharmakīrti's appeal to the nondeceptiveness of cognition. Again, this is due to the fact that a nondeceptive cognition, as understood by Dharmakīrti and his followers, is one that entails correctness or truth, whereas the properties of warrant and reliability are generally agreed to be fallible.[28]

It would be instructive to reflect on this point more formally. The standard analysis proclaims that three features are necessary and jointly sufficient for knowledge: (i) *p* is true, (ii) S believes that *p*, and (iii) S is justified in believing that *p*. The justification condition, (iii), can be replaced by some other condition, one specifying that the belief in question must possess some property Q. The property Q could be the property of warrant or the property of reliability, and so on. No matter what that property Q is, as long as it is logically independent of the belief's truth—that is, as long as the property Q is logically consistent with the falsity of belief—the property Q will not play a role analogous to that of nondeceptiveness, given how that latter property is understood by Dharmakīrti and his followers in the Buddhist tradition of epistemology. For, on the Buddhist account of knowledge episodes, the nondeceptiveness of cognition is a feature that guarantees truth or correctness.

In this way, no separate condition of truth or correctness of cognition is required for knowledge in the Buddhist tradition. As noted in the preceding section, having an episode of knowledge does indeed *entail* that one's cognition is true/correct, but knowledge episodes are not analyzed as cognitions that are true and meet some further condition independent of truth. Instead, an episode of knowledge is just a cognition having the quality of being nondeceptive, where this quality requires a law-like connection to the truth.

One consequence of such an understanding is that the Buddhist tradition of epistemology may not be susceptible to instances of the Gettier problem. The original examples provided by Gettier of cases where a person has a justified true belief and yet still (intuitively) lacks knowledge were situations that hinged on a person possessing other beliefs that are justified and yet false. But as Linda Zagzebski has noted, modified versions of the Gettier problem can be constructed in any account on which the truth requirement for knowledge is logically independent of whatever other property or set of properties a belief must possess in order to suffice for knowledge. As she points out, "If knowledge is true belief + x, it does not matter whether x is identified with justification, reliability, proper function, intellectual virtue, or something else . . . The problem arises out of the *relation* between x and the truth in any definition according to which it is possible to have a false belief that is x."[29]

What all of this means is that the Buddhist account of knowledge that stems from Dharmakīrti and is refined by later Buddhist epistemologists is one that cannot be assimilated to any analysis of knowledge in which *both* of the following are the case:

(a) the truth of one's belief/cognition is included as an independent necessary condition for knowledge, and
(b) the only additional property or properties required of beliefs/cognitions are ones that are logically consistent with falsity/error.

In turn, this implies that the Buddhist account not only does not fit with the justified true belief analysis of knowledge, it likewise cannot be assimilated to any reliabilist theory in which reliable belief is still fallible.

2.5. *Pramāṇa* and Reliabilism

The preceding point is one that needs to be emphasized. It has become somewhat common—though far from overwhelmingly so—within recent scholarship on Buddhist philosophy to characterize the classical Buddhist account of *pramāṇa* as a version of reliabilism. This view is found, most prominently, in the collection *Moonshadows: Conventional Truth in Buddhist Philosophy*, where the term *pramāṇa* is translated variously as "reliable epistemic instrument," "means of reliable cognition," or simply as "reliable cognition."[30] A similar translation of *pramāṇa* is adopted in Christian Coseru's *Perceiving Reality: Consciousness, Intentionality, and Cognition in Buddhist Philosophy*.[31] In that work, *pramāṇas* are described as "sources of reliable cognition" or as "reliable cognitions." The relationship between Buddhist accounts of *pramāṇa* and contemporary reliabilism is made explicit by Jay Garfield in his 2015 book *Engaging Buddhism: Why It Matters to Philosophy*. There, Garfield directly characterizes Buddhist *pramāṇa* theorists as "classical reliablists [*sic*]" and suggests that we might view their theory as a kind of process reliabilism.[32]

This assimilation of Buddhist accounts of knowledge episodes to contemporary reliabilist theories of knowledge is, I believe, a mistake. That is not to impugn, of course, the three books just referenced. They are all excellent works of scholarship on Buddhist philosophy. I also do not mean to deny that there are similarities between classical Indian appeals to "instruments of knowledge" and contemporary reliabilist appeals to "belief-forming processes." But we must be incredibly cautious about attributing a version of reliabilism to classical Buddhist epistemologists.

How widely the label of "reliabilism" can or should be extended to different theories of knowledge (or theories of warrant or justification) is up for debate. As Alvin Goldman notes, " 'reliabilism' is sometimes used broadly to refer to any theory that emphasizes truth-getting or truth indicating properties. More commonly it is used narrowly to refer to process reliabilism about justification."[33] Goldman's own (1975 and 1979) versions of process reliabilism should, without question, be considered reliabilist accounts of knowledge. Whether, however, all causal theories of knowledge count as versions of reliabilism is much less certain. Likewise, the label of reliabilism is sometimes extended to accounts like Robert Nozick's truth-tracking theory of knowledge, and sometimes also to the broader set of theories that endorse either a sensitivity or safety condition for knowledge. The question of whether these latter theories should be included as examples of epistemic reliabilism is far from easy to answer, except as a matter of *fiat*. Yet it is precisely because of this vagueness about how widely the term "reliabilism" can or should be extended that we should be careful about making attributions of "reliability" or "reliabilism" to Buddhist theories of knowledge. In particular, to speak of the Buddhist account of *pramāṇa* as a version of reliabilism may serve to obscure important features of the Buddhist account of knowledge, while also encouraging mistaken assumptions about the Buddhist approach toward epistemology.

The most standard version of reliabilism, Goldman's *process reliabilism*, appeals to the idea of a reliable belief-forming process, which he speaks of as a kind of functional operation that produces as its outputs states of belief. The reliability of such a belief-forming process consists in its "tendency . . . to produce beliefs that are true rather than false." Goldman is clear that this reliability is associated with a mere *tendency* to produce true beliefs and not with a logical guarantee that true beliefs are produced. As he puts it:[34]

> we might ask how reliable a belief-forming process must be in order that its resultant beliefs be justified. A precise answer to this question should not be expected. Our conception of justification is vague in this respect. It does seem clear, however, that perfect reliability isn't required. Belief-forming processes that sometimes produce error still confer justification. It follows that there can be justified beliefs that are false.

Similar claims along these lines can be found in other authors' versions of process reliabilism. In this respect, the most standard version of reliabilism is generally taken to be a *fallibilistic* theory, inasmuch as a belief can be reliably formed (and thus "justified" or "warranted") and yet also be false.

This all stands in sharp contrast to the Buddhist account of knowledge episodes that is associated with Dharmakīrti (and that is itself borne out of earlier Indian accounts of *pramāṇa*). Buddhist philosophers emphatically do not adopt a fallibilistic account of *pramāṇa* nor a fallibilistic conception of nondeceptiveness. As has been stated earlier, Dharmakīrti's notion of "nondeceptiveness" is one that entails the truth or correctness of one's cognition. Thus, to translate the term *pramāṇa* as "reliable epistemic instrument" or as "reliable cognition" may wrongly suggest that *pramāṇas* are cognitions that *tend* to be true/correct, but only fallibly so; and this is simply not an accurate account of what Buddhist epistemologists historically supported.

As I have stated already in section 2.3.4, the Buddhist account of *pramāṇa* is one in which the nondeceptiveness of a cognition can be said to consist in its *invariably tracking the truth*. Episodes of knowledge are cognitions in which there is a *law-like guarantee* of the cognitions' correctness. Now, in speaking of a law-like guarantee of a cognition's correctness, what I am suggesting is that there are broad similarities between the Dharmakīrtian account of knowledge episodes and David Armstrong's "thermometer" account of noninferential knowledge—an account that makes an explicit appeal to "a *law-like connection* between the state of affairs Bap [i.e., person *a*'s belief that *p*] and the state of affairs that makes 'p' true."[35] Armstrong pursues the analogy of knowledge being likened to the reliability of a thermometer. He acknowledges that a good or reliable thermometer may sometimes (in some environments) provide incorrect readings of the temperature. But when pressed on the question of whether knowledge requires *absolute* reliability or just a weaker form of probabilistic reliability (like that found in Goldman's theory), Armstrong finds himself compelled toward the former, infallibilist position. He opts for a strict account in which, whenever a person knows something (noninferentially, at least), there is a law-like connection between the person's belief and the state of affairs believed. As he puts it, "The moral I draw is that, for knowledge, the belief in question must strictly ensure truth."[36]

A similar position is adopted by Buddhist epistemologists. Cognitions are not, in general, infallible. After all, a person can have erroneous sensory cognitions and can form incorrect judgments about the world. But there are, according to the Buddhist account, a select subset of cognitions, those that are *pramāṇas*, which do carry with them the guarantee of truth or correctness. And in an important sense these *pramāṇas*, or episodes of knowledge, constitute a special type of cognition—a type that could not occur without being correct. This understanding of knowledge is, I would contend, importantly different from what is found in standard reliabilist theories of knowledge. It is much closer in structure to the *factive mental state* theory of knowledge that has been defended by Timothy Williamson. As Williamson states, "To know is not merely to believe while various other conditions are met; it is to be in a new kind of state, a factive one."[37] In fact, on this very point, Williamson's account reaches a conclusion that Armstrong himself had toyed with thirty years earlier, when Armstrong mused, "We might read it as 'Knowledge is a state of mind which as a matter of law-like necessity ensures that p.'"[38] It is this approach toward knowledge that bears the strongest resemblance to the Buddhist account of knowledge associated with Dharmakīrti and his followers.

Further Reading

For a clear treatment of how Dharmakīrti's definitions of *pramāṇa* are understood by his later interpreters, see Dreyfus, G. (1991). Dharmakīrti's definition of *pramāṇa* and its interpreters. In E. Steinkellner (Ed.), *Studies in the Buddhist epistemological tradition: Proceedings of the second international Dharmakīrti conference, Vienna, June 11–16, 1989*. Vienna: Austrian Academy of Sciences Press.

For a careful philological discussion of Dharmakīrti's purported definitions of *pramāṇa*, see chapter 2 of Franco, E. (1997). *Dharmakīrti on compassion and rebirth*. Vienna: Arbeitskreis für Tibetische und Buddhistische Studien.
For an earlier discussion of Indian epistemology in relation to the standard analysis of knowledge, see Potter, K. (1984). Does Indian epistemology concern justified true belief? *Journal of Indian Philosophy*, *12*, 307–327.

3
Perception

As has been mentioned repeatedly in the first two chapters, classical Buddhist epistemologists contend that there are two main types of knowledge episodes; there is perceptual knowledge and inferential knowledge. Though Buddhist epistemologists from the time of Dignāga onward are concerned with establishing that these are *the only* two *pramāṇas*, relatively little attention is given to *proving* that perception is a legitimate source of knowledge. Instead, it is largely taken for granted within the Indian tradition of philosophy that perception is indeed a source of knowledge. As such, when writing about perceptual knowledge, Buddhist epistemologists like Dignāga and Dharmakīrti are mainly concerned, first, with providing an explanatory account of how perceptual cognition works—that is, with detailing its central components—and, second, with demarcating the scope of perceptual knowledge.

A full presentation of the accounts of perception adopted by Dignāga and Dharmakīrti could fill several hundred pages. Given the introductory nature of this book, our focus shall be on the two broad topics just mentioned. In the first section of this chapter, I will talk through the basic features of the Buddhist account of perceptual awareness (*pratyakṣa*), discussing both the cognitive basis of perception and the objects of perception. The remaining sections of the chapter will be dedicated to exploring various questions about the scope of perceptual experience. This includes not just detailing the various forms of perception that are accepted by classical Buddhist epistemologists but also exploring possible cases of nonconceptual experience that fall outside the scope of perception.

Illuminating the Mind. Jonathan Stoltz, Oxford University Press (2021). © Oxford University Press.
DOI: 10.1093/oso/9780190907532.003.0003

3.1. Perception and Nonconceptual Awareness

3.1.1. Nonconceptual Cognition

As this chapter progresses, readers will see that Dignāga and Dharmakīrti do not agree on all details about the nature of perceptual cognition. In fact, they appear to disagree on some relatively fundamental points. Let us begin, however, with two basic points on which these two philosophers do agree. First, Dignāga, Dharmakīrti, and all their Buddhist followers agree that all cognitions have some object, in the broadest sense of the term "object." All cognitions are cognitions *of* something. This does not mean that the objects of cognition must be real things or that these objects must exist external to or independent of the mind; and they are certainly not committed to anything approaching a "Meinongian" treatment of objects' existence.[1] The point is simply that all cognitions have an object in the minimal sense that for all cognitions it is appropriate to speak of the object cognized.

With respect to the object of perception, Dignāga is fully clear in his view that perceptual cognitions differ from inferential cognitions in the kinds of objects that are cognized. Episodes of perceptual knowledge have as their objects *particular* entities (*svalakṣaṇas*), whereas episodes of inferential knowledge have as their objects *general* entities (*sāmānyalakṣaṇas*). Though Dignāga takes it for granted that there are only these two kinds of objects, and though he maintains that perceptual cognitions concern only the former type of objects—particular entities—he does not define perceptual cognitions in terms of the objects cognized. Rather, Dignāga's principal characterization of perception is formulated in terms of the specific *activities* that occur (or can occur) within that form of mentation. On this topic, the standard Buddhist view, which is shared by both Dignāga and Dharmakīrti, is that perceptual cognitions are mental episodes that are entirely free of conceptual construction (*kalpanā*). This is made explicit in the third verse of Dignāga's *Compendium of Knowledge*, where he categorically asserts that "Perception is free from conceptual construction."[2]

Immediately after characterizing perception as being free from conceptual activity, Dignāga goes on to tell his readers that conceptual construction is "the association of name, kind, etc."[3] This implies, at the very least, that in a moment of perceptual cognition, there can be no categorization of the cognition's object as being of any kind or type. For example, when perceiving a swatch of blue color, one is incapable of categorizing the perceived object as being 'blue' or as being 'sky blue.' These associations of color kinds require conceptual activities of the mind, and thus cannot occur in episodes of perception on Dignāga's account. Likewise, with respect to a perceptual cognition of a swatch of blue, linguistic attributions, such as calling the object "blue" or calling it "sky blue," could not occur, as these sorts of verbal attributions require conceptuality as well.

Insofar as perceptual cognitions are deemed to be entirely devoid of these sorts of conceptual activities, there is an important sense in which perception is, for Dignāga, a largely if not entirely *passive* process. Perceptual cognitions do *apprehend* an object, but additional active cognitive processes do not occur in episodes of perception. In this way, it is accurate to characterize perceptual knowledge—at least as understood by Dignāga—as an episode of *raw sensation*. It is "raw" in the sense that, while an object appears to or is apprehended by the cognition, no additional interpretive activities are carried out by the mind. When looking at a blue cloth, for example, a person's perception is constituted by the mere visual sense experience of blue, but without identifying or categorizing the object as being blue. To the extent that this is the case, some scholars have opted to translate the relevant Sanskrit term, *pratyakṣa*, not as "perception" but as "sensation."[4] The use of the term "sensation" does indeed help to communicate the fact that, for Dignāga, perception is a passive mental process that is devoid of conceptual activities. Yet, as we shall see later, for Dignāga as for all later Buddhist epistemologists, the category of perception includes not just cognitions tied to one's five senses but also other forms of nonconceptual mentation extending beyond the five senses. For this reason, I shall continue to speak of this general form of cognition as "perception." Nevertheless, it is important to keep track of the fact that, for Dignāga and other Buddhist epistemologists, perceptual knowledge is something along the lines of a raw sensing of an object.

With respect to Dignāga's characterization of perception as being "free from conceptual construction," it is critical to make one related note. Of the two forms of knowledge accepted by Buddhist epistemologists—perception and inference—perception is devoid of conceptual construction, whereas inferential cognitions necessarily involve conceptuality. But, as will be discussed in the next chapter, while all episodes of inferential knowledge involve conceptuality, not all conceptual cognitions are instances of inferential knowledge. There are, as we will see, plenty of conceptual cognitions that fail to deliver knowledge. With respect to nonconceptual cognitions, however, there is strong evidence that Dignāga understood *all* nonconceptual cognitions to be instances of perception—and, hence, episodes of knowledge. In short, on Dignāga's account, perception is *identified with* nonconceptual cognition (whereas inferential knowledge is only a proper subset of conceptual cognition). We will see momentarily, however, that Dharmakīrti and later Buddhist epistemologists move away from Dignāga's position on this matter.

3.1.2. The Objects of Perception and Metaphysics

Given the earlier discussion, we can see that perceptual knowledge, for Dignāga, consists in having a nonconceptual episode of cognition—a raw sensation. But this cannot be the whole story, for there must be some object that is cognized. On the one hand, Dignāga is clear that episodes of perception cognize particular entities (*svalakṣaṇas*). On the other hand, insofar as perception is a raw sensation, we might think that the objects of perception are thus to be understood as *sense-data*. Here, by "sense-data," I am referring to the objects of immediate awareness as described by proponents of the sense-data theory of perception found within the Anglo-American tradition of philosophy. The sense-data theory is generally treated as a form of *indirect realism* about perception, wherein it can be held that perceptual knowledge of extramental objects is attainable, but only indirectly, through one's interaction with sense-data. Indeed, a number of prominent scholars of Buddhist epistemology do characterize Dignāga's theory of perception as a kind of sense-data theory, and they also speak of the direct objects of perception being "sense-data." This view is defended, for example, by Richard Hayes in his excellent and detailed presentation of Dignāga's philosophical views.[5]

In standard Anglo-American sense-data theories of perception, the *direct objects* of perception, sense-data, are taken to be mental objects. But sense-data theories are consistent with the affirmation that real, external (i.e., extramental) things are the *indirect objects* of perception. And so it can be asked whether this is true of the Buddhist epistemological tradition as well. Do Dignāga and Dharmakīrti regard perception to provide humans with (indirect) access to external objects? It is here where we need to take a step back and confront a major element of complexity inherent in classical Buddhist epistemology.

Dignāga and Dharmakīrti are influenced by a broad range of philosophical predecessors in India, and the views that are propounded by those predecessors are not always consonant with one another. With respect to matters of metaphysics, some Buddhist philosophers defend a version of external realism in which (atomistic) external objects exist and can stand in causal relations with human minds and cognitions. This is the view adopted by proponents of the *Sautrāntika* system of Buddhist philosophy. Other Buddhist philosophers support an idealist metaphysics in which extramental objects do not exist, and in which the experience of a subject-object duality is derived from karmic tendencies internal to the mind. This kind of view is adopted by proponents of the *Yogācāra* system of Buddhist philosophy. It is not possible to reckon fully with Dignāga's and Dharmakīrti's accounts of the epistemology of perception without taking into account those philosophers' relationships to these two metaphysical systems.

Dignāga provides an account of perception in which the cognizer directly experiences only sense-data internal to the mind. But this leaves open the question as to whether such experiences of sense-data can provide one with (mediated) knowledge of external reality. To the extent that he is influenced by the views of the *Yogācāra* system, many scholars are now convinced that Dignāga does not think that perceptual knowledge can be had of extramental reality. Matters are much more ambiguous with regard to the views of Dharmakīrti, writing a century after Dignāga. In many places, it appears as though Dharmakīrti supports a version of external realism like that associated with the *Sautrāntika* system, and his explication of perception in many ways proceeds under the assumption of external realism. In some other places within his writing, however, Dharmakīrti appears to defend a *Yogācāra* interpretation in which perception is to be explained without any appeal to extramental reality.

As mentioned in chapter 1, this has led scholars in recent years to defend the position that Dharmakīrti must be understood as endorsing an "ascending scales of analysis" in which he does not exclusively write from the perspective of any single metaphysical system, but instead moves back and forth between external realism and idealism depending on the particular philosophical context at issue. Despite these "ascending scales of analysis," and despite the fact that most of Dharmakīrti's discussion is in alignment with the external realism of the *Sautrāntika* system, his ultimate position is that of the idealist. What is most important for our purposes, however, is the recognition that these background perspectives about the nature of reality have an important impact on how we are to understand Dharmakīrti's account of perceptual experience.

Dharmakīrti, like many other Buddhist philosophers, is inclined to support a causal theory of perception. On this sort of theory, a perceptual cognition is the result a causal process that depends on multiple causal conditions. These necessary conditions include the *object condition*, the *empowering condition*, and the *predecessor condition*.[6] Roughly speaking, these three conditions capture the essential roles played by (1) the object of perception, (2) the sense faculty, and (3) the immediately preceding cognitive episode, respectively. In order for a perceptual cognition to arise, there must be a real object—one that is causally efficacious—that interacts with a sense faculty. These two items, when combined with an immediately preceding moment of cognition, give rise to a perceptual experience.

More specifically, Dharmakīrti maintains that, owing to a causal process, the object cognized leaves an impression or "phenomenal form" (*ākāra*) on the cognition itself. This view that perceptual cognitions are imprinted with the phenomenal forms of their objects is widely accepted among Buddhist epistemologists, and it is also accepted by several non-Buddhist schools of Indian philosophy. It is natural to think of proponents of this view as being defenders of something akin to either a *sense-data* or *representationalist* theory of perception. Not all Indian schools accept such a view, however. Adherents to the Nyāya School of Indian logic defend an account of perception that does not involve an appeal to phenomenal forms or representations. As readers will see in a subsequent chapter, even some later Buddhist epistemologists in Tibet defend a naïve realist account of perception in which that form of cognition is explained without an appeal to phenomenal forms.[7] Dignāga, Dharmakīrti, and the vast majority of their Indian Buddhist followers, however, do support the view that the objects of perception leave a phenomenal imprint on a person's cognitions.[8]

This causal theory is important for a variety of reasons, at least two of which need to be addressed here. First, the causal theory cannot be delinked from one's understanding of the nature of reality external to the mind. Proponents of the *Sautrāntika* theory of external realism regularly elucidate the causal structure of sense perception, and the *object condition* that is necessary for such a perception, by way of an appeal to an external, and mind-independent, object. That is, it is frequently held that a perceptual cognition arises as a result of a real, external object interacting with a sense faculty.[9] The cognition that is produced has the phenomenal form of the external object that was its cause. Since the phenomenal form (*ākāra*), or sense-datum, that is produced is something that is mind dependent, this means that the direct object of perception is not an external object. Yet this causal theory allows that a real, external object can still be the indirect object of perception. That is, the causal theory is consistent with the view that one can perceive external objects, albeit indirectly. Expressed more carefully, and in accord with later Buddhist epistemologists, Dharmakīrti can maintain that, in an episode of perception, what is (directly) *experienced* is an internal sense-datum, but what is (indirectly) *apprehended* is an external object.

This all assumes, of course, a metaphysical framework in which mind-independent objects causally interact with sense powers. But for proponents of the idealist *Yogācāra* system of thought, this assumption is a nonstarter. A causal theory of perception can still be defended by metaphysical idealists, but the causal account does not involve a mind-independent object causally generating sense-data. Instead, the causal process is initiated solely by factors that are internal to the cognizer herself. In most places in his writing, Dharmakīrti espouses an account of perception that takes for granted the existence of external reality. Yet, in some other places, his arguments do not assume the existence of external objects and are supportive of an idealist metaphysical perspective.

As mentioned earlier, we need not fret over Dharmakīrti's prima facie inconsistent claims regarding the metaphysics of perception. Yet, because the vast majority of Dharmakīrti's claims about perception do appear to take for granted extramental objects, let us look at one additional, extremely important consequence associated with an indirect realist, causal account of perception.

3.1.3. Nonerroneous Cognition

Let us suppose for argument's sake that perceptual cognitions arise as a result of some sort of external object causally interacting with a sense power. This causal interaction, according to Dharmakīrti, gives rise to a cognition that is imprinted with the phenomenal form of the object that was its cause. But given this interpretation, perception consists of both a mental entity—a phenomenal form or sense-datum—and a mind-independent object. One might then ask about the nature of the relation between the internal phenomenal form and the external object. These two items are causally related, but to the extent that the phenomenal form is a representation of the external object, it is appropriate to ask whether that representation is (or must be) accurate.

More to the point, inasmuch as sense perception involves an external object as one of its causal conditions and an internal phenomenal form as part of the effect, perceptual experiences of this sort have what contemporary philosophers of mind call "accuracy conditions."[10]

Consider a hypothetical case in which a person has a visual experience as of a yellow conch shell. This experience is, let us assume, one in which the cognition is imprinted with a yellow phenomenal form. But let it further be assumed that this cognition was causally generated from an interaction with a real, mind-independent *white* conch shell. In short, a white external object has causally produced a yellow sense-datum. In such a circumstance there is a strong inclination to say that the cognition is inaccurate. But if it is an inaccurate visual experience—and yet still a nonconceptual experience—should it really be characterized as an episode of perception?

The philosophical point being raised here is a simple one. Given a causal theory of perceptual experience wherein external objects serve to causally produce cognitions imprinted with phenomenal forms, such cognitions can be assessed for accuracy. Yet it would appear to be possible for some of these causally generated cognitions not to be accurate. And if a given experience of this sort is not accurate, one might be strongly inclined to support the conclusion that the experience is not a genuine perception at all. (Such an experience is, perhaps, better classified as an instance of *sensory illusion*.)

Whereas Dignāga simply characterized perception as a cognition that is free from conceptual construction, Dharmakīrti modified his predecessor's characterization and instead defined perception as a cognition that is "*nonerroneous* and free from conceptual construction."[11] This qualifier that perception must be "non-erroneous" is, one can plainly see, a new addition. In the post-Dharmakīrtian period of Buddhist epistemology, this appeal to nonerroneousness becomes quite standard in philosophers' definitions of perception. Yet it is clear that Dignāga did not himself include this qualifier. Many scholars of Buddhist philosophy take this to indicate that Dignāga did not think that nonconceptual cognitions could be in error. Errors are possible, of course, but those errors must be, on this interpretation of Dignāga, tied to the conceptual activities of the mind. Examples of conceptual errors of this sort are not hard to identify. When looking at a coiled-up rope in the corner of a dark room, I may mischaracterize that rope as being a snake. Yet, when this mischaracterization occurs, the error is not due to my perceptual cognition. It is an error rooted in the conceptual judgment that I form subsequent to the sense experience.

Dharmakīrti, by contrast, is quite explicit in his view that nonconceptual cognitions can be erroneous. When, for example, a person with jaundice looks at a white conch shell, he may have a visual experience as of a yellow shell. According to Dharmakīrti, and setting aside any erroneous conceptual judgment that may be formed from this experience, the initial nonconceptual awareness this person has is in error as well. The process whereby a series of causal conditions—including the presence of an external object—leads to the production of an episode of cognition can sometimes be such that the object directly experienced fails to correspond with the external object that was its cause; and when this happens, the cognition is not an episode of perceptual knowledge at all.

Given an external realist metaphysics and a causal account of perception, it is not entirely surprising that Dharmakīrti deems it necessary to insert the qualifier "nonerroneous" within his definition of perception. Somewhat more surprising is the fact that Dignāga's definition, a century earlier, involved no reference to accuracy. This suggests that, on Dignāga's account, perception is not understood to be a representational state. From an idealist perspective, perception does not involve an external object at all, and thus there is no*thing* that is to be re-presented. On this idealist interpretation of Dignāga's account, perception does not even provide us with mediated knowledge of external reality; the only objects of perception are the sense-data themselves.

All this goes to show that the background presuppositions one has about the nature of reality have important impacts on philosophers' explications of perceptual cognition. But we should not let those presuppositions obscure a fundamental point: Dignāga's and Dharmakīrti's central concern is with articulating an adequate account of the *epistemology* of perception. Their accounts of perception are thus centrally focused on showing how perceptual knowledge arises and on determining the scope of perception. Matters pertaining to the metaphysics of perceptual objects are not unimportant, but they take on only a secondary importance for these philosophers in their epistemological treatises. This secondary status is reflected in the "ascending scales of analysis" interpretation of Dharmakīrti that is accepted by contemporary scholars. On that interpretation, Dharmakīrti moves from one ontological perspective to another—in some places accepting external realism, in other places supporting idealism—depending on the particular epistemological context in question. Alternatively, one could interpret Dharmakīrti's claims as supporting a single epistemological account, albeit one that seeks to be *consistent* with both external realism and idealism. Yet to the extent that this epistemological account is consistent with idealism, it could then be argued that knowledge of external reality thereby cannot be secured, which thus shows that the idealist position is the only ontological perspective that is fully defensible.[12]

3.2. Perceptual Judgment

Up to this point, it has been repeatedly emphasized that, according to Dignāga, Dharmakīrti, and their followers, perceptual cognitions are devoid of conceptual construction. While this position is widely accepted by Buddhist epistemologists, it is, to say the least, a controversial position—both within the Indian tradition of philosophy and in the contemporary analytic tradition of epistemology. Dignāga and Dharmakīrti craft their views of perception at least partly in response to the accounts of the Indian Nyāya School of philosophy. Recall that for Dignāga and his Buddhist successors, while I can, to take a basic example, perceive a blue object, I cannot in an episode of perceptual awareness *determine that* the object is blue. By contrast, proponents of the non-Buddhist Nyāya School of Indian thought contend that, while there are indeed still instances of raw sensation, there can also be episodes of perception that involve conceptual activity and have something like a propositional structure. For example, they allow that a person can perceive that an object is qualified by the universal 'blueness.' Even some Buddhist philosophers, albeit ones only tangentially connected to the Buddhist tradition of epistemology, appear to adopt the view that perceptions can be conceptual. The Buddhist thinker Candrakīrti (c. 570–640), for example, argues that, when we consider the ordinary ways in which people speak about perception, it makes little sense to proclaim (as Dignāga does) that perceptual knowledge is fundamentally nonconceptual.[13]

Within contemporary analytic epistemology, the central focus has long been on the status of propositional knowledge. This is true just as much for claims about perceptual knowledge as it is for rational judgments. It is common to see contemporary epistemologists proclaiming that, for example, a person can perceptually know *that there is a red barn along the side of the road*, or perceptually know *that there is a zebra in front of her*. Given this, the idea that perceptual knowledge must be nonconceptual is, in the minds of many analytic philosophers, a rather bizarre commitment. Classical Buddhist epistemologists do not, of course, deny that humans form concept-laden judgments as a result of sensory perceptions. What they deny is just that these judgments are genuinely instances of perceptual cognition.

It must be kept in mind that for Buddhist epistemologists what are at issue are momentary cognitive episodes. Instances of perceptual knowledge are held to be nonconceptual, but it is granted that these cognitive episodes can give rise to subsequent concept-laden judgments. For example, upon looking up toward a mountain pass I may have a perceptual cognition of smoke. This episode of perception is nonconceptual and, hence, the object perceived is not categorized as being a certain kind of thing—for example, as being smoke—nor are verbal attributions possible. Nevertheless, upon having such a perceptual experience, I may immediately thereafter form the judgment that there is smoke on the mountain pass. This judgment is indeed conceptual, and it can be characterized as being, roughly speaking, a kind of propositional cognition. Let us call these conceptual judgments that arise subsequent to episodes of perception *perceptual judgments*. Again, while I am characterizing these cognitions as "perceptual judgments," they are not, strictly speaking, instances of perception at all. Indian Buddhist epistemologists refer to these judgments as "ascertaining cognitions" or "determinate cognitions" (*niścayapratyaya*).

It is undeniable that perceptual judgments play a critical role in humans' cognitive lives. After all, these determinate cognitions serve an important function within ordinary processes of inferential reasoning. If I am cold and seeking warmth, the visual sensation of smoke coming from a chimney will serve me no practical benefit. I will be able to warm myself only after reasoning (inferring) that there is a fire burning in that location; and that reasoning makes use of the determinate cognition that there is smoke over there. Yet, despite the important role played by perceptual judgments in Buddhist epistemology, they are not, technically speaking, episodes of knowledge. The initial, nonconceptual visual experience of smoke is a *pramāṇa*—an episode of knowledge—but the subsequent conceptual judgment that there is smoke is not a *pramāṇa* at all.

That perceptual judgments do not qualify as episodes of knowledge is a consequence of the particular way in which the notion of a *pramāṇa* is understood in Buddhist epistemology. It may sound odd, for example, to affirm that the judgment that there is a white conch shell, formed immediately after visually sensing a white conch shell, is not an episode of knowledge. We must keep in mind, however, that on one standard interpretation a *pramāṇa* is understood to be a *source of knowledge*. Knowledge is attained in the initial (nonconceptual) perceptual cognition. The subsequent (conceptual) judgment that is formed a moment later is not a source of any new information. Recall also Dharmakīrti's second definition of *pramāṇa*, which states that an episode of knowledge is "the revealing of a state of affairs that is not [already] known." As was mentioned in chapter 2, this is interpreted by later Buddhist thinkers as indicating that episodes of knowledge must provide *new* information—but no new information is attained when a perceptual judgment is made immediately after a (nonconceptual) sensory cognition.

Much the same point can be made from a different angle by focusing on the causal activities of the cognitive episodes in question. Buddhist epistemologists maintain that it is the initial moment of (nonconceptual) perceptual experience that plays the dominant causal role in a person's subsequent actions toward the object cognized. For example, upon perceiving smoke, I (thereby) form the judgment that there is smoke on the mountain pass, deduce that there is fire on the mountain pass, and am thus positioned to act toward that object. Yet what prompts me to action, what plays the dominant causal role, is the initial, nonconceptual visual experience. It is that initial perceptual experience that serves to causally generate both my subsequent judgments and my action(s) to achieve the object desired, and thus it is just the initial perception that is the source of knowledge.[14]

This Buddhist understanding of perception, including its sharp distinction between the initial episode of nonconceptual perception and the succeeding episode(s) of concept-laden perceptual judgment, is quite different from how contemporary analytic philosophers understand perception. To the extent that contemporary epistemologists are focused on knowledge in relation to propositional attitudinal states—for example, the belief that *p*—there is a strong tendency to think of perception as a (perhaps multistage) process that essentially terminates in a propositional belief being formed. The perceptual belief-forming process also requires, presumably, some operation of one's sense faculties, but given the role played by propositional belief formation in this model of perceptual knowledge there is little attention paid to the distinction between nonconceptual (or preconceptual) processes and conceptual processes. The Buddhist account of perception stemming from Dignāga, by contrast, places significant weight on the contrast between nonconceptual episodes of cognition and episodes of cognition that contain conceptual construction.

It should also be pointed out that, in some cases, the conceptual judgment that a person forms immediately after some sensory experience can be mistaken or incorrect. For instance, when I peer into a dark room and look at what is actually a coiled-up rope, my visual experience may be perfectly accurate. But if I were to subsequently judge that there is a snake in the room, my judgment in such a case would be mistaken. Given that the judgment is incorrect, it cannot qualify as an episode of knowledge. By contrast, the kinds of cases that are at issue here, perceptual judgments, are assumed to be *correct* determinate cognitions; and the claim is that even these correct judgments do not qualify as episodes of knowledge.

3.3. Four Types of Perception

Thus far, our discussion of perception has focused entirely on sensory cognitions—on cognitive episodes produced in dependence on any of a person's five basic sense faculties: vision, hearing, smell, taste, and touch. This is not surprising. The most intuitive examples of perception are those involving knowledge tied to one's five senses, and especially to visual sensation. Appeals to visual perception are exceedingly common both in contemporary analytic philosophy and in traditional Buddhist epistemological treatises. Though, as we will see shortly, Buddhist epistemologists accept the existence of various forms of perception above and beyond the five senses, the most standard examples of perceptual cognitions that are provided in Buddhist texts are sensory cases. In particular, the "go to" examples tend to be episodes like *seeing* the color blue and *hearing* a sound.

Nevertheless, given that episodes of perceptual knowledge are simply defined as (nonerroneous) nonconceptual cognitions, there is nothing that prohibits additional forms of perception above and beyond those that are tied to the five senses. In the post-Dharmakīrtian period of Buddhist epistemology in India and Tibet, there is widespread agreement that four distinct forms of perception can be identified:

1. Sense perception
2. Mental perception
3. Reflexive perception
4. Yogic perception

Though this fourfold division of perception has long been standard in Buddhist epistemology, there is still a great deal of historical disagreement about the origins of this typology. In particular, while Dharmakīrti is explicit in his acceptance of these four forms of perception, it is far from clear whether his predecessor Dignāga agreed to this same typology. The dispute hinges on the status of reflexive perception (*svasaṃvedana*)—frequently called "self-awareness"—and on whether Dignāga believed it to constitute a distinct type of perception, or whether self-awareness is merely to be understood as a feature or quality present in all cognitions. If the latter is the case, then Dignāga can be interpreted as propounding a threefold division of perception—one consisting of sense perception, mental perception, and yogic perception.[15]

How we are to understand the status of reflexive perception in Dignāga's system is partly a philosophical question, but it is also, to a large extent, a *philological* question. Much of the dispute is tied to interpretive difficulties in understanding what Dignāga meant by self-awareness, mental perception, and the relationship between the two. Contributing to this interpretive difficulty is the fact that Dignāga's writing is incredibly terse—and especially so on this issue. Furthermore, there is some question as to whether Dignāga's original language concerning these forms of perception was faithfully reproduced in later transcriptions and translations of his *Compendium of Knowledge*.

Related to this dispute over whether there are three or four distinct kinds of perceptual cognition is the question of how we are to understand the operation of mental perception. It is standard in Buddhist philosophy to conceive of the sense faculties as being sixfold: the five external sense faculties—vision, hearing, smell, taste, and touch—plus an internal, mental sense faculty. Given this basic framework, it is reasonable to think of mental perception as the kind of perception that arises in dependence on the mental sense faculty. But this does not entirely resolve the status of mental perception, for it does not indicate what objects are known or knowable via mental perception. On an external realist account of perception, the five standard sense faculties provide knowledge of external objects. By parallel reasoning, one could hold that mental perception is the form of cognition whereby a person gains knowledge of "internal" objects—such as one's mental events. Something in the neighborhood of this understanding appears to be accepted by Dignāga, for whom mental perception includes a person's awareness of his or her own acts of mentation. These mental events include, according to Dignāga, things like desires, pleasures, and pains.

Matters are understood differently by Dharmakīrti, for whom the very relationship between mental perception and reflexive perception is quite different. Our awareness of our own mentation comes, for Dharmakīrti, through the operation of reflexive perception and not from mental perception. Mental perception, on Dharmakīrti's view, is restricted to a person's nonconceptual episode of awareness that follows immediately after an instance of (external) sense perception. For example, suppose that I perceive blue via my visual sense faculty. That initial cognitive awareness of blue then serves as a causal factor for the production of a subsequent moment of (nonconceptual) awareness—a mental perception.[16]

Much like in the case of mental perception, the epistemological status of yogic perception is also subject to various interpretations. At its simplest, yogic perception is an episode of nonerroneous awareness that arises not as a result of a causal interaction between an object and the senses, but instead as a result of the cultivation of certain meditative activities. Although the contemplative process that leads up to an episode of yogic perception will no doubt involve instances of conceptual reasoning, the adept's meditation culminates in a nonconceptual awareness of the object that is cognized.[17] The standard example that Dharmakīrti provides of an object known by an adept through yogic perception is the seeing of the Four Noble Truths.

As described, yogic perception is quite unlike standard cases of sense perception, where the particular object that is cognized plays a direct causal role in the production of the cognition. Nevertheless, these yogic cognitions have two features that ensure their status as episodes of knowledge. First, any yogic perception must be a "correct" cognition; and as such it is a *nonerroneous* cognition. In addition, according to Dharmakīrti's account, yogic perception reveals its objects with a distinctness or vividness that is incompatible with conceptual construction; and so it is regarded to be a form of *nonconceptual* cognition. Since these yogic cognitions are both nonerroneous and nonconceptual, they are, therefore, to be characterized as episodes of perception.

To be clear, yogic perception is not merely an accidentally correct intuition about reality. Given its status as a *pramāṇa*, it must be a nondeceptive cognition—one that invariably tracks the truth. Yet one might think that this is controversial claim to make. It is far easier to see how sensory perception can yield a cognition that invariably tracks the truth. In the case of sense perception the cognition is produced as a result of a causal interaction between the object and the sense faculty. That such a causal process can generate a truth-tracking cognition is not so mysterious. But in the case of yogic perception there is no causal interaction between the object and any sense faculty. And yet, according to Dharmakīrti, the cognitive awareness of the meditative adept is such that his or her apprehension of certain objects and states of affairs somehow still invariably tracks the truth.[18]

Given what has been said earlier, some readers may be skeptical of attributing positive epistemic status to yogic perception. In fact, this skepticism may be similar to that which many contemporary analytic epistemologists display toward hypothetical cases of reliable clairvoyance. Buddhist accounts of yogic perception are, it must be pointed out, quite different from contemporary epistemologists' expositions of clairvoyance, but skeptical worries about these two purported sources of knowledge may be seen as similar. Some contemporary philosophers, especially those who are critical of reliabilist accounts of knowledge, entertain examples of persons possessing clairvoyant powers whose beliefs (on certain matters) reliably track the truth, but for whom the reliability therein is portrayed as a kind of mystery.[19] Clairvoyance is presented as a kind of intuitive apprehension of the truth that comes neither from sensory awareness nor from logical reasoning. Critics of epistemic reliabilism point toward theoretical cases of clairvoyance so as to show that there is something fundamentally insufficient about a belief-forming process that delivers reliably correct beliefs but does so with a total lack of evidential backing.

Concerns about yogic perception in the Buddhist tradition are not altogether different from these worries about clairvoyance. Dignāga, Dharmakīrti, and other Buddhist epistemologists agree that yogic perception is nondeceptive and thus a form of knowledge, but its status as a nondeceptive cognition that invariably tracks the truth was controversial within India. Various non-Buddhist thinkers in India rejected Dharmakīrti's claims about yogic perception. The Mīmāṃsā philosopher Kumārila Bhatta, for example, argued that the Buddhist's yogic perception cannot be a *pramāṇa*, for the cognitions would seem to arise in much the same fashion as do episodes of hallucination. After all, in yogic perception there is no direct causal contact with the object that is said to be cognized. Thus, yogic perception appears to have a status much like that of hallucination. Indeed, Dharmakīrti does himself note the similarities between yogic perception and hallucination or the confused visions of a deranged person.[20] Yet Dharmakīrti contends that, by virtue of the precise ways that yogic meditation works, the adept's meditative practices culminate in experiences that prove to be efficacious, and thus are reliably correct, unlike the experiences of a deranged person.

3.4. Reflexive Perception and Self-Awareness

While mental perception and yogic perception play only a small role in the broader context of Buddhist epistemology, matters are completely different with respect to reflexive perception (*svasaṃvedana*). This form of cognition has an outsized role in Buddhist accounts of the mind. From the time of Dignāga onward, Buddhist epistemologists have stood in agreement that all episodes of cognition have a kind of reflexive character to them. In addition to apprehending its object, each episode of cognition serves to reveal itself. What there is disagreement over is how precisely this self-revelatory aspect of cognition is to be understood. As we have already seen, Dharmakīrti explicitly conceives of a cognition's ability to reveal itself as a distinct form of perception—reflexive perception. It is far less clear whether Dignāga shared this understanding. Dignāga agrees that all cognitions are reflexively aware of themselves, but it is not obvious that he conceived of the self-revelatory aspect of cognition as itself constituting a discreet kind of cognition.

Dharmakīrti, however, very clearly treats reflexive awareness as a distinct form of perceptual cognition. It is, as Dharmakīrti explicitly states, the kind of perception that reveals the mind and all mental factors. Given this understanding of reflexive perception, and given that all cognitions have this reflexive dimension, there is a temptation to think of reflexive perception as a specific form of cognition that accompanies all episodes of cognition. For example, when forming the concept-laden judgment that there is a fire on a far-off mountain pass, this conceptual cognition is, on this view, accompanied by the (nonconceptual) reflexive awareness of one's conceptual cognition of fire on the mountain pass. While no single cognition can, on pain of contradiction, be both conceptual and nonconceptual, it is possible to accommodate the co-occurrence of one conceptual cognition and one nonconceptual cognition by thinking of these as two discreet, but simultaneous, cognitions.

An understanding along the earlier lines does appear to be accepted by various Indian and Tibetan Buddhist epistemologists, but this interpretation is neither universally accepted nor without philosophical difficulties. An alternative view is to understand the reflexivity found in all cognitions not as a distinct type of cognition (nor type of perception) but merely as a *feature* that is universally present in cognition. It is generally agreed by Buddhist epistemologists that all cognitions—correct and incorrect cognitions, conceptual and nonconceptual cognitions—are inherently self-aware in the sense that they reveal themselves. But this property of being inherently self-aware need not imply that self-awareness is a sui generis type of cognition. This latter understanding, which interprets self-awareness as not as a distinct type of perception but just as a pervasive feature of cognition, has in recent years been characterized as capturing a "*constitutive* understanding of self-awareness."[21]

Regardless of whether one adopts the constitutive understanding or the perceptual understanding of reflexivity, Buddhist epistemologists agree that all cognitions have a dual role. There is both the apprehension of an object of cognition and the apprehension of the cognition itself. This twofold apprehension is explained by Dharmakīrti as involving two kinds of phenomenal aspects (*ākāra*)—an objective aspect and a subjective aspect. The subjective aspect of cognition is the cognition's appearance to itself—its self-awareness. The objective aspect of cognition is the appearance of the phenomenal form that represents a (potentially) external object. As explained in section 3.1 earlier, Buddhist epistemologists like Dignāga and Dharmakīrti deny that external objects are experienced directly. At best, they are known indirectly by way of internal phenomenal forms, which are the objective aspects of cognition. But it is not merely these objective aspects that appear to cognition, for the cognition itself appears; and that appearance is by way of the subjective aspect.

Scholars' understandings of Buddhist accounts of reflexive perception (or self-awareness) have advanced markedly in the past twenty years or so. Be that as it may, the topic is one for which a better understanding is still needed. There is nothing close to a consensus scholarly view on how exactly to understand the views of Dignāga and Dharmakīrti on this issue. This is, to be completely fair, not terribly surprising, given that Buddhist epistemologists in India and Tibet writing in the centuries after Dharmakīrti did not necessarily share any broad agreement on how the reflexivity of cognition is to be understood. Recent scholars of Buddhist philosophy have suggested possible Western analogs for Buddhist account of self-awareness. Dan Arnold has proposed that the Buddhist's self-awareness be understood along the lines of Immanuel Kant's notion of *apperception*.[22] Christian Coseru, by contrast, thinks of the reflexivity of cognition as being similar to Merleau-Ponty's understanding of *embodied self-awareness*.[23] It is far beyond the scope of this book to make any assessment about the viability of either of these interpretations. The point, rather, is to show that current understandings of the Buddhist notion of reflexive perception (*svasaṃvedana*) are still incomplete and thus subject to a wide range of possible analogs.

3.5. Perception, Illusion, and Hallucination

In Indian epistemology, as understood by both Buddhists and non-Buddhists, perception is a success term: Given its status as a *pramāṇa*, all episodes of perception must be correct cognitions. Yet, as we have seen earlier in this chapter, since perceptual cognitions are typically understood to be the outcomes of causal processes, it may be possible for these causal processes to result, on occasion, in *incorrect* cognitions. It is, therefore, not surprising that Dharmakīrti and later Buddhist epistemologists speak of perception as a *nonerroneous* form of nonconceptual cognition. Nonconceptual cognitions that are erroneous, however, align with what are now typically called illusions and/or hallucinations.

As portrayed by contemporary philosophers of mind, the broad category of 'perceptual experiences' consists of three subcategories: (veridical) perceptions, illusions, and hallucinations. Veridical perceptions are the success cases. Illusions are experiences for which there is a genuine external stimulus, but in which the experience—or the representational character of the experience—does not correspond to the reality of object that was its cause. For example, a person falls prey to an illusion when two tabletops of identical size appear as being differently shaped (one longer and narrower than the other) due to their particular (vertical vs. horizontal) orientations. Hallucinations, by contrast, are understood to be cases of perceptual error where there is no external stimulus at all responsible for one's experience. This could happen as a result of, perhaps, the degeneration of one's sense organs—as with Charles Bonnet syndrome—or as a result of taking psychedelic drugs, and so on.[24]

In the case of Buddhist epistemology, while perceptions are by necessity veridical experiences, philosophers from the time of Dharmakīrti onward believe that nonconceptual error is possible. The examples of nonconceptual error that Dharmakīrti provides include both instances of illusion and of hallucination, though no such explicit distinction is made between these two kinds of cases. Among the most commonly cited examples of nonconceptual error in later Buddhist epistemological literature are those of (a) a white conch shell appearing yellow to a person with jaundice and (b) trees appearing as though they are moving to a person traveling down a river on a boat. Both of these examples fall into the category of illusion, for there is in both these cases an external object that brings about the nonveridical experience in question. In the first case the error is due a defect in the sense faculty itself—that is, a defect associated with the jaundiced person's eyes. In the latter example, the error is due to the situational context—one's visual faculties are working properly, but the movement of the boat makes it appear as though the trees are moving.

To be clear, in both these cases, Dharmakīrti would regard the visual errors to be nonconceptual. This means that the erroneous experiences are generated not by conceptual activities of the mind, but entirely due to the causal genesis of the experience. This is, admittedly, easier to acknowledge in the case of the white conch shell appearing yellow. One's experience of a yellow conch shell is caused, in part, due to the presence of a white conch shell, and in part due to the (mis-)operation of the jaundiced person's visual faculties.[25] Even before any conceptualization occurs, the visual experience itself is erroneous and fails to conform to its object.

That such errors are nonconceptual is, to be sure, controversial. In fact, it is controversial both in the Buddhist tradition of epistemology and in contemporary philosophy of mind. Dignāga, as has been repeatedly stated earlier in this chapter, does not include the expression "nonerroneous" as part of his definition of perception. This is not because he believes that perceptions can be erroneous, but instead because he apparently regarded cognitive errors to be entirely due to conceptual construction. It can be argued that in cases of erroneous cognition a person *superimposes* upon reality certain qualities that are not genuinely present. Yet the very activity of superimposition can legitimately be construed as a process that relies on conceptuality.

Even within the Buddhist tradition itself, some philosophers have maintained that Dignāga simply failed to consider the possibility that errors sometimes can be due *not* to conceptual superimposition, but instead due to things like defective sensory faculties. This is the argument that is made by Śāntarakṣita, who addresses this dispute (between Dignāga and Dharmakīrti over the definition of perception) while writing in the eighth century. He and many other Buddhist epistemologists agree with Dharmakīrti's assertion that the qualifier "nonerroneous" is needed in the definition of perception. Even if we grant that perceptual experiences are passive processes devoid of conceptual activity, it is still possible that certain factors causally contributing to a sensory experience—such as defective sense faculties—can give rise to an erroneous cognition.

In the earlier paragraphs I have been emphasizing that there is a close connection between (a) granting the existence of phenomenal forms (*ākāra*) or sense-data, on the one hand, and (b) the existence of erroneous sensory experience—illusions and hallucinations—on the other.[26] As I have expressed matters, it is the acceptance of a causal theory of perceptual experience, wherein external objects produce internal sense-data, that leaves space for the very possibility of error in the form of inaccurate mental representations. This link between (a) granting a place for sense-data and (b) countenancing erroneous sensory experience is something that is recognized by contemporary analytic philosophers as well, though it is common to see the explanatory connection reversed. In particular, it is commonly argued that the brute existence of illusions and/or hallucinations provides us with compelling reasons to conclude that (veridical) perceptions can never provide humans with direct access to external objects. Instead, all perceptual experiences must be mediated by (internal) sense-data. This view is codified in the widely expressed "Argument from Illusion" and "Argument from Hallucination."

Homing in on the argument from illusion, the standard claim is that this argument serves as a refutation of direct realist accounts of perception. We can represent the basic line of argumentation as follows:

Consider two cases, α and β.

Case α: I have an illusory experience as of a yellow conch shell (though it is actually a white conch shell).

Case β: I have a (veridical) perception of a yellow conch shell.

Argument:

(1) The experience of yellow in α is indistinguishable from the experience of yellow in β.
(2) Thus, the yellow object that I (directly) experience in α is identical to the yellow object that I (directly) experience in β.
(3) Nothing yellow exists external to the mind in α.
(4) Therefore, the yellow object that I (directly) experience in β cannot be something that exists external to the mind.
(5) So, in general, what are (directly) experienced in veridical perceptions are not objects external to the mind.

The argument from illusion is commonly used to show not just that a direct realist account of perception is untenable, but also that all perceptual experiences must be mediated by mental entities of some sort—for example, sense-data.

Objections to the argument from illusion are possible, however. Premise (3) of the argument is true by hypothesis—that is, it is true just based on how case α has been described. Premise (1) is often taken for granted, but there are some philosophers who object to the very assumption that illusory experiences can be qualitatively indistinguishable from veridical sense experiences. Far more controversial in the argument from illusion, however, is the inference from (1) to (2). That specific inference is controversial in at least two respects. First, while premise (1) is about *experiences* being indistinguishable, (2) is ostensibly about the *objects* that are experienced. It may be denied, however, that there is any object at all that is experienced in these cases. For example, proponents of the adverbial theory of perception, who reject the view that experiences should be described in terms of relations to objects at all, would deny the inference from (1) to (2). Likewise, proponents of contemporary intentionalist theories of perception can reject the view that indistinguishable experiences share any mental *object* in common. Rather, the intentionalist account maintains that such experiences have identical *representational contents*. In both α and β something is represented as being yellow. But the intentionalist theory of perception is not committed to the assumption that sensory experiences involve any mental objects (such as sense-data) at all.

More relevant for our purposes is a second objection that could be made concerning the inference from (1) to (2). Even if we grant that perceptual experiences do involve connections to objects, we need not further grant that indistinguishable experiences must, thereby, be experiences of the same object. Proponents of the disjunctivist theory of perception argue that even if some illusion is fully indistinguishable from a veridical perceptual experience, perceptual and illusory experiences can still be fundamentally different in kind.[27] In a similar vein, a disjunctivist could maintain, theoretically at least, that a perception of a yellow conch shell and an illusion as of a yellow conch shell, even if indistinguishable, are experiences constituted by fundamentally different objects. On this view, in perception one directly experiences an external object, whereas a completely different (mentally constructed) entity is encountered in cases of illusion.[28] A version of this view is, in fact, adopted by some Tibetan Buddhist epistemologists in the twelfth century. In contrast to Dharmakīrti and most of his Buddhist followers in India, these Tibetan philosophers endorse a direct realist account of perception in which there is no role to be played by sense-data. Instead, the objects experienced in episodes of perception and illusion are held to be fundamentally different in kind.[29]

For Dharmakīrti and most other Buddhist epistemologists, by contrast, the possibility of illusions—and of erroneous nonconceptual experiences more generally—goes hand in hand with their support for a sense-data theory of experience in which the only objects directly experienced are phenomenal forms (*ākāra*) internal to the mind. Both veridical perceptions and erroneous illusions/hallucinations have in common the production of internally accessible phenomenal forms. Given that this is the case, however, it threatens one's ability to gain knowledge of external reality. After all, even if the phenomenal forms that immediately appear within a given cognition are, in fact, caused by real objects external to the mind, a person is in no epistemic position to know that that's the case. For all the person knows, the phenomenal forms could be causally generated by internal, karmic tendencies as is supported by proponents of the *Yogācāra* system. Thus, given that all nonconceptual experience is mediated by phenomenal forms or sense-data, and given that nonconceptual experiences can be erroneous, this makes it difficult to account for how such experiences can garner knowledge of external reality. It is therefore not surprising that Dharmakīrti finds it necessary to adopt a *Yogācāra* perspective within such contexts.

Further Reading

For an English translation of, and careful discussion about, Dignāga's presentation of perceptual cognition, see Hattori, M. (1968). *Dignāga, on perception*. Cambridge, MA: Harvard University Press.

For a more extensive discussion of the different forms of perception accepted by Dignāga and Dharmakīrti, see Yao, Z. (2004). Dignāga and four types of perception. *Journal of Indian Philosophy*, *32*, 57–79.

For a detailed presentation of Buddhist epistemological accounts of perception and how those accounts developed over time, see chapters 19 to 26 of Dreyfus, G. (1997). *Recognizing reality: Dharmakīrti's philosophy and its Tibetan interpretations*. Albany: State University of New York Press.

4
Inference

Buddhist epistemologists all agree that perception is a source of knowledge. Yet it is clear that humans' knowledge of reality extends beyond mere perceptual knowledge. I know, for example, that 2 + 2 = 4 and that all bachelors are unmarried. These kinds of truths—mathematical truths and "analytic" truths—can be known, but it is doubtful that they are known directly via sense perception. How then do I know these two claims to be true? One common response is to say that they are known via *reason*. Alternatively, we could say that these truths are known by virtue of one's *intellect*. Here, reason/intellect is spoken of as though it is a special power or faculty—one analogous to my sense faculties—that makes it possible for me to recognize the undeniable truth of propositions such as 2 + 2 = 4. What do we really mean, though, by "reason" or "intellect"? Do these notions genuinely pick out inerrant instruments of knowledge, or is reasoning fallible in much the same way that our vision or hearing might be fallible?

Dignāga, Dharmakīrti and their Buddhist followers share the consensus view that more can be known than just that which can be perceived. Knowledge of certain matters that are fundamentally imperceptible can be secured through a process of *inferential reasoning* (*anumāna*). Explaining how inferential reasoning works in the Buddhist tradition, and defending inferential cognition's status as a legitimate *pramāṇa*, is of critical importance, but it is also a matter that cannot be addressed here in as much depth as the topic deserves. Buddhist accounts of inferential reasoning developed substantially over time and so a full treatment of the issue would demand that we be attentive to the subtle differences between various thinkers' presentations. In addition, just as is the case in the Western tradition of philosophy, the Buddhist account of inference involves a *logical* dimension, a *psychological* dimension, and an *epistemological* dimension. All three aspects are relevant to this chapter, but a full accounting of these different dimensions would require a book-length work on Buddhist theories of inference.

Illuminating the Mind. Jonathan Stoltz, Oxford University Press (2021). © Oxford University Press.
DOI: 10.1093/oso/9780190907532.003.0004

4.1. Two Forms of Inference

Not unlike the case of perception, when Buddhist epistemologists lay out their presentations on inference, they do so by breaking down the general category of inference into various different subtypes. Yet there are several different ways in which these categories of inference can be delimited. In this chapter we will look at two fundamentally different strategies for distinguishing subtypes of inferential reasoning. One strategy, which is documented as early as the time of Dignāga in the early sixth century, is to distinguish inferences by way of the *persons* who are to benefit from them—inferences for oneself and inferences for others. A century later, Dharmakīrti popularized a second strategy for how to think about and categorize inferences. He focuses on the role played by *evidence* in inferential reasoning, and subdivides inference based on the different forms of evidence that are employed. These two approaches are not incompatible with each other, and in later Indian and Tibetan Buddhist accounts of inference, both of these categorizations are frequently used. A discussion of the role of, and different subtypes of, evidence in inferential reasoning will be detailed later in this chapter. Let us begin, however, by framing the topic of inference around the distinction between inference for oneself and inference for others.

4.1.1. Inference for Oneself and for Others

At the very beginning of the second chapter of his *Compendium of Knowledge*, Dignāga distinguishes two forms of inference: that *for the sake of oneself* and that *for the sake of others*. The second chapter of his text is then devoted to laying out the relevant details of inference for oneself, and the third chapter focuses on inference for others. Why this distinction? In short, there is a recognition that reasoning is an activity that takes place not only inside a single person's mind but also in interpersonal discourse between two or more parties.

Inference for the sake of oneself refers to the process of inferential reasoning that takes place within the mind of a single cognitive agent. A person may, to take a basic example, observe smoke rising from a house's chimney and, based on that information, infer that there is a fire burning in the house. When a person reasons in this way, he or she can be said to be engaging in inference for the sake of oneself. We can and do, however, additionally speak of "reasoning" and "inference" as performative gestures that occur when interacting with other people. In particular, an argument might be given in an attempt to persuade someone else to accept some conclusion. Practically speaking, this might happen in a classroom (e.g., a teacher may present an argument to his or her students), or it could happen in a courtroom (e.g., an argument could be presented by lawyers and aimed at convincing the jury of a person's guilt) or in any number of different places. The central domain of "inference for others" in the Indian context, however, is linked to the role played by inferential argumentation in (formal and informal) *debates*.

Argumentative debate has a long history in ancient India, and the impact that formal debate had on the development of Indian epistemology cannot be overstated. Indian philosophers, centuries before the time of Dignāga and Dharmakīrti, developed intricate accounts of topics pertinent to the nature of argumentation and debate. For example, they distinguished honest forms of debate from spurious, trickster debates—that is, those in which a person cheats, since his or her principal goal is to win at all costs. They also developed detailed accounts of how argumentative demonstrations are to be presented, how examples are to figure in such demonstrations, and so on. Given this early emphasis on argumentative reasoning within the context of debate, we should not be surprised to find Dignāga and his Buddhist followers taking up these sorts of topics within their own presentations. Buddhist philosophers shared an interest in formal, demonstrative argumentation, and in standardizing concepts such as those of "proof" and "refutation." All of these matters fall loosely under the topic of "inference for (the sake of) others."[1]

The topic of inference for the sake of others is both important and interesting, but our central concern in this book is with the *epistemology* of inferential reasoning, and that is something that is most directly linked to the cognitive faculties or cognitive processes that an individual person employs to gain knowledge of objects and states of affairs. As such, in this chapter the presentation shall largely be restricted to Dignāga's "inference for (the sake of) oneself"—that is, inference as an episode of knowledge occurring as the result of a cognitive process within the mind of a single person.

4.1.2. The Logic and Psychology of Inference

Dignāga's distinction between inference for oneself and inference for others lays bare the dual role that reasoning plays in our lives: reasoning both undergirds rational argumentation and debate (qua public phenomena) and it allows us to draw inferential conclusions (qua private mental processes). It is not uncommon to find contemporary scholars of Buddhist epistemology proclaim that the distinction between inference for oneself and inference for others is not of particular importance, as these two forms of inference share the same general structure. When these claims of structural similarity are made, however, what scholars are really pointing out, intentionally or not, is the fact that the *logical structure* of inferential reasoning is the same in cases of inference for oneself and inference for others. Yet, in emphasizing this logical similarity, it is possible to lose sight of the important *psychological* differences that exist between inference for oneself and inference for others.

The eighth-century Buddhist epistemologist Dharmottara argues that inference for oneself and inference for others are fundamentally different, and that, as such, there cannot be any single definition of inference that covers both of these categories.[2] My own belief is that Dharmottara is fundamentally correct in this assessment. Inference for oneself is, after all, an essentially psychological phenomenon, involving episodes of (concept-laden) cognition. Inference for others, however, is primarily a verbal matter, tied to (oral) presentations of arguments. The logic that underpins these two forms of inference is indeed shared in common, but it would be a mistake to zoom in exclusively on the logic of inferential reasoning at the expense of its psychology and epistemology.

In contemporary philosophy there is an analogous, but often unstated, contrast between two ways of thinking about argumentation and inference. Over the course of the twentieth century it became incredibly common to characterize an argument as a collection of propositions (one of which is the conclusion of the argument, and the others of which constitute the argument's premises). When presented in this way, the validity of an argument is a matter involving the logical relation between the propositions that compose the argument. Yet there is a second, much older, way of understanding arguments wherein an argument is a kind of performative activity—viz., an argument is the *presentation* of a set of statements, some of which (the premises) are claimed to support the truth of another statement (the conclusion).[3]

There is little question that, at least within analytic philosophy, the project of *depsychologizing logic and argumentation*—a project that was taken up in earnest within the pioneering work of the late nineteenth- to early twentieth-century logician Gottlob Frege—has been so successful that many present-day students of philosophy have a difficult time even grasping the idea of logical arguments as psychological processes.[4] Yet to the extent that we are interested in the *epistemology* of inferential reasoning, it is of critical importance that the psychological dimension of argumentation not be forgotten. Inference is not simply a logical process. It is, for Buddhist epistemologists, a psychological process that results in a concept-laden judgment. Our central task in this chapter is to determine what conditions need to be met in order for such a judgment to be warranted—that is, in order for it to be a *pramāṇa*.

4.2. Inference and Conceptual Cognition

As we have already seen in the preceding chapter, perceptual cognitions are claimed to be entirely devoid of conceptual construction. Inferential cognitions, by contrast, are inherently conceptual. Recall that, for Dignāga, conceptual cognition is defined in terms of the applicability of "name, kind, etc."[5] Later Buddhist epistemologists take this claim to imply that there is a strong link between conceptual thought and language. Dharmakīrti, for example, defines conceptuality as "cognition where what appears can be associated with language."[6] In turn, this implies that inferential cognitions can be associated with language and vocalization in a way that perceptual cognitions cannot.

Relatedly, Buddhist epistemologists from the time of Dignāga onward argue that words do not denote individual, particular objects. For instance, the word "cow" is not the name of (nor does it denote) any specific entity at all. Instead, words can only serve to pick out "general" or "universal" entities. This idea is rooted in Dignāga's assertion that there are only two kinds of objects, particular entities (*svalakṣaṇas*) and general entities (*sāmānyalakṣaṇas*)—the former of which are real, transitory, and causally effective, and the latter of which are unreal, conceptually constructed entities. Conceptual cognitions—and, as such, words as well—can operate on general entities only. Insofar as this is the case and insofar as all inferential cognitions are conceptual, that means that inferential reasoning likewise operates on unreal, general entities and not real, particular objects.

Synthesizing the points just made, Buddhist presentations of conceptual cognition fall roughly into two groups. There is *the linguistic depiction* of conceptuality, where conceptual cognition is principally linked to the applicability of *language* and *word meaning*. But there is also a *mentalistic depiction* of conceptual thought that focuses much more squarely on the *objects* that are associated with those cognitions. These two depictions are by no means independent of or inconsistent with each other, and they can be seen as, perhaps, two sides of the same coin. The groundwork for these two depictions of conceptuality can be identified already in the writing of Dignāga and Dharmakīrti, but it becomes increasingly evident in the writings of later Buddhist epistemologists that placing a greater emphasis on the mentalistic depiction of conceptual thought makes it easier to answer some of the most tricky philosophical puzzles associated with how knowledge is possible in cases of conceptual cognition. Let us briefly walk through two of these puzzles.

The first and most pressing question is this: *Can (or How can) inferential cognitions provide humans with knowledge of real objects and states of affairs in the world?*

Reality consists of momentary, spatio-temporally discrete objects (be they individual atoms, collections of atoms, or ordinary compound objects). But conceptual cognitions only operate on unreal, general entities. I might have, for example, the thought that fire is hot or the thought that sound is impermanent. If these thoughts make reference only to unreal, general entities (such as the concept or idea of fire), how can conceptual thought be used to garner knowledge about real things in the external world around us? Dignāga and Dharmakīrti construct their epistemologies around the idea that inferential reasoning, and conceptual cognition more broadly, involves only general entities (*sāmānyalakṣaṇas*). But given that this is so, how can inferential knowledge be gained of individual, real things? We expect inferential reasoning to be capable of providing us with knowledge of reality, but it isn't obvious how this is possible given the traditional Buddhist understanding of conceptual cognition. Buddhist studies scholar Georges Dreyfus has identified this, in fact, as "the greatest difficulty in Dharmakīrti's system."[7]

Elucidating the various strategies that Buddhist epistemologists employ to resolve this difficulty is well beyond the purview of this book and requires the development of a full-throated philosophy of mind, including an account of intentionality, and so on. Suffice it for our purposes here to point out that philosophers writing after Dharmakīrti introduce a series of distinctions—both with respect to the activities involved in conceptual cognition and with respect to the kinds of objects that are associated with those cognitive activities—that allow them to defend the position that, in one sense, conceptual thought makes use of unreal, conceptually constructed entities, but, in another sense, conceptual thought still engages, epistemologically speaking, real, particular objects in the external world. In this way, inferential judgments, which are conceptual, can indeed yield knowledge of real things and states of affairs.

There is a second, and somewhat overlapping, puzzle about the relation between conceptual thought and knowledge. In the Buddhist epistemological tradition of Dignāga and Dharmakīrti, one particularly important assertion about conceptual cognition is that all these cognitions are fundamentally *erroneous* (*bhrānta*). That said, Buddhist thinkers over the centuries adopt subtly different views about how the "error" of conceptuality is to be understood. The overarching idea is that while, on the one hand, conceptual cognitions systematically make use of mentally constructed general entities that do not exist in reality, on the other hand, it is additionally the case that all conceptual thought involves the *projection* of these mentally constructed entities onto reality. When, for example, I have the thought that fires are hot, I conceive of the property of heat, or universal 'hotness,' as having an objective existence—which, according to classical Buddhist philosophy, is a mistake. Later Buddhist epistemologists sometimes express this point as reflecting the mistake of *conflating* conceptually constructed entities with real things.[8]

Given this view of conceptual thought, the key question thus becomes: *How can all conceptual cognitions be erroneous, and yet still, in at least some cases, yield knowledge?*

Buddhist epistemologists agree that inferential knowledge is possible. But inferential cognitions are conceptual and, as such, fundamentally erroneous. It is thus imperative for thinkers in the Buddhist epistemological tradition to explain how knowledge can be obtained via a form of cognition that is erroneous. Just as with the first puzzle, a detailed answer to this second puzzle cannot be presented here.[9] Oversimplifying, the solution involves (that most basic philosophical move of) drawing a linguistic/conceptual distinction. Erroneous cognitions (*bhrānti-jñāna*) must be distinguished from nondeceptive cognitions (*avisaṃvādi-jñāna*). The former can be explained in terms of how objects appear or how objects are apprehended. The latter feature, nondeceptiveness, is the true mark of knowledge. But nondeceptiveness has, as we have seen in chapter 2, an important pragmatic dimension for Buddhist epistemologists. Conceptual cognitions may involve a form of error, but they can still provide us with pragmatic success. The knowledge, via inference, that there is a fire on a nearby mountain pass, for example, allows us to receive the pragmatic benefit of receiving warmth from the fire.

For the purposes of this book, the most important point here is to keep in mind that though all conceptual cognition is said to be erroneous, Buddhist epistemologists contend that this error does not impinge on our ability to acquire knowledge. It is affirmed that erroneous cognitions can still be nondeceptive cognitions—and it is this latter notion that is most relevant to Buddhist epistemology.

4.3. The Structure of Inferential Reasoning

As noted earlier, psychologically speaking, inferential knowledge is held to be a species of conceptual cognition. Not all conceptual cognitions are instances of inferential knowledge, however. As such, one key task for Buddhist epistemologists is to determine the conditions under which a given conceptual cognition qualifies as an instance of inferential knowledge. Let us now examine some of the key features of inferential cognitions.

First and foremost, Buddhist epistemologists uphold the view that inferential knowledge is an *indirect* form of knowledge. This stands in contrast to perceptual knowledge which is *direct*. Most commonly, Buddhists capture this indirectness by saying that inference provides knowledge of objects that are "hidden," in the sense of being not directly manifest to the cognizer. It may additionally be claimed that inferential knowledge is indirect in the sense of being derived from or dependent on other bits of knowledge that we already possess. This second way of putting things can be formulated more clearly by describing inferential knowledge in terms of its relationship to *evidence*. Within the Buddhist tradition of epistemology, instances of inferential knowledge are described as those episodes of (nondeceptive) cognition that arise in dependence on (good) evidence. It is through a reliance on evidence that a person is able to gain knowledge of that which is hidden from the cognitive agent.

Much of the Buddhist discussion of inferential reasoning, especially due to contributions by Dharmakīrti, focuses on providing details about the nature of, and role played by, evidence (*hetu*). Making sense of the nature of evidence is an important topic, and one that will be covered in greater detail in the next segment of this chapter. In this section, however, our main concern is to provide a clear sketch of the various component elements involved in inferential reasoning. Evidence is one component of inferential reasoning, but it is by no means the only important feature that needs to be explicated.

4.3.1. Elements of Inferential Cognitions

In the preceding chapter we saw that perceptual cognitions take as their objects real things. A person can have perceptual knowledge of the color white, or might perceive the moon, but a person cannot have an episode of perceptually knowing *that the moon is white*. Such 'propositional' knowledge, or 'knowledge *that*,' is beyond the scope of perception. Matters are different in the case of inferential cognition. Because these cognitions are conceptual, something roughly approximating propositional knowledge is possible. To take two standard examples within the Buddhist tradition, a person might be said to gain inferential knowledge *that sound is impermanent* or knowledge *that there is fire on the mountain pass*.

Now, because our goal is to delineate the central characteristics of *inference for oneself*, and hence to understand inferential knowledge qua an episode of cognition, there is still an important sense in which these inferential cognitions take an *object* as their contents. One way of putting this is to say that in a case of inferential judgment the object of one's cognition is an *aggregate* of two (or more) items. For example, when it is said that a person infers *that sound is impermanent*, the object of the inferential cognition is, in one respect, the aggregate of 'sound' and 'impermanence.' Or, to be even more careful, the object of cognition is a given *subject* or *locus* qualified by a property. When, for instance, a person infers that there is a fire on the mountain pass, this can be more formally expressed as a cognition that apprehends a location ('on the mountain pass') as being qualified by a property ('fire').

Though inferential judgments can be said to take as their objects an aggregate of two items, those elements play two importantly distinct formal roles. One is the *subject* or *locus* (*pakṣa*) of the inference. It can be understood as that about which the reasoner is trying to gain knowledge. The other constituent element is the *property to be proven/inferred* (*sādhyadharma*). It is what the reasoner is trying to establish about the subject of the inference. Putting these two elements together, when a person has an episode of inferential knowledge, she has a cognition of the subject being qualified by the property to be proven.

In what follows, instead of speaking of a "subject qualified by a property," I shall just speak for the sake of simplicity of inferential cognitions taking *states of affairs* as their objects. We can say that in a case of inferential reasoning a person judges that some state of affairs is the case. For example, consider a person who infers that there is a fire on the mountain pass. In such a case, we can say that the person has a cognition apprehending the state of affairs that on the mountain pass there is a fire.

Thus far, matters have been described from the perspective of inference as an episode of cognition—which is to say, from the perspective of *inference for oneself.* But inference can also be (and frequently is) understood in terms of argumentative reasoning and the processes associated with *inference for others.* When understood in this second way, it is most natural to describe the constituent elements of inference in linguistic terms. The *thesis* in a case of inferential reasoning is a statement to the effect that the subject has the property to be proven. In this way, a person's inferential knowledge of a given state of affairs—such as that sound is impermanent—can be seen as running parallel to an instance of verbal inferential reasoning wherein a given thesis is established—for example, the thesis that sound is impermanent.

Though inferential knowledge is a form of conceptual cognition, not all conceptual cognitions that apprehend a given state of affairs are instances of knowledge. First of all, some cognitions can be mistaken in the sense of apprehending states of affairs that do not exist. In other words, false or incorrect cognitions are possible, and these cognitions are not instances of knowledge. But even among conceptual cognitions that apprehend states of affairs that are in accord with reality—that is, true states of affairs—not all of these cognitions will qualify as instances of inferential knowledge. In addition to apprehending a true state of affairs, all episodes of inferential knowledge necessarily rely on an appeal to *evidence.* In order for a person to have an instance of inferential knowledge, his or her cognition must be one that arises from and is supported by other cognitions that make an appeal to evidential considerations.

Consider the two examples of inferential judgments cited earlier. In the one case, a person judges that there is a fire on the mountain pass. This cognition does not simply arise spontaneously. Instead, it is a cognition that, in a successful case of inference, is (epistemically) supported by and (causally) generated from an appeal to evidence. In this particular example, the existence of *smoke* on the mountain pass might be put forward as the evidence for judging that there is fire on the mountain pass. In one sense, the evidence can be understood to be the object or property itself—viz., smoke. In another sense, however, the evidence can be thought of as a state of affairs—for example, the fact that there is smoke on the mountain pass. In this latter sense, what is actually being referenced is the subject/locus of the inference (*pakṣa*) being qualified by the evidential property (*hetu*). That state of affairs—that there is smoke on the mountain pass—can be said to be evidence for inferring that there is fire on the mountain pass.

So as to avoid confusion, I shall standardly refer to evidence qua individual object/property (in this example, 'smoke') as the "evidence," and I will speak of evidence qua state of affairs (here, 'the existence of smoke on the mountain pass') as the "reason." This latter term is used more frequently in contexts of linguistic, argumentative inferences. For example, a person may argue:

> "There is fire on the mountain pass because there is smoke there."

In this case, it is the latter clause, "there is smoke there [on the mountain pass]" that functions as the *reason* for concluding that there is fire on the mountain pass. The *evidence* cited when putting forward such a reason is the property of 'smoke.'

Once again, not all appeals to evidence or reasons result in an instance of inferential knowledge. Sometimes evidential appeals are mistaken or inconclusive. Let us imagine a scenario in which I reason that there is a fire on the mountain pass because there is *a tree* there. In such a case, it would be foolish to think that the presence of a tree could serve as an adequate epistemic support for my belief that there is a fire on the mountain pass. Buddhist philosophers from at least the time of Dignāga onward would surely agree that the existence of a tree on the mountain pass is not sufficient evidence for coming to know that there is a fire on the mountain pass. A major project in the history of Buddhist epistemology is determining exactly what conditions must be satisfied in order for some appeal to evidence to be sufficient for genuine inferential knowledge.

4.3.2. The Three Characteristics

Dignāga provides the foundation for all subsequent Buddhist accounts of evidence, and of inferences grounded in evidence. In particular, he maintains that in order to achieve knowledge via inference, the evidence must meet three conditions—the "three characteristics" (*trairūpya*):[10]

1. The evidence must (be ascertained to) be a property of the subject/locus of the inference.

2. The evidence must (be ascertained to) occur in "similar instances" (*sapakṣa*).
3. The evidence must (be ascertained to) be absent from all "dissimilar instances" (*vipakṣa*).

It will be valuable to discuss these three conditions individually. Before doing so, however, let us first note that each of these three conditions includes both a *factual* requirement and an *epistemic* requirement—indicated by my use of parentheses. For instance, and focusing on the first condition, factually speaking, the evidence must be a property of the subject of the inference. But, epistemologically speaking, the cognitive agent must ascertain that this factual requirement is met. The factual requirements inherent in these three conditions capture the logical, or ontological, prerequisites for successful inferences. Meeting these factual requirements is certainly not sufficient for a person gaining *knowledge* via inference, however. In addition to the factual conditions being met, the cognizer must recognize or "ascertain" that those conditions are met.

The first condition requires the evidence to be a property of the subject of the inference and also that the cognizer ascertains this to be so. Using the basic example of a person who cites smoke as his or her evidence for inferring that there is a fire on the mountain pass, it must first be established that the subject of the inference—in this case, the mountain pass—has the property of 'smoke.' In other words, it must be established that there is smoke on the mountain pass. The determination that there is smoke on the mountain pass is something that comes from sense perception. As we saw in the preceding chapter, on the Buddhist account, the episode of knowledge in such a case would be the raw sensory experience of smoke, not the (conceptual) judgment that there is smoke on the mountain pass. Yet this latter judgment may very well be induced by the episode of perceptual knowledge, and it is the ascertainment that there is smoke on the mountain pass that pertinent to the first of the three characteristics.

The second and third conditions in Dignāga's account of proper evidence involve appeals to two technical terms: "similar instances" and "dissimilar instances" (*sapakṣa* and *vipakṣa*, respectively). How these two notions are to be understood is a matter of long historical dispute within the Buddhist tradition of epistemology. A "similar instance" is an item (an object or property) that is said to be "similar to the subject"—similar in that it possesses the property to be inferred. In our central example, since the property to be proven is that of 'fire,' an item similar to the subject—where the subject of the inference is 'on the mountain pass'—could be loci such as 'in a kitchen' or 'in an oven.' A "dissimilar instance," by contrast, is an item dissimilar from the subject insofar as it does not possess the property to be inferred ('fire'). For instance, an acceptable dissimilar instance could be the locus 'in the middle of the lake.'[11]

With these brief characterizations of similar and dissimilar instances in place, let us now see how they apply to the second and third conditions for adequate evidence. The second condition states that the evidence must be found in similar instances, and the third condition states that the evidence must not be found in any dissimilar instances. The similar instance 'in a kitchen' is indeed a location in which the evidential property 'smoke' can be found, and the dissimilar instance 'in the middle of a lake' is a location where the evidential property 'smoke' is absent. Moreover, it seems reasonable to think that any dissimilar instance—any place or object where fire is absent—will likewise be a place or object where the evidential property, 'smoke,' is absent. Assuming that this is the case, the factual requirement associated with Dignāga's third condition is satisfied.

This appeal to similar and dissimilar instances may strike readers as a bit odd. It is here where the contrast between a *logical* interpretation of inference and a *psychological* interpretation of inference is particularly important. The fact that Dignāga appeals to similar and dissimilar instances, which function as examples in support of one's inferential judgments, suggests that he is concerned principally with grounding the psychology of inference. Philosopher Jonardon Ganeri has convincingly argued that Dignāga's understanding of inference can be seen as impacted by earlier Indian philosophers' proclivity toward inductive arguments and inferences that rely on what Ganeri terms "extrapolation," where reasoning by extrapolation is a taken to be a version of inductive sampling.[12]

In terms of the logic of inferential reasoning, the use of examples and sampling may not seem particularly powerful. Yet psychologically and epistemologically speaking, appeals to similar and dissimilar instances may very well put within reach certification of the conditions deemed necessary for a warranted judgment regarding the state of affairs that is to be inferred. For instance, it could be argued that it is simply not humanly possible to establish the truth of the universal claim that 'wherever there is smoke there is fire.' But perhaps a person could be in position to establish the more limited claim that she has never encountered 'smoke' in any location where 'fire' is absent.

Nevertheless, in the generations after Dignāga, Buddhist epistemologists advance more and more toward crisp *logical* interpretations of inference, and gradually reinterpret Dignāga's second and third conditions for adequate evidence. In particular, a growing emphasis is placed on the idea that there must be a relation of *universal entailment* (*vyāpti*) between the evidence (*hetu*) and the property to be inferred (*sādhyadharma*).[13] It is asserted that everything having the evidential property must also have the property to be proven. In other words, the evidence must *entail* the property to be proven, where this entailment is grounded in there being an *invariable dependence* (*avinābhāva*) of the evidence on the property to be inferred. This concept of invariable dependence will be taken up in much more detail in chapter 8, where an extension of the concept will be deployed in the articulation of a sensitivity requirement on knowledge.

This appeal to a relation of universal entailment finds its footings in the works of Dharmakīrti—as will be seen in the next section—and becomes even more thoroughly entrenched in the writing of later Indian and Tibetan Buddhist epistemologists. Yet, if we think of Dharmakīrti's notion of universal entailment in purely logical (or even set-theoretic) terms, it would appear that what is critical for establishing a universal entailment relation between the evidence and the property to be proven is just Dignāga's third characteristic—that is, (3)—and not the second characteristic. After all, if it is indeed true that the evidential property is entirely absent from the class of "dissimilar instances," then the evidence does, logically speaking at least, entail the property to be inferred. For example, consider the inference that "clay pots are impermanent because they are produced by humans." On the assumption that the property 'produced by humans' can never be coinstantiated with the property 'being permanent,' it would indeed follow that whatever is produced by humans is impermanent, which is to say that the evidence would entail the property to be proven.

The possibility that the second of Dignāga's three characteristics of adequate evidence may, logically speaking, be entirely dispensable was not missed by later Buddhist epistemologists, nor by contemporary scholars. Logically speaking, what is necessary for a legitimate inference to the conclusion *that S has P* (i.e., that the subject has the property to be proven) is just:

(i) S has E (i.e., the subject has the evidential property) and
(ii) E entails P (i.e., the evidence entails the property to be proven).

Of course, for inferential knowledge to be gained, it must not only be the case that these two conditions hold as a matter of fact, but also that the cognizer actually *ascertain* that these two conditions are satisfied. As the centuries passed by, and especially in the later epistemological tradition in Tibet, it became more and more common for Buddhist writers to express support for Dignāga's "three characteristics," but then to argue that there are essentially only two conditions that must be met for inferential knowledge by way of evidence:

(PD) (*pakṣadharmatā*) the evidence must be a property of the subject/locus of the inference and
(V) (*vyāpti*) the evidence must entail the property to be proven.

That said, if the epistemology of inference does indeed require universal entailments between the evidence and the property to be proven, it needs to be asked why one should think that there are such entailments, and, if there are, how they can be established.

4.4. Evidence and Entailment

One of Dharmakīrti's most important contributions to epistemology has to do with his account of evidence's role in inferential reasoning, and in providing an ontological framework for understanding the relationship between the two properties that are essential to any and all inferences—the evidential property and the property to be inferred.[14] In this way, he succeeds in improving upon the epistemological groundwork that had been laid by Dignāga. As important as Dignāga's appeal to the "three characteristics" of adequate evidence was, his account left largely unanswered the deeper questions of how the second and third characteristics are to be established or ascertained. It is here where Dharmakīrti's account of the nature of evidence proves helpful.

Dharmakīrti provides a theory of inferential reasoning in which there are three distinct types of inferences, ones that are based on three different forms of evidence that can be employed in an argument. By delineating these three forms of evidence, it becomes possible to capture more clearly the relationship between the evidential property and the property to be inferred, which will thus put one in the position to show that the former property entails the latter property. These three forms of evidence are identity evidence (*svabhāva-hetu*), causal evidence (*kārya-hetu*), and nonobservation evidence (*anupalabdhi-hetu*). Let us discuss each of these individually.[15]

4.4.1. Identity Evidence

Suppose I were to deduce that there is a deciduous tree in my backyard from my already knowing that there is a maple tree there. Given that I both (1) know there is a maple tree in my yard, and (2) know that maple trees are deciduous, one might think it reasonable to conclude that I (am at least in the position to) inferentially (3) know that there is a deciduous tree in my yard. This sort of inference is featured prominently in analytic accounts of epistemology. One way of expressing this point is to say that there is an *analytic entailment* from the proposition 'There is a maple tree in my backyard' to the proposition 'There is a deciduous tree in my backyard.' It might also be claimed that the property of 'being a maple tree' *ontologically entails* the property 'being a deciduous tree.' Regardless of how exactly this point would be expressed by contemporary philosophers, it is this same sort of relationship that is to be captured by Dharmakīrti's identity evidence (*svabhāva-hetu*; literally, "own nature evidence").

For Dharmakīrti, this form of evidence is linked to the existence of ontological relation between two properties—a dependence of one property on another that is rooted in having an "identical essence" (*tādātmya*). The two properties of 'being a maple tree' and 'being a deciduous tree' share the same essence in the (admittedly restricted) sense that anything having the property of being a maple tree is also going to be something that has the property of being deciduous. The maple tree that I know to exist in my backyard is not a different object from the deciduous tree. There is only one tree, a single thing that is both a maple and a deciduous tree. Moreover, any object that does not have the property of being a deciduous tree will also not have the property of being a maple tree. In this respect, the property of 'being a maple tree' *ontologically depends* on 'being a deciduous tree.'[16]

4.4.2. Causal Evidence

The second form of evidence that Dharmakīrti argues in support of is causal evidence (*kārya hetu*; literally, "effect evidence"). This is the kind of evidential property that is used in the stock example of inferring the existence of fire on a mountain pass by evidence of the presence of smoke on the mountain pass. In the Indian tradition, fire is said to be the cause of smoke, in the sense that fire is a necessary condition for smoke. As such, this means that "wherever there is smoke, there is fire." Of course, even if fire exists in every location where smoke exists, that does not mean that the properties of fire and smoke are instantiated in the same objects. Fire and smoke do not, in other words, stand in the relation of "identical essence." Yet these two properties are claimed to be metaphysically related; they are causally related to one another. To be more precise, Dharmakīrti maintains that the evidential property stands in the relation of causal dependence (*tadutpatti-saṃbandha*) on the property to be inferred.

Just as in the case of essential identity, the relation of causal dependence is an asymmetric one. The effect (e.g., smoke) depends on the existence of its cause (fire), but not necessarily vice versa. Fire is deemed to be a necessary condition for smoke, but it is not held to be a sufficient condition. As such, when two properties stand in the relation of causal dependence, the cause can be inferred from the effect, but the converse is not necessarily the case. In turn, this means that what is to be put forward as evidence for inferring some property x must be the effect of x. Because smoke is the effect of fire, it is capable of playing the role of evidence in support of inferring the existence of fire in a given location.[17]

It should be clear why these first two dependence relations—causal dependence and ontological dependence in the form of the "identical essence" relation—are so valuable to Dharmakīrti. They are both, first and foremost, relationships that would appear to be capable of grounding the existence of universal entailments between a given inference's evidential property and its property to be inferred. If the existence of one property ontologically depends on a second property, it follows that whenever (and wherever) the first property exists, the second property must exist as well. Likewise, if one property causally depends on a second property, the existence of the first property guarantees the existence of the second property. In turn, each of these entailments will indirectly ensure that, factually speaking, Dignāga's third condition for adequate evidence will be satisfied.

How a person is to *ascertain* that two properties stand in the relation of identical essence or the relation of causal dependence is a more difficult matter. With regard to the relation of ontological dependence, it might be thought to be roughly analogous to the problem, common in post-Kantian philosophy, of how a person is to gain knowledge of *analytic* truths. As for establishing the relation of causal dependence, there is the well-known problem of induction. Buddhist epistemologists must likewise confront the challenge of determining how these universal entailments can be known to be true. It has been argued by B. K. Matilal that these relations can be known only through experience. As he states, "The relation between such genuine properties can be either identity or causal dependence. These relations between genuine properties, on Dharmakīrti's view, hold necessarily but are knowable only a posteriori." [18] As helpful as the distinction between a priori and a posteriori knowledge might be, it is not obvious that such a distinction is made by Buddhist epistemologists. What we can be sure of, however, is that ascertainment of the universal entailments that are critical to inferential reasoning could only come from one or the other of the two *pramāṇas*—perception and/or inference. Dharmakīrti and his followers do indeed hold that the ascertainment of universal entailments comes from applications of perceptual cognition. In this respect, Matilal is correct in affirming that universal entailments are knowable only a posteriori.

4.4.3. Nonobservation Evidence

The third form of evidential reasoning supported by Dharmakīrti operates rather differently from the first two forms. While identity evidence and causal evidence each make use of a particular dependence relation between two properties, there is no third form of dependence associated with nonobservation evidence. Instead, this third and final form of evidence indirectly makes use of those first two relations, but does so in order to draw a *negative* inference—an inference concluding that something is *not* the case or does *not* exist. Recall our earlier example of inferring that there is a deciduous tree in my backyard from my knowing that there is a maple tree in my backyard. What if, instead, I were to reason that there is no maple tree in my backyard because there are no trees in my backyard? Here, the property to be inferred is a kind of absence or nonexistence—that is, there not being a maple tree. Strictly speaking, this is an example of what is classically termed by Buddhist philosophers a "nonaffirming negation." Now, in a sense, this inference relies on an entailment that is the contrapositive of the original claim that the property 'being a maple tree' entails 'being a deciduous tree.' But the evidential property in this case is not something affirmative; it is only an absence. These inferences are termed "nonobservational" owing to the fact that, in a situation in which all the requisite conditions for observing some object or property are met, that object/property nonetheless fails to be observed. In such a circumstance, Dharmakīrti argues that it is appropriate to draw an inference to the absence of some other property whose existence depends on the former, unobserved one.

The earlier example in which it is inferred that there is no maple tree in my backyard, because there are no trees in my yard, exhibits just one inferential structure among many different inferential forms that fall under the category of inferences based on nonobservation evidence. In most cases, the evidence to which the reasoner appeals is the absence of an object or property, but this is not always the case. Dharmakīrti also describes, for instance, a case where a person infers that there is no sensation of cold in a given location by evidence of the fact that there is a fire in that location. In this example, the evidential property, fire, is something that *is* positively observed. This is nevertheless considered an inference based on nonobservation evidence owing to the fact that the inferential judgment that is reached is not affirming a positive state of affairs but only the nonexistence of something—viz., there is no sensation of cold in that location.

4.5. Epistemic Closure

For Buddhist epistemologists, inference is a *pramāṇa*. Inferential cognitions are episodes of knowledge. But whereas perceptual knowledge is, in a sense, a *basic* source of knowledge, inferential knowledge is not—it is a *derived* form of knowledge. Inferential knowledge is derived from, and depends on, earlier episodes of perceptual and/or inferential cognition. Inasmuch as this is the case, it is worth exploring in more detail the epistemological relationship between the resultant judgment in a process of inferential reasoning and the cognitions via which that inferential judgment is reached. In particular, we should examine the question of whether Buddhist philosophers are committed to any epistemic closure principles of the sort that are now commonly discussed by contemporary analytic philosophers.

4.5.1. The Closure of Knowledge

One standard formulation of the *principle of epistemic closure* runs as follows:[19]

For any propositions *p* and *q*, and any person S, if

1. S knows that *p*
   and
2. S knows that *p* entails *q*
   then
3. S knows that *q*.

This argument schema captures one way of expressing the basic claim that knowledge is closed under known entailments.

The Buddhist account of inferential knowledge, when boiled down to its essential logical principles, runs roughly as follows:

For a subject/locus *s*, evidential property E, and property to be inferred P, if

(i) S knows* that E(*s*)
(i.e., S knows the subject has the evidential property)
(ii) S knows* that $(x)(E(x) \supset P(x))$
(i.e., S knows the evidence entails the property to be inferred)
then
(iii) S knows that P(*s*)
(i.e., S knows that the subject has the property to be inferred).

When expressed in this way, it would appear that the Buddhist approach toward inferential reasoning is very much in accord with the classical principle of epistemic closure.

There are, it should be acknowledged, some relevant constraints on the applicability of this principle of closure within the Buddhist context—constraints that are tied, for the most part, to the episodic nature of cognition in the Indian context. First of all, one psychological constraint on epistemic closure is that there must actually be a "desire to know" on the part of the cognitive agent. According to Buddhist epistemologists, if a person has already ascertained the thesis to be inferred, P(*s*), or if she has no intellectual curiosity about it, then even if (i) and (ii) are true, the person may not form the judgment that P(*s*). It must additionally be kept in mind that, in the Buddhist tradition of epistemology, what is at issue are momentary episodes of knowledge, and not dispositional states of knowledge. As such, what is necessary in order to arrive at inferential knowledge that P(*s*) is actually, as stated earlier in the chapter, the person *ascertaining* that E(*s*) and *ascertaining* that property E entails property P. These ascertainments may or may not constitute episodes of knowledge in the sense of satisfying Buddhist definitions of *pramāṇa*, but in this context "ascertainment" plays a role analogous to that played by knowledge in contemporary treatments of epistemic closure in analytic epistemology. I have used the notation "knows*" to indicate that we are talking about ascertainment or knowledge in an informal sense, since the cognitions constituting (i) and (ii) may not technically be episodes of knowledge/*pramāṇas*.

4.5.2. The Counterclosure of Knowledge

Much more interesting than the question of whether Buddhist epistemologists accept the principle of epistemic closure is that of whether they would support the converse principle, which I shall call the *principle of epistemic counterclosure*.[20] Roughly stated, the principle of epistemic counterclosure affirms that:

(CC) S can come to inferentially know that q, via an inference from p_1, p_2, . . . p_n, *only if* S knows that p_i for all i.[21]

In particular, and applied to the case of inference in the Buddhist tradition that proceeds from Dignāga and Dharmakīrti, the principle of epistemic counterclosure would maintain that:

For a subject/locus *s*, evidential property E, and property to be inferred P,

(i) S inferentially knows that P(*s*)
only if both
(ii) S knows* that E(*s*)
(iii) S knows* that $(x)(E(x) \supset P(x))$

It is this principle, and not the earlier principle of closure, that is directly implicated in Buddhist accounts of inferential knowledge. Recall that Dignāga's "three characteristics" are deemed to boil down to the requirement that two conditions, (PD) and (V), are satisfied. In particular, these two conditions must not only be factually true but also ascertained to be true.

As long as the reference to "knows*" in this principle is understood as a broad assertion that the cognizer *ascertains* (PD) and (V), it would appear that this principle of epistemic counterclosure is indeed endorsed by Buddhist epistemologists. Ascertainment of both (PD) and (V)—namely, that the evidence is a property of the subject and that the evidence entails the property to be inferred—is held to be *necessary* for inferential knowledge; and this is precisely what the principle of epistemic counterclosure asserts.

But is this principle correct? Counterclosure has increasingly been called into question over the past fifteen years or so by some analytic epistemologists. In particular, it has been argued that it is possible to gain knowledge from falsehoods. That is, it has been argued that inferential knowledge can be secured even in cases where one (or more) of the premises on which that inferential belief depends is itself false, and so, a fortiori, not known. Here is a popular example that is provided by Ted Warfield:[22]

> Counting with some care the number of people present at my talk, I reason: 'There are 53 people at my talk; therefore my 100 handout copies are sufficient'. My premise is false. There are 52 people in attendance—I double counted one person who changed seats during the count. And yet I know my conclusion.

This is a case of inferential belief—believing that 100 copies of the handout is sufficient for the crowd at the talk. Yet this belief is derived from another belief that is mistaken. The person believes that there are 53 people at the talk when there are actually 52 present. Nevertheless, Warfield contends that this false belief does not prevent the person from knowing that 100 copies will be sufficient.

There are, perhaps, numerous details that can be disputed in Warfield's example and, as such, larger questions about the general thrust of these attacks on the principle of epistemic counterclosure. The current debates over counterclosure in contemporary epistemology are intriguing and are by no means fully settled. What I wish to address in the remainder of this chapter, however, is the question of whether Buddhist epistemologists *ought to* accept counterclosure, or whether they should grant that a person can have an episode of inferential knowledge even in a situation where he or she either does not know* (PD) or does not know* (V).

One way of thinking about Warfield's example is that it shows that even if a belief is false, it may be close enough to the truth so as to allow the inferred proposition to be known. The person is mistaken in her belief that there are 53 people at the talk, for there are actually 52, but why should that small error prevent a person from knowing that 100 handouts are sufficient for the attendees? It looks like the warrant for the inference is secure enough, even though it relies on a false belief.

To the extent that cases like Warfield's are at all persuasive, it would seem that relevantly similar examples could be given in the Buddhist context. Let us, therefore, consider an example that fits the Buddhist model of inference, but in which (PD) is not satisfied. Suppose that a person spies a vase on the table in front of her and judges that it is a terra-cotta vase. She also knows that terra-cotta vases are impermanent things. As such, she deduces that there is an impermanent thing on the table. But let us further suppose that the person is mistaken. What appears to be a terra-cotta vase is actually a (superbly produced) plastic vase. Is it right to say that her cognition that there is an impermanent thing on the table is *not* an episode of (inferential) knowledge? Her perceptual judgment was mistaken—there is no terra-cotta vase—but that judgment might still be deemed close enough to the truth for the relevant purposes of the inference in question.

Formally, the person's "inference" runs as follows:

(i) S knows* that there is a terra-cotta vase on the table.
(ii) S knows* that all terra-cotta vases are impermanent.
Thus,
(iii) S (inferentially) knows that there is an impermanent thing on the table.

In this case, (i) is incorrect. S does not know* that there is a terra-cotta vase on the table, because that judgment is mistaken. There is, in fact, no terra-cotta vase on the table at all. But must the falsity of (i) prevent S from knowing that there is an impermanent thing on the table? According to adherents of the principle of epistemic counterclosure, the answer has to be yes. One of the necessary conditions for an instance of inferential knowledge has not been satisfied.

Indeed, there is, in the writings of Buddhist epistemologists in the centuries following Dharmakīrti, ample evidence indicating that these Buddhist thinkers would be committed to the view that the person simply *cannot* gain inferential knowledge in a case like this. According to standard Buddhist epistemological accounts, this example suffers the fault of having an "unestablished reason" (*asiddha hetu*); and because the reasoning suffers from this fault, it is deemed to be incapable of resulting in an instance of knowledge.

There is little question that reasoning suffering from the fault of having an unestablished reason would, in many cases, clearly not result in an episode of knowledge. If, for example, I were to reason that 'there is a fire on the mountain pass because there is smoke on the mountain pass'—when, in reality there is no smoke on the mountain pass at all, only a patch of fog—this judgment would intuitively fail to be an instance of knowledge, even under the assumption that there is, in fact, a fire on the mountain pass. Here, the fact that there is an "unestablished reason" does provide solid grounds for concluding that the person lacks knowledge of there being a fire on the mountain pass.

So, what is the difference between the first case, where I would contend that it could be reasonable to grant that the person could gain knowledge that there is an impermanent thing on the table, and this latter case, where the person more obviously does not gain knowledge? One possible explanation of the difference, already mentioned in relation to Warfield's parallel example, is that in the first case, but not the second, the false belief is sufficiently close to the truth of the matter as not to infect the inferred belief that there is an impermanent thing on the table. We might say that, in first case but not the second, the inferred belief is *safe* in the sense of being highly unlikely to be false in relevantly similar circumstances. Alternatively, we might express the point by saying that the inferred belief is nonaccidentally true in the first case, but that in the latter case if it turned out to be true at all, it would be merely accidentally true.

My central point here is not that the Buddhist epistemological tradition's support for the principle of epistemic counterclosure is in error. Instead, it is to call attention to the fact that their account of inference—reliant as it is on an acceptance on the principle of counterclosure—places significant restrictions on what can be known via inferential reasoning, and that these restrictions thereby exclude from the realm of knowledge some inference-like judgments that could intuitively be considered instances of knowledge. If so, that suggests that there may be some tension between the Dharmakīrti's defining conditions for knowledge (i.e., his definition(s) of *pramāṇa*) and the conditions he deems necessary for inferential knowledge. There is little question that the standard understanding of inferential cognition in the post-Dharmakīrtian Buddhist epistemological tradition is one that would accept the principle of epistemic counterclosure. But it is far from clear whether Dharmakīrti's general definition of *pramāṇa*, a knowledge episode, must likewise restrict (inference-like) knowledge to just those cases where counterclosure is satisfied. It is thus important to examine more carefully the relationship between the conditions for knowledge, on the one hand, and the conditions for perceptual and inferential knowledge, on the other hand. It is that precise topic that will form the basis for chapter 8.

Further Reading

For a careful treatment of Dignāga's theory of inference, see (particularly, chapter 4 of) Hayes, R. (1988). *Dignaga on the interpretation of signs*. Dordrecht: Kluwer Academic.

For a brief overview of Dharmakīrti's theory of inferential reasoning, see Gillon, B. (1986). Dharmakīrti and his theory of inference. In B. K. Matilal & R. Evans (Eds.), *Buddhist logic and epistemology* (pp. 77–87). Dordrecht: D. Reidel Publishing Company.

For a broader treatment of Indian logic, a treatment that contextualizes the importance of Dignāga and Dharmakīrti within the broader Indian tradition of logic, see Matilal, B. K. (1998). *The character of logic in India*. Albany: State University of New York Press.

5
Testimony

Much of the knowledge that I now possess lies far outside the direct, perceptual realm. For example, I know that the American Declaration of Independence was signed on August 2, 1776; and I know this even though I wasn't born until two hundred years after this event took place. I know that Neil Armstrong was the first person to walk on the Moon; and I know this even though, having not yet been born, I was not in any position to grasp this fact through direct perception at the time of the event. More generally, I want to claim that a large proportion of the facts that I and others know about the world comes not from perception, but from the testimony of others. It could be testimony contained in books, or the testimony of teachers and other "persons of authority." Regardless, there is a persuasive case to be made that my knowledge of the world is supplemented by information that I receive through the testimony of others.

Though testimonial knowledge plays an important role in our lives, there has been surprisingly little ink spilled on the epistemology of testimony in the Western tradition of philosophy, especially in comparison to perceptual and inferential knowledge. There are, undoubtedly, many reasons why testimonial knowledge has been consigned to a backseat in discussions of epistemology. On the one hand, much of Western epistemology, especially since the time of Descartes, has proceeded under a framework wherein the key question is that of how knowledge can be generated and secured within oneself. Questions of the justification of one's beliefs, including whether and how those beliefs can be grounded in other beliefs, have stood at the heart of the European project of epistemology. Testimonial knowledge, on the other hand, is rarely thought of as knowledge that is generated within oneself. One standard view holds that testimony does not generate knowledge at all; it merely *transmits* or *transfers* knowledge from one person to another. In this way, concerns about the status of knowledge by testimony have largely been relegated to a background role in European and Anglo-American epistemology.

Illuminating the Mind. Jonathan Stoltz, Oxford University Press (2021). © Oxford University Press.
DOI: 10.1093/oso/9780190907532.003.0005

Matters are somewhat different within the Indian philosophical context. Because the Indian tradition frames questions of knowledge in terms of different sources of knowledge, it has long been quite normal for Indian philosophers to think of testimony as a distinct form of knowledge—one that is secured by an instrument different from both perception and inferential reasoning. This does not mean that *Buddhist* epistemologists in India accepted testimony as a separate *pramāṇa*. They did not. But it does mean that the views of Buddhist epistemologists in India were shaped by the broader Indian tradition of epistemology and its attentiveness toward the status of testimonial knowledge.

It is not just Buddhist epistemologists whose views of testimony were shaped by the broader Indian tradition, however. Yes, the question of whether testimony constitutes a separate source of knowledge, a separate *pramāṇa*, has long been at the heart of Indian investigations of testimonial knowledge. But over the past twenty-five years this question of whether testimony is an irreducible source of knowledge has seeped into contemporary analytic discussions of epistemology. In particular, it is now quite common in analytic epistemology to frame questions of testimony in terms of *reductive* versus *nonreductive* approaches. Though that framing has a basis in the history of European epistemology, the debate between reductive and nonreductive theories of testimonial knowledge has become all the more central to contemporary epistemology due to a growing awareness of the nonreductive theory of testimony endorsed by the Nyāya School of philosophy in ancient India. Indeed, contemporary philosophical discussions of the epistemology of testimony, and especially of the split between reductive and nonreductive accounts of testimony, became much more common following the publication of the book *Knowing from Words: Western and Indian Philosophical Analysis of Understanding and Testimony* in 1994. The articles in that book went a long way toward exposing Anglo-American philosophers to the value of Indian schools of epistemology. But they also had a lasting effect on how contemporary philosophers think of testimonial knowledge—bringing into focus the question of whether testimony is or is not a separate, irreducible source of knowledge.

5.1. The Nyāya Account and the Buddhist Response

I have already mentioned that Buddhist epistemologists in India deny that testimony is a separate means of knowledge. Many Buddhists, however, do wish to accommodate the thesis that persons can gain knowledge through scriptural testimony, and so their position is not that there is no such thing as knowledge by testimony. The claim, instead, is that testimony is not an irreducible form of knowledge separate from perception and inference. The goal of this chapter is to make sense of the Indian Buddhist account of testimonial knowledge and to raise some philosophical concerns about their epistemology of testimony. None of this can be accomplished, however, without first describing the theory of testimonial knowledge that was endorsed by the Nyāya School of philosophy in India, for it is this account to which Buddhist epistemologists, either directly or indirectly, are responding.

5.1.1. The Nyāya Account of Testimony

Let us keep in mind that in Indian philosophy, a *pramāṇa* is a means or instrument of knowledge. The central question of this chapter is whether testimony (*śabda*) is a separate, irreducible *pramāṇa*. Proponents of the Nyāya School of Indian philosophy maintain that testimony is a separate means of knowledge, whereas Buddhists do not; they contend that it is merely a form of inference. The *Nyāya-Sūtra* defines testimony as "the instructive assertion of a reliable person."[1] Or, as translated by Stephen Phillips, testimony is "the (true) statement of an expert."[2] Here, the concept of an "expert" or "reliable person" or "credible witness" (in Sanskrit, *āpta*) plays a critical role.[3] In order to gain knowledge via testimony, the source of the testimony must be reliable, or an "expert." This is to say that an adequate authority must, at the very least, be *knowledgeable* on that which he or she is speaking/writing. But the testifier's knowledge alone is not sufficient for testimonial knowledge, for a knowledgeable person might intentionally deceive another person. Thus, in addition to being knowledgeable, a testifier must have a *desire to communicate* the truth that he or she knows. These two factors combine to make a testifier trustworthy.

Obviously, the requirement that the testifier is a trustworthy source limits the scope of testimonial knowledge in several ways. For starters, not all beliefs formed based on testimony will be instances of knowledge, even if the beliefs that I form are true. If a fraudster were to tell me that the watch I am looking at is a real Rolex, and, unbeknownst to the fraudster himself, the watch happens to be a genuine Rolex, my (true) belief that there is a Rolex watch in front of me would not be an instance of knowledge by testimony.

That is because the testifier was not knowledgeable and did not have a desire to communicate truthfully to me. So, too, if a person in a museum were to spontaneously exclaim, "Oh, how beautiful!" while standing in front of a Rembrandt painting, it is possible that I could come to know that *this person thinks the Rembrandt painting is beautiful*, but my knowledge would not qualify as an instance of knowledge by testimony. This is because, in this case, the speaker had no desire to communicate information to me when making the relevant exclamation.

This is all well and good, but there is certainly more to testimony than just factual information about the testifier. Also important are grammatical elements of the sentence(s) uttered by the testifier. For example, later Nyāya writers claim that the sentence that is uttered must itself meet a number of conditions. In particular, the elements of the sentence must be properly presented and they must be syntactically well formed.[4]

Up to this point, all of these conditions for testimonial knowledge are focused on the testifier. Surely, however, accounting for knowledge by testimony requires not just placing restrictions on the *testifier* and his or her words but also requires certain events to occur on the *hearer's* part. That the Nyāya School focuses so much on speaker conditions for testimonial knowledge is, perhaps, not surprising. They are defending the view that testimony is a separate means of knowledge, and defending the status of testimony as an irreducible source of knowledge requires specifying the conditions under which the speaker is indeed trustworthy. But testimony cannot be a means of knowledge unless it results in the right kind of belief or cognition on the part of the hearer. Indeed, Nyāya writers affirm that the testimony in question must, through a causal process, result in the hearer forming a true belief concerning the statement expressed by the testifier's utterance. Importantly, the claim is *not* that the result of this causal process is the hearer forming the belief *that the speaker has testified that p* (for whatever proposition, *p*, is expressed by the testifier). Instead, in cases of testimony the hearer comes to believe the statement *p* itself. Nor is the claim that the hearer comes to believe *p by virtue of* first believing that the speaker has testified that *p*. Rather, the hearer's belief that *p* is formed directly from hearing the speaker's utterance.

What is most important about this Nyāya account of testimonial knowledge is that the hearer's belief is not generated through an inferential process. Though certain conditions must obtain concerning the testifier and his or her utterance, it is denied that the hearer draws an inference to the conclusion that *p* is true from first having established that the speaker has asserted *p* and then establishing that the speaker meets the conditions necessary for trustworthiness. It is certainly possible that (in some cases) the hearer could entertain such inferential considerations, but doing so is not at all essential for testimonial knowledge according to Nyāya epistemologists. In light of their broader externalism about knowledge, these philosophers are careful to distinguish the conditions necessary for the possession of knowledge from the conditions necessary for *certifying* knowledge. To think that testimony could only yield knowledge through an inferential process is to confuse knowledge with its certification.[5]

Insofar as the Nyāya view of testimonial knowledge does not require the hearer to draw any explicit—or even implicit, or subconscious—inferences regarding the trustworthiness of the testifier, it has been argued that this kind of account is "an epistemic charter for the gullible and undiscriminating."[6] It is a charter for the gullible, according to Elizabeth Fricker, because the Nyāya account relies on the "presumptive right" to trust a speaker. The Nyāya account grants that knowledge can be obtained from testimony even without verifying that the speaker is a reliable, trustworthy source. I will have more to say about the merits of the Nyāya account later in this chapter. Before discussing those merits, however, let us tackle the Buddhist account of knowledge by testimony.

5.1.2. The Buddhist Account of Testimonial Inference

We have seen earlier in this book that Buddhist epistemologists as early as Dignāga defend the claim that there are only two *pramāṇas*, perception and inference. In fact, Dignāga's reasoning on this matter, which distinguishes *pramāṇas* by way of their objects, guarantees that there could not possibly be more than two *pramāṇas*, for there are only two kinds of objects, particular entities and general entities. Thus, if testimony is to be a genuine source of knowledge, there is no question that it must be subsumed under one of the two established forms, perception or inference. And as was mentioned earlier, Buddhist philosophers do argue that knowledge by testimony—or scripturally based knowledge—is to be treated as a form of *inferential knowledge*.

Let us look, then, at the account of scriptural knowledge that is endorsed by Dharmakīrti, and which forms the basis for much of the Buddhist epistemological tradition that follows. To start off, Dharmakīrti explicitly restricts the domain of testimonial or scripturally based knowledge to facts that are inaccessible to perception and ordinary inference. Let us call these "radically inaccessible" facts.[7] If a statement can be established empirically (through perception) or through ordinary (nonscriptural) inferential reasoning, then such a statement is not one that should be established through scripturally based inference. Expressed differently, the only kinds of truths that can be established through scriptural testimony are those that pertain to religious matters that transcend the empirical and rational realms.

Dharmakīrti goes on to state that a threefold analysis is to be applied to the scripture, *s*, from which one wishes to draw a scripturally based inference:

(a) *s* cannot be contradicted by ordinary perception.
(b) *s* cannot be contradicted by ordinary inferential reasoning.
(c) *s* cannot contain any internal contradictions with respect to its pronouncements on radically inaccessible matters.

In cases for which it is observed that these three conditions are met, a person is in the position to accept, inferentially, the truth of the radically inaccessible statements made in the scripture *s*.

As presented, it looks as though Dharmakīrti is putting forward a form of scripturally based inferential reasoning that is inductive in character. Let us assume that a scripture, *s*, contains a radically inaccessible pronouncement, *p*, and that *s* meets conditions (a) through (c). One cannot, strictly speaking, thereby deduce that statement *p* is true. At best, all we know is that the assertions in scripture *s* (including *p*) are mutually consistent and that the empirically and rationally verifiable statements in *s* have not been shown to be false. But even if all that is so, it does not deductively entail that *p* is true.

In an ordinary inference, as was examined in chapter 4, the evidence or reason bears an invariable relation to the property to be proven. That is, there is a logical or causal connection between the evidence and the property to be proven that guarantees that the inference will be deductively valid. It is additionally true, however, that a purely objective fact undergirds these standard inferences—namely, that the argument's subject possesses the evidencing property. For example, the objective fact that the mountain pass possesses smoke undergirds the inferential cognition that the mountain pass possesses fire. In short, ordinary inferences proceed *by the power of real entities*.

Dharmakīrti's scripturally based inferences, by contrast, seem not to operate through the power of real entities at all. They appear to proceed *by the power of words*. Scripturally based arguments claim that some radically inaccessible statement *p* is true because scripture *s* states that *p* and scripture *s* passes tests (a) through (c). But, again, the fact that the scripture asserts *p* (and that the scripture passes these tests of consistency) is not at all objective evidence capable of guaranteeing *p*'s truth. In this regard, it does not seem that scripturally based inference is a genuine form of inference at all.

Indeed, Dharmakīrti himself recognizes that scriptural inferences are not genuine inferences, owing to the lack of an objective entailment from the words of scripture to the statement's actual truth.[8] Instead, scripturally based inferences are said to be warranted simply because there is no other way to gain knowledge of these radically inaccessible religious matters. Dharmakīrti says of scripturally based knowledge that "The cognition is said to be an inference because there is no other way to know that object."[9]

Thus, the Buddhist epistemologist is faced with a quandary. If we are to grant that one can obtain knowledge through scriptural testimony, and also grant that this knowledge fails to come from an irreducible *pramāṇa*, then it would follow that testimonial knowledge must be a form of inferentially obtained knowledge. But, in fact, scripturally based inferences fall short of the formal requirements that must be met for genuine inferential knowledge. Nevertheless, reliance on scripture is necessary if one hopes to acquire knowledge on matters that transcend the empirical and rational realms.

Let us take a step back for a moment. In contrast to the Nyāya School, Buddhists like Dharmakīrti wish to maintain that testimonial/scriptural knowledge is merely a form of inference and not a separate means of knowledge. That distinction between these two traditions is clear. But there is a second difference between these two main accounts that has yet to be emphasized. All three of the conditions—(a) through (c)—that Dharmakīrti places on scripturally based inference are conditions involving the statements within the scripture. Nothing at all has been said, thus far, about whether the *author* of the scripture in question is a reliable authority or credible witness (*āpta*). Expressed differently, Dharmakīrti's account focuses on 'content conditions' necessary for scriptural knowledge but not on 'testifier conditions' for scriptural knowledge. By contrast, the Nyāya account focuses quite a bit on 'testifier conditions' for scriptural knowledge, for it is the very idea that someone must be a trustworthy source or expert that stands at the heart of the Nyāya account of testimonial knowledge.

The fact of the matter is, however, that Dharmakīrti *does* entertain 'testifier conditions' for scriptural knowledge. Immediately after presenting the earlier described account, Dharmakīrti goes on take up an alternative account of testimonial knowledge—an account that appeals to the idea of a credible authority. When a person, such as the Buddha, has shown himself to be credible on the most important of matters, such as the Four Noble Truths, this person can be deemed trustworthy on other radically inaccessible matters as well.

There is some uncertainty among scholars as to the intended relationship between these two approaches toward scripturally based knowledge—the first involving 'content conditions' necessary for knowledge and the second involving 'testifier conditions' necessary for knowledge. It looks like the first account, relying on 'content conditions' is Dharmakīrti's actual theory of how knowledge is attained through scriptural inference. But it also appears that he is endorsing the idea that scriptural inferences involve an appeal to a credible authority. It has been argued that Dharmakīrti's second, alternative account of testimonial knowledge may be an attempt to "bridge the gap" between the Buddhist approach toward testimony and the traditional Nyāya approach.[10]

With that said, Dharmakīrti goes on, in the very next verse, to reject the view that one could ever actually determine whether a testifier (e.g., an author of scripture) is a credible authority. Determining the credibility of a testifier would appear to be incredibly difficult. After all, one is seeking to determine a testifier's credibility on matters that are inaccessible to empirical and rational proof. Thus, there is no practical means by which to assess the credibility of the testifier on these radically inaccessible matters. Dharmakīrti states, "But if one is to act on the basis of examining the person, one would not act at all because one cannot know whether or not that person has those kind of extraordinary qualities."[11]

These criticisms by Dharmakīrti would not be seen as persuasive to Nyāya epistemologists. First of all, Dharmakīrti's concern that the credibility of a testifier cannot be established is an objection that only makes sense on the assumption that testimonial knowledge arises as a result of inferential reasoning. But this is explicitly denied by the Nyāya School. Second, as we have already seen, although the Nyāya School's account of testimony *does* require that the testifier be a trustworthy authority, their account *does not* require the hearer to *know* or *be aware* of the fact that the testifier has the quality of being trustworthy. On the Nyāya, nonreductive account of testimonial knowledge, all that is required on the part of the hearer is that the appropriate belief gets formed through the appropriate causal process. Yes, the speaker must, as a matter of fact, be an "expert" or trustworthy authority, but there is no separate condition that demands the hearer to validate that trustworthiness.

Framed in a completely different way, the criticism raised by Dharmakīrti—that a person cannot practically establish whether a person is a trustworthy authority on radically inaccessible matters—assumes an *internalist* approach toward testimonial knowledge acquisition. Since, for Dharmakīrti, testimonial knowledge is a form of inference, one must identify that the testifier is a trustworthy authority in order to make a warranted inference. But the Nyāya account of testimonial knowledge does not involve drawing an inference at all, and it is one that makes sense only under an *externalist* approach toward testimonial knowledge. To better appreciate the weight of the disagreement here, let us explore in more detail another distinction—the distinction between reductive and nonreductive theories of testimonial knowledge.

5.2. Reductive and Nonreductive Theories of Testimonial Knowledge

As a first approximation, we might say that *nonreductionists* uphold the view that testimony (from a person, scripture, etc.) is a distinct source of knowledge, irreducible to other means of knowledge. *Reductionists*, on the other hand, maintain that testimony is not a distinct means of knowledge. They would assert that knowledge gained by testimony—assuming there is such knowledge—is in some way or other reducible to knowledge gained through other means, such as perception and/or inference.[12] Expressed by philosopher Peter Strawson,[13]

> The question is whether we are to regard testimony, so understood, as a direct and immediate source of belief based upon it or whether we are to regard belief so based as being, in the last resort, essentially the product of other, more fundamental sources of knowledge, or, in brief again, is testimony, as a source of knowledge (or belief), *reducible* to these other sources?

This distinction between reductionism and nonreductionism can be articulated a bit differently by expressing it in terms of *warrant*, where warrant is understood to be whatever conditions are necessary to make some true belief an instance of knowledge. When a speaker, S, testifies that *p*, that testimony provides some measure of epistemic support for hearer H's belief that *p*. The reductionist position is that this testimony is *never by itself* sufficient to warrant H's belief that *p*. According to the reductionist, some additional support is needed if the hearer is to be warranted in believing *p*. The nonreductionist, by contrast, contends that in certain contexts (perhaps even the vast majority of contexts) the speaker's testimony alone is sufficient for H attaining a warranted belief that *p*. So, for example, when a high school mathematics teacher tells her students that $\sqrt{2}$ is irrational, the nonreductionist might proclaim that this testimonial assertion alone is all the evidence needed to warrant her students in believing that $\sqrt{2}$ is, in fact, irrational. (Of course, this is consistent with there being other cases in which testimonial assertions could fail to provide adequate evidential support for a proposition. For example, while the testimony of a single eyewitness to a murder at a drug house could provide some evidence about the guilty party, it is still open to the nonreductionist to maintain that, in *that* circumstance, the testimonial evidence would need additional corroboration to warrant a jurist's belief about who is guilty of the murder.) The main point is simply that the nonreductionist grants that there are some situations in which testimony alone provides grounds sufficient to warrant beliefs, whereas the reductionist denies this.

As has been spelled out earlier, members of the Nyāya School of Indian philosophy endorse a nonreductive account of testimonial knowledge. They not only maintain that testimony is a distinct source of knowledge, irreducible to other forms of knowledge, but they also adopt the stance that, provided that there are no grounds for concluding that a given testimonial source is untrustworthy, a person can be warranted in accepting the testimonial claims of that source. This nonreductionist position is rejected by Dharmakīrti and other Buddhist thinkers in India. They support a reductive conception of testimonial knowledge. Within the Western tradition of philosophy, Thomas Reid is frequently put forward as the paradigmatic representative of nonreductionism, while David Hume offers a view emblematic of the reductionist position.[14]

To be clear, the disagreements between Nyāya and Buddhist epistemologists over the status of testimonial/scriptural knowledge involve more than just a disagreement over nonreductive versus reductive conceptions of testimony. Nevertheless, the dispute between reductionism and nonreductionism is of central importance to this Indian disagreement. Buddhist epistemologists believe that one cannot gain knowledge through scripture unless that knowledge is grounded in a process of inferential reasoning. The Nyāya School disagrees. They contend that testimony is an irreducible *pramāṇa*, and that the beliefs generated through this *pramāṇa* are not arrived at inferentially at all.

It must be emphasized, again, that this dispute between reductive and nonreductive approaches to testimonial knowledge in Indian epistemology arises, in part, because the very notion of a *pramāṇa* takes on a different meaning within the Buddhist tradition than it does in the Nyāya tradition. For the Nyāya School, a *pramāṇa* is a means or instrument of knowledge, and that school believes that testimony is a bona fide means for obtaining knowledge. Buddhists, by contrast, conceive of *pramāṇas* principally as episodes of cognition—viz., knowledge-laden cognitions. For the Buddhist, there are only two kinds of knowledge-laden cognitions: those that apprehend particular entities (perceptual cognitions), and those that apprehend general entities (inferential cognitions). When conceived of in terms of this dichotomy, testimonial-based knowledge only makes sense as a form of inferential cognition, since a cognition or belief that arises through an appeal to scripture must—as a cognition capable of being mixed with language—be one that apprehends general entities.

The preceding paragraph suggests that the different approaches toward testimonial knowledge taken by the Nyāya School and the Buddhists can be accounted for by examining the broader foundations (and origins) of their epistemological programs. But it may additionally be the case that there are *teleological* explanations for why the Naiyāyikas would be nonreductionists, and the Buddhists reductionists, about testimonial knowledge. In short, Buddhist and Nyāya philosophers very likely have different conceptions of *what testimony is for*. On one ordinary conception of testimony, it is a direct means by which to pass knowledge from one person to another. One person, who possesses knowledge on a particular topic, may have an interest or intent to pass that knowledge on to others. This transfer of knowledge might happen, for example, when a teacher tells her students that there will be a test the following day, or when a person walking down the street provides directions to a lost traveler. These sorts of cases can be classified as instances of *informal testimony*—cases where it might be thought that the information transfer from speaker to hearer is direct and not tied to inferential considerations on the part of the hearer. The hearer simply accepts as true what the speaker has said.

On a different conception of what testimony is for, its goal is to provide indirect evidence of that about which one is testifying. This conception is associated with cases of *formal testimony*, such as those that regularly occur in courtroom interrogations of a witness. A courtroom attorney may be intent on convincing the jury that the defendant committed murder, and he or she may cite as evidence of the defendant's guilt a witness who has testified to that effect. In a case like this, there is no presumption on the attorney's part that the witness's testimony will be directly transferring knowledge from the witness to the jury. Instead, in cases of formal testimony, the expectation is that the jury will treat the witness's assertion(s) as just one piece of evidence that (together with other corroborating evidence) inferentially supports the conclusion that the defendant did indeed commit murder.

The Nyāya School's characterization of testimonial knowledge shares more in common with the aforementioned instances of informal testimony, whereas the Buddhist account of testimonial knowledge is much more closely aligned with applications of formal testimony. Dharmakīrti's claims about testimony, for example, are focused squarely on the question of how religious scriptures should be used. Just as in cases of formal courtroom testimony, Dharmakīrti is concerned with the question of how we are to assess the reliability of scriptural assertions—where those scriptures are assumed to be composed by authors who may, for all we know, be fallible. Any belief arising from what is testified in such a scripture would only be warranted indirectly, through an inferential process that appeals to the general trustworthiness of the scripture in question. Given this emphasis on the formal assessment of religious scriptures' trustworthiness, it is no surprise at all that Buddhist epistemologists adopt a reductive account of testimony.

Just as instances of formal testimony are more readily assimilated to reductive conceptions of testimonial knowledge and instances of informal testimony are more readily assimilated to nonreductive conceptions of testimonial knowledge, the distinction between reductive and nonreductive accounts of testimonial knowledge is also linked to two different conceptions of what conditions need to obtain in order for someone to gain testimonial knowledge. In particular, we can distinguish 'speaker conditions' for testimonial knowledge from 'hearer conditions' for testimonial knowledge. Roughly stated, in order for a hearer to gain knowledge via testimony, a specific set of conditions must obtain on the part of the speaker/testifier, and a separate set of conditions must obtain on the part of the hearer. For example, the Nyāya School proclaims that one speaker condition for testimonial knowledge is that the testifier be a credible witness. Buddhists like Dharmakīrti, however, maintain that testimonial knowledge requires the recipient of testimony to verify the reliability of the scripture in question—which is a hearer condition on testimonial knowledge. Broadly speaking, nonreductive accounts of testimonial knowledge, like that of the Nyāya School, are primarily focused on speaker conditions for knowledge, whereas reductive accounts of testimonial knowledge, like that supported by Buddhists, tend to focus more on hearer conditions for knowledge.

Which approach toward testimony is the correct one—the Nyāya, nonreductionist account or the Buddhist, reductionist account—is actually not among the most important questions to be answered. In fact, Jennifer Lackey, in her deep dive into the epistemology of testimony, argues that *both* reductionism and nonreductionism are inadequate. And in her view, recognizing why they are both inadequate provides us with information necessary for constructing a more accurate account of the necessary and sufficient conditions for testimonial knowledge. In particular, she argues that reductionism and nonreductionism each fail because they too narrowly constrain the necessary conditions for testimonial knowledge. As she notes:[15]

> Reductionists, on the one hand, focus entirely on the hearer in a testimonial exchange . . . all of the epistemic work needs to be shouldered by the hearer since it is precisely her positive reasons that are supposed to provide the reductive base. . . . Non-reductionists, on the other hand, capture the work that needs to be done by the speaker in a testimonial exchange, but neglect the positive contribution that a hearer needs to make.

Lackey thus argues in defense of what she calls "dualism" in the epistemology of testimony, an approach that combines together both speaker conditions and hearer conditions for testimonial knowledge.

5.3. Speakers, Hearers, and Knowledge

From the foregoing discussion, we are now in the position to synthesize, and express more perspicuously, a number of the scattered points made earlier in this chapter. At least four different conceptual factors serve to distinguish the Buddhist account of testimonial knowledge from the Nyāya account:

1. The *pramāṇa* contrast—whether a *pramāṇa* is to be understood principally as (a) a means/instrument of knowledge or as (b) a knowledge-laden cognition
2. The *reductive status* contrast—whether testimony is (a) an irreducible form of knowledge or (b) reducible to inferential reasoning
3. The *warrant* contrast—whether testimonial knowledge makes use of (a) an externalist or (b) an internalist conception of warrant
4. The *testimonial locus* contrast—whether the central figure in instances of testimonial knowledge is (a) the speaker or (b) the hearer of testimony

The Nyāya theory of testimony—which sides with option (a) for each of the four factors above—starts with the assumption that what are of central concern are the various means or instruments of knowledge (*pramāṇa*), and thus affirms that testimony is an irreducible means of knowledge. As an irreducible means of knowledge, it is granted that testimonial knowledge is generated in a hearer owing to the fact that this knowledge is already possessed by a credible testifier (the speaker). The speaker or testifier (together with his or her testimony) must meet a number of conditions in order for the hearer to gain testimonial knowledge, but because these conditions are all tied to the speaker and his or her utterance, this knowledge requires no internally accessible evidence to be collected or assessed by the hearer.

The Buddhist account—which accepts option (b) for each of the four factors listed earlier—as espoused by Dharmakīrti, is grounded in a different conception of epistemology, one in which what is at issue is not so much separate instruments of knowledge as it is different types of knowledge-laden cognitive episodes. In cases of testimonial belief, because these sorts of cognitive episodes are conceptual in nature, the question of whether they count as episodes of knowledge is determined in a manner similar to that occurring for other episodes of (inferential) conceptual cognition. As such, testimonial knowledge is held to be reducible to a form of inference. So, too, since the *pramāṇa* is a knowledge-laden cognition of the hearer, the determinative factors for this sort of knowledge are conditions associated with the hearer of the testimony. In much the same way, whether the hearer meets the relevant conditions for knowledge depends on whether he or she possesses—and has access to—the relevant evidence necessary to ground one's inference.

The disagreement between the Nyāya School and Buddhist epistemologists over the status of testimonial knowledge, then, is not simply a disagreement over the question of whether this form of knowledge is or is not reducible to (perception and) inference. It is, more accurately, a disagreement about the nature of epistemological speculation, and about what the central focus of these speculations should be. If, as the Nyāya School believes, epistemology is primarily an investigation of the various means of knowledge, then the epistemology of testimony should rightly be focused on the speaker/source of a testimonial pronouncement. But if, as Buddhists believe, epistemology is principally an investigation of the kinds of cognitive episodes that impart knowledge, then the epistemology of testimony should be centered on the hearer/recipient of a testimonial pronouncement.

5.4. The Transmission Theory of Testimony

One additional topic in the epistemology of testimony that is impacted by the question of whether the speaker or the hearer of testimony is to be the central focus of these investigations is that of whether testimony is capable of imparting knowledge in a hearer *without* the speaker/testifier having that knowledge. Defenders of the *transmission theory of testimony* argue that testimonial knowledge is transmitted (or transferred) from a speaker to a hearer. More specifically, it is proclaimed that a hearer can gain knowledge by testimony only if the testifier has or had that knowledge himself or herself. As one proponent of the transmission theory, Robert Audi, pithily states, "What I do not have, I cannot give."[16] Expressed more fully, defenders of the transmission theory of testimony maintain that one necessary condition for hearer H to obtain (from speaker S) the testimonial knowledge that *p* is that S knows that *p*.

Before addressing the question of whether classical Buddhist epistemologists accept, or should accept, the transmission theory of testimony, let us note that its validity has been called into question in recent years within the analytic tradition of epistemology. Jennifer Lackey has developed a series of examples that are designed to show the failure of the transmission theory.[17] On her view, pace Audi, testimony can *generate* knowledge—in the sense that the hearer can obtain knowledge, via testimony, that the testifier does not possess. The details of Lackey's arguments cannot be repeated here, but her main line of reasoning involves identifying cases where a speaker, who testifies that *p*, fails to be justified in what she attests (and thus lacks knowledge), but where the hearer nonetheless comes to form a justified true belief from that speaker's testimony.

For example, Lackey considers a case where a person asks for directions to the nearest coffee shop. The person asked, speaker S, believes that the closest coffee shop is just around the corner, and testifies as such. However, this person S is, unbeknownst to the hearer, in the throes of Cartesian skepticism and—though she *believes* that to which she has testified—is convinced that none of her beliefs about the external world could be *justified*. Given this self-skepticism, Lackey maintains that S's belief about the location of the coffee shop has defeaters that prevent said belief from being justified, and thus ensure that S lacks knowledge. The hearer of this testimony, however, has no such skeptical concerns herself and has no reasons to believe that the testifier is consumed with skepticism. As such, her belief about the location of the coffee shop could be both justified and true, and thus an instance of knowledge.

Following Dharmakīrti's lead, Buddhist epistemologists adopt a reductive account of testimonial knowledge. But do they accept—or *would* they accept—the transmission theory of testimony? When a person comes to know something from an appeal to a scriptural source such as the word of the Buddha, must it be the case that the testifier, the source of the scripture, possess knowledge of that about which he is testifying?

This topic is not taken up explicitly within Buddhist philosophical texts. So to determine whether the transmission theory would be accepted within that tradition, we must look for clues indicating whether the theory is presupposed in epistemologists' reasoning about testimony. First, I will explore this question by reflecting on the relationship between testimonial knowledge and inferential reasoning. That discussion will be followed by a consideration of Buddhist appeals to credible authorities, including their discussions of the Buddha himself as an epistemic authority.

5.4.1. The Transmission Theory and Inference

Let us begin by reflecting on the threefold analysis that Dharmakīrti proposes regarding scriptural knowledge. This analysis involves, as explained earlier, verifying that no claims in the scripture are contradicted by perception or (ordinary) rational inference. Additionally, there can be no internal contradictions (within the scripture) on matters that transcend perception and ordinary inference. When these three conditions are passed, a person may permissibly draw an inference that a "radically inaccessible" pronouncement made within the scripture is true. As has been pointed out earlier, these three conditions for scripturally based inference are all 'content conditions' on testimonial knowledge. That is, in contrast to 'testifier conditions' like those adopted by the Nyāya School, the 'content conditions' that are a part of Dharmakīrti's account place no explicit restrictions on the person who is testifying. The author of the scripture may (or may not) possess knowledge of that about which he or she is testifying, but the epistemic status of the author does not directly figure into Dharmakīrti's threefold analysis of scriptural inference.

Insofar as this is the case, it would appear that Dharmakīrti's account of scriptural inference is at least consistent with a rejection of the transmission theory of testimony. In other words, a scripture can pass the threefold analysis and usher forth an inference from that scripture, even in cases where the author of the scripture does not him/herself possess knowledge of that about which he or she is testifying. More dramatically, it would appear to be possible for a scripture to pass Dharmakīrti's threefold analysis, and yet for the radically inaccessible statements within the scripture to be *false*. (To be clear, an ordinary human drawing such an inference from scripture would be in no position to recognize the falsity of these statements. Those statements are, after all, "radically inaccessible.") Given this possibility, the whole idea of a "scriptural inference," within Dharmakīrti's system of thought, appears to function rather differently from ordinary inferences like those described in chapter 4.

As we saw in chapter 4, in standard inferences, which proceed by an appeal to the power of real entities—as opposed to by an appeal to words/scripture—a person cannot (inferentially) come to know a proposition (e.g., that 'S has P') unless she already knows both that 'S has E' and that 'E entails P.' Expressed in a manner that is more in accord with typical Western portrayals of inference, the standard Buddhist view is that an inferential conclusion, viz., that the subject S has property P, cannot be known unless all the essential premises of that inference are also known to be true. In this respect, it could fairly be said that knowledge is not created via inferential reasoning as much as it is preserved or "passed on" from the premises to the conclusion. This reflects the assumption by Buddhist epistemologists that ordinary inferences not only *preserve* truth (from the premises to the conclusion) but also *depend on* having true premises.

It is less than fully clear, however, whether scriptural inferences have these same logical features. In particular, given that the thesis to be proven in an instance of scriptural inference is something that is radically inaccessible, it is not at all clear that an ordinary person could ever be in the position to know both that 'S has E' and that 'E entails P.' To see why, suppose that both 'S has E' and 'E entails P' are capable of being known via ordinary applications of (perception and) inference. If this is the case, then so, too, is the thesis 'S has P' capable of being known via an ordinary application of inference. The contrapositive claim should also hold: if the conclusion of a scriptural inference is something radically inaccessible, then so, too, must at least one of the "premises" of that inference be radically inaccessible. But provided that this is the case, it threatens the very possibility of an ordinary person ever possessing knowledge of the truth of both premises. In short, it would appear that there is some credence to Dharmakīrti's contention that "this kind of inference is not without problems."[18]

Remarkably, in the later Tibetan Buddhist tradition of epistemology, there is a movement toward the view that scriptural inference is no less certain than ordinary applications of inference—viz., that scriptural inference is "inference like any other."[19] This shift is remarkable not only because it reflects a clear departure from Dharmakīrti's own views on scriptural inference, but also because the Tibetan position appears to be in conflict with the basic line of reasoning that was put forward in the preceding paragraph. The late fourteenth- to early fifteenth-century Tibetan scholar Tsongkhapa argues that in scriptural inferences the "three characteristics"—and, in particular, both conditions (PD) 'S is E' and (V) 'E entails P'—*are* capable of being established through ordinary, objective reasoning. It is for this very reason that he regards scriptural inference as "inference like any other." For Tsongkhapa, what makes something a scriptural inference is simply the fact that the thesis to be proven, the conclusion, is radically inaccessible.

There is, in my estimation, an inconsistency in such a combination of views, however. If we are to grant that the "three characteristics" can all be established through ordinary reasoning, that very fact should entail that the conclusion is not radically inaccessible at all. Though I am not persuaded that Tsongkhapa's "inference like any other" account of testimonial inference is tenable, his approach can, nonetheless, be seen as a way to ensure that testimony never results in knowledge (via inference) on the part of the hearer unless the "premises" of that inference are themselves known. As such, if Tsongkhapa's account of scriptural inference is accepted, testimony does not create knowledge, and the transmission theory of testimony can be preserved.

Yet the typical way in which the transmission theory of testimony is understood is one that prioritizes the relationship between the speaker and the hearer of testimony. Dharmakīrti's threefold analysis does not lend itself easily to accommodating that relationship, as it focuses entirely on 'hearer conditions' for testimonial knowledge. What, though, of Dharmakīrti's subsequent appeal to "credible persons"? Perhaps his appeal to credible persons sheds light on whether the transmission theory of testimony is to be accepted within the Buddhist epistemological tradition.

5.4.2. The Transmission Theory and Persons of Authority

Dharmakīrti's discussion of credible persons or experts focuses largely on his worry that *determinations* of a testifier's credibility are not possible. As such, his attention, once again, is on 'hearer conditions' for knowledge and the difficulties associated with satisfying those conditions. Nevertheless, Dharmakīrti's discussion of credibility—and the difficulty of establishing that credibility—does appear to presuppose various ideas about the nature of credible persons. At the very least, his account appears to presuppose that a credible person would speak *truthfully*. It also seems that Dharmakīrti presupposes that credible persons are *generally* knowledgeable. These two features do not guarantee that the transmission theory holds within Dharmakīrti's account, but they do lend credence to the view that he was predisposed to grant something like the transmission theory.

There is a second line of evidence, as yet unaddressed, that may provide additional support for the conclusion that Dharmakīrti and other Buddhist epistemologists implicitly endorse the transmission theory of testimony. It stems not from Dharmakīrti's arguments about testimony as a form of inference (contained in chapter 1 of his *Commentary on [Dignāga's Compendium of] Knowledge*), but instead from his claims about *the authoritativeness of the Buddha* (which are found in chapter 2 of that same text). Dharmakīrti's forerunner, Dignāga, began his *Compendium of Knowledge* with a salutation to the Buddha and refers to the Buddha as "one who has become a *pramāṇa*" (*pramāṇabhūta*).[20] This epithet is not uncommonly interpreted as an affirmation that the Buddha is a *pramāṇa* in the sense of being a *reliable authority*. Dignāga's salutation forms the basis for a full chapter of Dharmakīrti's

Commentary on Knowledge, and many subsequent Buddhist epistemologists attempted to further elucidate the claim that the Buddha is or has become a *pramāṇa*. There has been an outpouring of secondary scholarship over that past thirty-plus years devoted to tackling the question of what was intended by referring to the Buddha as *pramāṇabhūta*.

On the strongest reading, the Buddha is to be considered a *pramāṇa* full stop—that is, as a source of knowledge. Understood in this way, the Buddha—or the word of the Buddha—should be treated as a third means of knowledge over and above perception and inference. On a weaker reading, the Buddha is *likened to*, or has a *similarity to*, the two *pramāṇas* of perception and inference. The Buddha himself is, after all, not literally a cognition or an episode of knowledge, but he can be metaphorically likened to the two kinds of knowledge episodes. Whatever the appropriate reading, this invocation by Dignāga suggests that, at the very least, we can understand the Buddha—if not other religious teachers as well—as *a person of authority*. And if the Buddha can be treated as such, then we could think of the teachings of the Buddha as a form of authoritative testimony capable of transmitting knowledge (of radically inaccessible matters) to others. In the context of the transmission theory of testimony, the question to be addressed is whether being a person of authority (in the sense of "one who has become a *pramāṇa*") implies an acceptance of the transmission theory. More formally, the question is whether Dignāga, Dharmakīrti, and their followers accept thesis (TT):

(TT) For any radically inaccessible state of affairs p^*, hearer H can know that p^* (on the basis of speaker S's testimony that p^*) only if S knows that p^*.

Given the likelihood that Dignāga was speaking metaphorically when referring to the Buddha as one who has become a *pramāṇa*, it is not entirely clear what he would have regarded to be the necessary and sufficient conditions for someone to qualify as such a person. Yet, when later Buddhist epistemologists explicate Dignāga's (and then Dharmakīrti's) remarks on this topic, there is every indication that these writers proceed from the assumption that the Buddha did or does himself have knowledge of the radically inaccessible truths that are announced in the *sūtras*. For example, on Dharmakīrti's understanding, the Buddha is an authority in part because he is the *sugata*, where this epithet is taken to imply that he has acquired knowledge of these radically inaccessible truths. As expressed by Eli Franco, "before becoming a protector he has to acquire the adequate knowledge, i.e., to become '*sugata*'. . . and in consideration of the three meanings of *su-*, *sugata* is said to state that the Buddha's knowledge is true, definitive and complete."[21] In this way, Dharmakīrti argues that the Buddha's authority, his having "become a *pramāṇa*," is partly explained by his being the *sugata* who has acquired this knowledge for the benefit of others.

Considerations of this sort give credence to the view that Dharmakīrti does indeed take for granted the thesis that, in the case of the Buddha's teachings, knowledge is transferred or transmitted from an authority who, himself, has that knowledge. To this extent, there is reason to believe that Dharmakīrti's account is in conformity with the transmission theory of testimony: testimony does not create knowledge; it merely transmits it from one person to another.

Further Reading

For much more on Indian theories of testimonial knowledge and their relationship to recent philosophical accounts of testimony, readers are strongly encouraged to consult Matilal, B. K., & Chakrabarti, A. (Eds.). (1994). *Knowing from words: Western and Indian philosophical analysis of understanding and testimony*. Dordrecht: Springer Science+Business Media.

For careful presentations of several puzzles relating to the epistemology of testimony in the Buddhist tradition, see chapters 1–3 of Tillemans, T. (1999). *Scripture, logic, language: Essays on Dharmakīrti and his Tibetan successors*. Boston: Wisdom Publications.

For a more extensive take on the notion that the Buddha is a person of authority, and on how Buddhists understood that claim, see Seyfort Ruegg, D. (1995). Validity and authority or cognitive rightness and pragmatic efficacy? On the concepts of *pramāṇa*, *pramāṇabhūta* and *pramāṇa(bhūta)puruṣa*. *Asiatische studien/Études asiatiques*, *49*(4), 817–827.

6
Ignorance

As an intellectual ideal, all beliefs aspire toward knowledge.[1] Not all beliefs, however, will deliver on this aspiration, for ignorance is an inevitable feature of human existence. Here, by "ignorance," what is meant is just the absence of knowledge—and more specifically, beliefs or cognitions that do not yield knowledge. A recognition of the inevitable ignorance of ordinary humans is prominent not only in Western philosophy but within the Buddhist epistemological tradition as well. Epistemologists rightly focus their attentions on the conditions necessary for accruing knowledge, but part of this epistemological project involves distinguishing the cases of success (knowledge) from cases of failure (ignorance). In fact, one of the best ways to understand *what knowledge is* comes from examining the various ways in which beliefs can *fail* to yield knowledge.

This chapter explores in greater depth those forms of cognition that do not impart knowledge. As we have seen earlier in this book, Buddhist epistemologists are intensely interested in detailing the parameters of perception and inference. To understand these two *pramāṇas* fully, however, one must appreciate how perception and inference differ from other forms of cognition that fall short of knowledge. Though Indian Buddhist epistemologists long recognized this point, it is in the Tibetan Buddhist tradition of epistemology from the eleventh century onward where we find the richest accounting of the assorted ways in which a cognition might fall short of knowledge. This chapter will detail a selection of these forms of *ignorant cognition* that are cataloged by Tibetan Buddhist epistemologists.

As the scholarly study of epistemology took hold in central Tibetan Buddhist monasteries beginning in the late eleventh century, among the most important works that informed the accounts developed by Tibetan scholars were the epistemology treatises written by the eighth-century Indian philosopher, Dharmottara. Two of Dharmottara's commentaries on Dharmakīrti's earlier texts gained significant traction with followers of the Tibetan scholar-translator, Ngog Lotsawa, in the eleventh and twelfth centuries.[2] These Tibetan philosophers did not always agree with Dharmottara's

Illuminating the Mind. Jonathan Stoltz, Oxford University Press (2021). © Oxford University Press.
DOI: 10.1093/oso/9780190907532.003.0006

views on epistemology, but his writings formed the basis for numerous epistemological developments made by Tibetan epistemologists in the eleventh and twelfth centuries.[3]

In particular, Dharmottara attempted to provide an accounting of various forms of cognition by showing how they can be reduced to more basic categories like "mistaken cognition" and "doubt." Tibetan philosophers, following Ngog Lotsawa's lead, disagreed with Dharmottara's reduction and instead offered much more detailed and systematic typologies of cognition. On this Tibetan account, there are still two forms of cognition that are accepted as instances of knowledge: perception and inference.[4] But there are numerous other forms of cognition that do not provide knowledge—various forms of ignorant cognition—some of which are, nonetheless, correct or true cognitions. In this chapter I will zoom in on three of these forms of ignorant cognition—(1) *mistaken cognition*, (2) *nonascertaining perception*, and (3) *factive assessment*—to give readers a clearer picture of how these Tibetan Buddhist epistemologists distinguished knowledge from its absence.[5]

6.1. Mistaken Cognition

What might appear to be the simplest form of ignorance is that of holding a false belief. As we saw in chapter 2, philosophers standardly maintain that truth is a necessary condition for knowledge. Thus, in any case in which a person forms a false belief, we can say that the person is ignorant on the matter in question. In standard parlance, in order to know that *p*, what is believed—the proposition *p*—must be true. Throughout much of this chapter the focus will be on specific forms of cognition that, even though "true," nonetheless fail to impart knowledge. I shall begin, however, by examining the most basic kind of ignorance—that of holding a belief that is false, or, in terms more relevant to the Buddhist context, *having a cognition that is mistaken.*

As we have seen in previous chapters, what are at issue in Buddhist epistemology are not (dispositional) beliefs but (episodic) cognitions, and the contents of these cognitions are frequently nonpropositional objects. Be that as it may, there is little question that in the Buddhist context something analogous to the truth of belief is still essential for knowledge. In chapter 2, this was termed a 'truth constraint' on knowledge. Pinning down the precise meaning of this truth constraint is not a simple matter. As we have seen in earlier chapters, from the time of Dharmakīrti onward, it has been maintained that episodes of knowledge are cognitions that are *nondeceptive* (*avisaṃvāda*). But, while nondeceptive cognitions satisfy the truth constraint, it is also acknowledged that some nondeceptive cognitions can be "erroneous" (*bhrānta*). In fact, as we saw in chapter 4, all conceptual cognitions—and, as such, all episodes of inferential knowledge—are held to be erroneous. It is thus worth examining more carefully the question of what conditions must obtain in order for a cognition to satisfy the 'truth constraint' on knowledge.

6.1.1. Nonconceptual Mistaken Cognition

Consider first the case of *nonconceptual* cognitions. Cognitions of this sort, according to Buddhist epistemologists, cannot possibly apprehend or engage any sort of propositional contents. How then should the truth constraint on knowledge be understood in the case of nonconceptual cognitions? One promising possibility would be to say that a cognition is "true" or "correct" only if the cognition *accurately represents* its object. For example, a visual cognition of a conch shell would be "true" only if the way the cognition represents the conch shell corresponds to the way the conch shell is in reality. The process of representation could be captured through some sort of causal mechanism wherein it is the real, external object that is the cause of the mental representations occurring within a person's cognition. This approach, which approximates the standard *Sautrāntika* account of perception, and which is frequently, if tacitly, endorsed by Dharmakīrti, relies on a version of correspondence or accordance between (a) the representation or phenomenal form (*ākāra*) in one's mind and (b) the real object itself. If, for example, a white conch shell is represented as yellow (or apprehended through a yellow aspect), then we should say that the cognition has failed the truth condition required for perceptual knowledge. Let us call this the 'accurate representation' interpretation of the truth constraint on perception. It would be fair to say that something in this neighborhood is one of the most common portrayals of the truth constraint on nonconceptual knowledge within the Buddhist epistemological tradition.

This way of understanding the truth constraint on knowledge is not without its difficulties, however. First, it presupposes a representationalist understanding of perception. Though Dharmakīrti and many other Buddhist epistemologists accept the idea that perceptual experiences involve the presence of mental aspects or representations, such an account could not be extended to those philosophers who deny that nonconceptual experience proceeds by way of representations.[6] Second, it is far from obvious what it even means for a representational aspect to correspond to its object, given that the aspect is something internal to the mind, whereas the object that is being represented may very well not be. It is, thus, no trivial matter determining what should count as an accurate versus inaccurate representation.

There is also the question of what to say about episodes of nonconceptual awareness in which the representation is partially accurate and partially inaccurate. Let us suppose, as supposed earlier, that a white conch shell is visually apprehended as yellow. That is, let us suppose that a person represents an external object (one that is actually a white conch shell) as being a conch shell and as being yellow. Surely, since the color is inaccurately represented, we should say that the person does not have perceptual knowledge of yellow (or of a yellow object). But what about the conch shell? Does the person perceive a conch shell? In this case there is a conch shell that is represented as a conch shell, and so it looks like it is an accurate representation in that regard. Should we thus say that the person has perceptual knowledge of a conch shell?

This matter is debated in the Indian Buddhist epistemological tradition, with some thinkers—in particular, Jinendrabuddhi—arguing that in such a circumstance the person does have perceptual knowledge of the conch shell.[7] Yes, the object is misrepresented as being yellow, but at least with respect to its being a conch shell, the object is accurately represented. Many other Buddhist epistemologists disagree with Jinendrabuddhi's position. Dharmottara, for example, argues that since the cognition is inaccurate (a *white* shell is represented as being *yellow*), it simply cannot meet the necessary requirement of representing accurately. In short, it is held that there is no such thing as a partially accurate perception. In order for one to have perceptual knowledge, the cognition must be fully accurate.

To add even more complexity, as I said earlier, not all Buddhist epistemologists even adopt a representationalist account of perceptual experience. Soon after the time that indigenous epistemological texts started to be written in Tibet in the eleventh century, a number of Buddhist thinkers adopted *direct (nonrepresentational) realist* accounts of perception. While these Tibetan writers—including the twelfth-century scholar Chaba Chokyi Senge and his followers—certainly did not shy away from describing mistaken cognitions in terms of a failure of correspondence with the actual state of affairs, the fact that nonconceptual experiences were asserted *not* to involve a process of representation makes it more difficult to see how this correspondence is supposed to work. On this Tibetan direct realist account, the truth constraint cannot be grounded in a correspondence between mental representations and the objects themselves, for Chaba denied the existence of any such representations.

What we see instead in these early Tibetan Buddhist epistemologists is the claim—standard among naïve realists—that perceptual cognitions are simply those whose apprehended objects are the real (and paradigmatically external) objects themselves. In short, veridical sense perceptions directly apprehend real, external objects; and those nonconceptual cognitions that apprehend something other than a real object are mistaken cognitions. This direct realist reading thus eschews the 'accurate representation' understanding of the truth constraint on knowledge and replaces it with what we might call the 'unmediated apprehension of real things' understanding. On this latter approach, mistaken cognitions are ones that do not apprehend real objects but instead apprehend "superimpositions." That is, they apprehend items that are not real but are merely superimposed on reality by the mind.

There are yet additional ways in which one can characterize what it takes for a nonconceptual cognition to satisfy the 'truth constraint' on knowledge—characterizations that cannot be addressed here. Suffice it to say that in any case in which a nonconceptual cognition fails this 'truth constraint,' the cognition in question is "mistaken" and so not an episode of knowledge. But again, what exactly it means for a cognition to be mistaken depends on further factors concerning the relationship between cognitions and their objects. Proponents of a representationalist account of perception will standardly claim that mistaken cognition is tied to having an inaccurate representation. Proponents of a direct realist theory of perception will argue, instead, that a mistaken cognition is one that does not apprehend a real thing. Whatever the case, when a nonconceptual cognition misfires in one of these ways, it is, thereby, an instance of ignorant cognition.

6.1.2. Conceptual Mistaken Cognition

When we turn to conceptual cognitions, the truth constraint on knowledge is still relevant, but it will need to be understood differently. Though Buddhist epistemologists all regard genuine inferential cognitions to be nondeceptive, these thinkers also maintain that all conceptual cognitions involve the apprehension of unreal, general entities (*sāmānyalakṣaṇas*). After all, in conceptual cognition, one is not experiencing real objects directly. Instead, a person is entertaining general, conceptual entities, which are used so as to gain, indirectly, knowledge of the world. But since the conceptual entities that factor into these episodes of cognition are not real, Buddhist epistemologists maintain that all conceptual cognitions are *erroneous* (*bhrānta*). It is thus critical for Buddhist epistemologists to give an account of how the 'truth constraint' on knowledge can be satisfied by inferential cognitions given that all these cognitions are nonetheless "erroneous."

To see what is at stake here, let us consider an example, such as a person's conceptual cognition *that there is a fire on the mountain pass* in a case where the person takes as evidence 'smoke,' even though there is not actually smoke; what was observed was really just a plume of dust. Let us further assume that the cognition or judgment is incorrect, and that there is actually no fire on the mountain pass. Here, it would be convenient to say that the cognition of there being a fire on the mountain pass fails the truth constraint on knowledge because there is no fire on the mountain pass. But what is it about this judgment that shows it to fail the truth constraint on knowledge?

Its failure cannot be explained by the fact that there is no universal 'fireness' on the mountain top, for such in re universals are widely rejected, full stop, in the Buddhist epistemological tradition. As a consequence, the question of whether a conceptual cognition passes or fails the truth constraint cannot be answered by making an appeal to any correspondence between the unreal, conceptual entities that are entertained in one's mind and universal properties existing in the external world. Beginning as early as the time of Dignāga in the sixth century, a nominalist *theory of exclusion* (*apoha*) is proposed by Buddhist philosophers as a means by which to bypass any commitment to real universals. The word "cow," for example, can be successfully used to refer to cows not by virtue of there being some universal 'cowness' existing in cows, but rather because the word "cow" serves to *exclude* all those things that are noncows. Though this may appear to suffer from a problem of circularity, Dignāga, Dharmakīrti, and their followers go to great lengths to argue that the exclusion theory is viable.[8] While the central purpose of the Buddhist theory of exclusion is to account for the nature of word meaning (in a world devoid of real universals), one might also expect that the theory could play a role in Buddhist accounts of conceptual knowledge. After all, as we saw in chapter 4, there is on the standard Buddhist account an intimate connection between conceptual cognition and language.

Tibetan epistemologists in the twelfth century do indeed maintain that the truth constraint relevant to conceptual knowledge is one that critically involves a process of exclusion. In particular, Chaba maintains that conceptual mistaken cognitions are precisely ones that, from the perspective of excluding what is other, affirm something that is not the case and deny something that is the case.[9] With respect to the example offered earlier, of a person who wrongly believes there to be fire on the mountain pass (even though there is not), Chaba would maintain that the cognition in question is one that *excludes* conceiving of the mountain pass as not containing a fire. Though Chaba and many of his followers frequently describe these mistaken conceptual cognitions in terms of a lack of correspondence with what is to be cognized, this lack of correspondence can be fleshed out in terms of excluding the actual state of affairs.

Although there are many more details that could be provided about what it means for a cognition to fail the 'truth constraint' on knowledge, and thus to be a mistaken cognition, those details need not be pursued here. The question of truth is an important one, philosophically speaking—and it is particularly important in relation to varying Buddhist accounts of ontology—but it is not the most central concern of epistemologists. This is true not just in the analytic tradition of epistemology but also in the Buddhist tradition. In fact, within Buddhist epistemology texts very little space is devoted to discussions of mistaken cognitions.

6.2. Ignorant Perception

Let us, therefore, set aside the case of mistaken cognitions and turn to a presumably more controversial case: episodes of nonconceptual awareness where the truth constraint on knowledge *is* satisfied. Should we grant that all veridical perceptual experiences—that is, all perceptions proper—are thereby instances of knowledge? To the extent that perceptual cognitions are episodes of awareness that are generated through causal processes operating flawlessly, and thus that the phenomenal forms or representations appearing to the perceiver are in accord with the objects to be apprehended, it would seem that perceptions are fully reliable sources for apprehending reality. As such, this lends weight to the view that all perceptual cognitions are *pramāṇas*—that is, instances of knowledge. This was, no doubt, the overwhelming consensus position within the Indian Buddhist epistemological tradition, and some account along these lines was endorsed by Dharmakīrti himself.

There may be some reasons to call into doubt the overall tenability of this understanding of perceptual knowledge, however. Just because there is a causal process that begins, let us suppose, with light bouncing off a conch shell, then entering into one's eye, and then ultimately resulting in a (veridical) experience of a conch shell, must we thereby conclude that this resultant experience of the conch shell suffices for knowledge? In essence, the question is whether a *causal* theory of perceptual experience adequately supports the conclusion that whenever a person has a veridical perceptual experience (caused in the appropriate way) that experience is tantamount to knowledge.

6.2.1. Discriminatory Power as a Requirement for Knowledge

In chapter 2, while elucidating Dharmakīrti's definition of knowledge episodes, it was emphasized that in the post-Dharmakīrtian tradition, Buddhist philosophers recognized that a cognition's merely being true/correct is insufficient for knowledge. To have an episode of knowledge requires that one's cognition invariably tracks the truth. Though this is most evident in the case of inference-like beliefs (to be described later, in section 6.3), it could also be the case that some veridical perceptual experiences may fail to be truth-tracking cognitions. In particular, it could be argued that perceptual knowledge requires not merely that an experience is veridical, but also that the cognizer possesses some sort of *discriminatory ability* whereby he or she can distinguish the object perceived from contrary alternatives to that object. This is a topic that will be addressed again more fully in chapter 8, when I undertake a deeper examination of the truth-tracking constraint on knowledge episodes and how that truth-tracking constraint is connected to the twin theses of *cognitive sensitivity* and *perceptual discrimination*. Nevertheless, the topic of perceptual discriminatory ability is of utmost importance here as well.

In the 1970s, the epistemologist Alvin Goldman developed a series of arguments to show that even if a person has a veridical visual experience, such as of a red barn—an experience resulting in a belief that has been generated through a trustworthy causal process involving the red barn itself—we should deny that the person has knowledge if he or she cannot distinguish red barns from relevant contrary alternatives, such as papier-mâché barn facades in an environment where such facades are common. In short, Goldman argued that perceptual knowledge requires not just having a correct belief with an appropriate causal connection to what is perceived but also the ability to distinguish the perceived object from relevant alternatives. Tibetan Buddhist epistemologists writing in the twelfth century adopt a position somewhat similar to that held by Goldman. On this Tibetan account, perceptual knowledge—of, for example, a mother-of-pearl shell in water—requires not just that one's cognition is veridical but also that the cognition is incompatible with contrary superimpositions—such as the superimposed property 'silver.'

There are important differences between Goldman's account in which perceptual knowledge requires the ability to distinguish the actual state of affairs from relevant alternatives and the twelfth-century Tibetan account in which perceptual knowledge is restricted to those cognitions that counter the capacity to produce contrary superimpositions. Foremost among these differences is one pertaining to the contrast between conceptual and nonconceptual cognitions. While Buddhist epistemologists, including Chaba and his Tibetan followers, are adamant that perceptual cognitions must be entirely nonconceptual, there is little question that Goldman would hold a different view. On his account, the relevant perceptual beliefs are ones that arise as a result of (unstated) cognitive factors, at least some of which likely involve conceptual capacities. Relatedly, Goldman represents these perceptual beliefs as having propositional contents, a perspective that would not be shared by Buddhist epistemologists. At least in part because perceptual cognitions are held to be nonconceptual, what is perceived is not an abstract proposition or state of affairs, but just a particular object.

In the pages that follow, I shall zoom in on the account of perception that was articulated by Chaba in the twelfth century. On his account, all perceptions apprehend real objects; and they do so directly, without the presence of representations. But Chaba contends that there are three distinct subtypes of perception, only one of which is a *pramāṇa*. The subtype of perception that is a *pramāṇa* we can call "perceptual knowledge." But there are two other forms of perceptual awareness—cases in which a person directly, and nonconceptually, apprehends a real object—that do not impart knowledge. One of these can be called "perceptual postknowledge cognition" and the other "nonascertaining perception."[10] Of these two forms of perception that are not instances of knowledge, the most pertinent here is the category of nonascertaining perception.

6.2.2. Nonascertaining Perception

On Chaba's account, nonascertaining perceptions are instances of perception—and this, again, means that they directly apprehend real objects—but they nonetheless fail to be instances of knowledge because, as Chaba puts it, they are "compatible with opposite superimpositions."[11] We have already encountered one core example: a person looks into a body of water and correctly apprehends (indeed, *perceives*) mother-of-pearl. Yet, in part because of the resemblance between mother-of-pearl and silver, the person could be induced to form the determinate judgment that there is a piece of silver in the water. In such a scenario, the fact that this perceptual experience of a mother-of-pearl shell could be accompanied by the superimposition 'silver' or could give rise to a subsequent judgment that it is a piece of silver shows that the perception was "compatible with opposite superimpositions." In other words, the perception, though veridical, was incapable of ruling out contrary alternatives (such as its being a piece of silver), and so it does not suffice for an episode of perceptual *knowledge*.

Chaba actually delineates two different subtypes of nonascertaining perception (and, surprisingly, the example of mother-of-pearl and silver doesn't squarely for into either of his two subcategories). One variety consists of cases where an object is veridically perceived, but where (so Chaba contends) some of the properties of the object are "nonmanifest" and thus fundamentally incapable of being known via perception. For example, suppose that a person visually perceives a white conch shell. Such a conch shell is, according to Buddhist philosophers, an impermanent thing—it is changing moment by moment. On Chaba's account, given that the person is perceiving a white conch shell, he or she is also, thereby, perceiving an impermanent thing. In fact, based on earlier reasoning by Dharmakīrti concerning the properties that appear in perceptual experiences, Chaba maintains that the person *perceives* the shell's impermanence. Yet Chaba contends that the person *cannot* have perceptual knowledge of the conch shell's impermanence, for the property of impermanence is "nonmanifest." The person can have perceptual knowledge with respect to the property of being white, but cannot have perceptual knowledge with respect to the property of being impermanent.

(Knowledge of the shell's impermanence, according to Chaba, is something that can only be obtained from a inferential cognition.) Expressed more succinctly, the cognizer *perceives* the shell's impermanence and yet is *ignorant* of the shell's impermanence.

A second variety of nonascertaining perception described by Chaba involves cases where a person is *inattentive*. Consider, for example, a case where a person has her eyes open, and visually perceives something blue, but where the person is utterly absorbed in her own thoughts, contemplating, let's say, some deep mathematical theorem. Chaba would say that the person in this case does indeed perceive blue, but also that due to her inattentiveness the perceptual experience is not sufficient for knowledge of blue. Similarly, a person sitting in a coffee shop reading a book may hear (and, as such, perceive through hearing) two people conversing at the table next to him. And yet, provided that the person is absorbed in the book he is reading, the sounds heard would not constitute (auditory) perceptual knowledge. In short, on Chaba's account, to perceive *x* does not always entail that one has knowledge of *x*.

Expressed differently, Chaba's contention is that that merely having a veridical perceptual experience is insufficient for knowledge. Needless to say, such a view is anathema to what is directly supported by Dignāga, Dharmakīrti, and other Indian Buddhist epistemologists. In particular, Chaba's proclamations that some perceptions could be "nonascertaining" would have been seen as highly peculiar to earlier Indian Buddhist epistemologists—not because they would disagree, but because they would have denied that activities such as "ascertainment" or "determination" could be present in any nonconceptual cognition, including perception.[12] Traditionally, Buddhist epistemologists like Dignāga and Dharmakīrti maintained that perception is a passive process that does not determine its object. Such determinations can occur only in conceptual cognitions. It is true that Chaba and other Tibetan epistemologists in the same broad time period would have agreed that perceptions cannot be determinate cognitions. Yet they did uphold the view that some (and only some) perceptions are "ascertaining"—provided that they can actively eliminate the presence of superimpositions. This, too, would have been emphatically denied by earlier Buddhist epistemologists like Dignāga and Dharmakīrti, however. The standard position in the Indian Buddhist tradition would have been to claim that the elimination of superimpositions is something that can be carried out in conceptual cognition alone.

To be fair, these Tibetan epistemologists, living high on the Tibetan plateau, were not simply creating the category of nonascertaining perception out of thin air. There is good reason to think that Tibetans' formalization of the category of nonascertaining perception derives from their readings of certain statements made by the eighth-century Indian philosopher Dharmottara. Yet it is only in the eleventh and twelfth centuries that this idea of nonascertaining perceptual cognitions becomes formalized as a distinct, irreducible type of cognition.[13]

What I want to do in the remainder of this section, however, is set aside the fact that Chaba's account of nonascertaining perception marks a radical departure from earlier Buddhist theories and instead focus on the philosophical implications of his contention that perceptual cognitions are episodes of knowledge only in cases where the cognition is incompatible with the presence of superimpositions. Chaba's claim is that knowledge requires more than just having a veridical cognition that directly apprehends its object. Additionally required for knowledge is the condition that the cognition be incompatible with the presence of (or the arising of) contrary, superimposed qualities. As will be noted again in chapter 8, this account has at least superficial affinities to the interpretations of knowledge that flowed from Alvin Goldman's discriminatory power interpretation of perceptual knowledge.

As suggested by examples like the "red barn" case mentioned earlier, it is now commonly agreed by contemporary epistemologists that a person wouldn't know, for instance, that something is a pine tree unless that person could distinguish pine trees from relevantly similar objects, such as spruce trees and fir trees. Using a more typical Buddhist example, we might say that in order to know that something is mother-of-pearl, a person would need to be capable of distinguishing mother-of-pearl from silver. In particular, to have perceptual knowledge of mother-of-pearl, the cognition that visually (and veridically) apprehends mother-of-pearl must be incompatible with, among other things, the superimposition 'silver.'

Again, this capacity to exclude or eliminate superimpositions, such as the superimposition 'silver,' is understood by Chaba to be fully explicable in nonconceptual and nonpropositional terms. To have perceptual knowledge of mother-of-pearl does not mean that she knows *that* the object is mother-of-pearl, nor *that* the object is not silver. Instead, on this Tibetan account, what it means for someone to have perceptual knowledge of mother-of-pearl is just that she directly apprehends mother-of-pearl and that the cognition that apprehends mother-of-pearl counters the capacity to produce superimpositions like 'silver.' When this capacity to produce contrary/opposite superimpositions has been countered, it should imply that the perceptual cognition of mother-of-pearl cannot be accompanied by the superimposition 'silver' nor give rise to a subsequent (conceptual) judgment that the object is silver.

One additional important difference between the discrimination theory of perceptual knowledge as proposed by Alvin Goldman and the earlier-described account put forward by Chaba is the fact that Goldman's account only requires the ability to rule out *relevant* alternatives. No parallel restriction is made by Chaba or other Tibetan epistemologists. On their view, cognitions must be incompatible with all directly contrary superimpositions in order for that cognition to be an instance of knowledge. This raises the question of whether this restriction on perceptual knowledge that is imposed by Chaba and his followers may be too restrictive—whether it will deny knowledge to episodes of perceptual awareness that, intuitively, should still have the status of being instance of knowledge. For example, it might be worried that Chaba's account would give a counterintuitive diagnosis in a case where a person perceives a zebra, but where the perceptual cognition is compatible with the superimposition of 'being a mule cleverly painted to look like a zebra.' As long as the object's being a mule cleverly painted to look like a zebra is an extremely remote (and thus irrelevant) possibility, Goldman would contend that even though, counterfactually, if the object had been a cleverly painted mule, the person would have still believed it to be a zebra, this does not prevent the person from perceptually knowing that there is a zebra in front of her. On Chaba's account, by contrast, it might appear that the inability to eliminate the superimposition 'mule cleverly painted to look like a zebra' would prevent the person from having perceptual knowledge—even when the person is actually perceiving a zebra.

I believe this worry about the Tibetan account is misplaced. Whereas Goldman's relevant alternatives restriction on his discrimination theory of perceptual knowledge proceeds by considering what one would believe in the relevant counterfactual situations, Chaba's account of perceptual knowledge, by contrast, does not involve any assessment of counterfactual cases. This is a key difference in how these two traditions' accounts of perceptual discrimination work, and one that tamps down concerns that Chaba's "countering of superimpositions" requirement places too great a restriction on perceptual knowledge.

To see more clearly why this is so, let us consider again the case in which a person peers into a body of water and has a perceptual cognition of mother-of-pearl; that is, the object that she visually apprehends is indeed a mother-of-pearl shell. Now, Chaba's position is that this episode of perception would be a *pramāṇa* only provided that the person's cognition of mother-of-pearl is incompatible with directly contrary superimpositions, including the superimposition 'silver.' But this account is silent about what would happen in the relevant counterfactual scenario. Perhaps if the object under water had been a piece of silver, the person would (wrongly) have had a cognition as of mother-of-pearl. But even if that were so, this counterfactual information is, on Chaba's account, irrelevant to the question of whether her actual perception of a mother-of-pearl shell in water qualifies as knowledge.

Now, the truth of the matter is that whereas Goldman and other contemporary epistemologists tend to focus their examples on cases of (perceptually) discriminating between objects that could very well be nearly indistinguishable—or perhaps only distinguishable by experts—those sorts of cases are rarely what is at stake in the parallel Tibetan examples. To be sure, the example of experiencing mother-of-pearl versus silver is a close analog to what we find in contemporary analytic epistemology, and Tibetan authors frequently use the near indistinguishability of silver and mother-of-pearl so as to exemplify the absence of perceptual knowledge. Some of Chaba's followers explicitly endorse the position that an initial perception of mother-of-pearl, from a distance, may fail to be an instance of knowledge (owing to the inability to counter the superimposition 'silver'). But this position is consistent with the further contention that, were the person to get a closer glimpse of the object (the mother-of-pearl), he or she could then be in the position to eliminate the superimposition 'silver,' and thus would have perceptual knowledge.

In most cases, however, the Tibetan category of nonascertaining perception does not involve (near) indistinguishability. As described earlier, the two central types of nonascertaining perception involve cases of "nonmanifest" properties and cases of perceptual inattentiveness. What is at stake in these sorts of cases is not an inability to distinguish the object or properties perceived from relevantly similar alternatives. Rather, these are cases where the perceptual cognition, though veridical, does not effectively constrain the conceptual activities that can occur within the cognizer. When a person who is utterly absorbed in her own thoughts perceives a white conch shell, and thus has a mere nonascertaining perception of the color white, the problem is not really that she cannot distinguish 'white' from 'nonwhite' (or from, 'blue' or 'black'). Instead, the problem, speaking loosely, is that she doesn't *notice* (or "ascertain") the color of the shell. Her perception was accurate but also compatible with the presence of mistaken conceptual imputations.

The central takeaways from these Tibetan examples are twofold. First, even with respect to nonconceptual cognitions, there is an avenue for upholding the position that the veridicality of one's experience does not necessarily entail that the experience should qualify as an instance of knowledge. The second takeaway from this Tibetan theory is their recognition that *knowledge* in perceptual cases may be better explained by the possession of a certain kind of *discriminatory power*—for Chaba, the capacity to eliminate superimpositions—than it is by the existence of a *causal process* involving the object apprehended and the cognition that apprehends that object. If this is right, it shows that there can be such a thing as "ignorant perception."

6.3. Ignorant Veridical Conception

Much less controversial than the status of ignorant perception is that of veridical conceptual cognitions that fail to be episodes of knowledge. Such cases are comparable to the positing of true beliefs that fall short of knowledge. Few contemporary philosophers question the presumption that there can be true beliefs that, nonetheless, fail to impart knowledge. This view is just as prominent in the Buddhist epistemological tradition. Some conceptual judgments can be true or correct and yet fail to be instances of knowledge. In the remainder of this chapter I will discuss two such forms of conceptual cognition that are formalized by Tibetan Buddhist epistemologists in the eleventh and twelfth centuries: "postknowledge cognitions" and "factive assessments."

6.3.1. Postknowledge Cognition

The first form of conceptual cognition that is veridical and yet not an episode of knowledge is that of postknowledge cognition. This category of cognition is taken, by Chaba and his immediate followers in Tibet, to include both nonconceptual episodes of awareness and conceptual episodes. Our focus here is just on *conceptual* instances of postknowledge cognition. But even here, Chaba mentions two different forms of conceptual postknowledge cognition.

One variety is essentially that of memory or recollection. Episodes of recollection, where persons form cognitions of that which is already known, do not qualify as *pramāṇas*. In one sense, this is the case because attributions of knowledge are taken to require, following Dharmakīrti, that the cognitions impart *new* information. Memories or recollections do not meet this requirement of novelty, and so they are not episodes of knowledge. Relatedly, while our focus has largely been on *pramāṇas* as episodes of knowledge, they can also be thought of as *sources* of knowledge. But memories and recollections are not at all *sources* of knowledge, and so they do not qualify as *pramāṇas*.

The other form of conceptual postknowledge cognition discussed by Chaba is that of determinate judgments subsequent to perception. An instance of perceptual (and, hence, nonconceptual) knowledge—for example, perceptual knowledge of a white conch shell—may give rise, a moment later, to the conceptual judgment *that there is a conch shell.* This conceptual judgment is, according to Chaba and other Tibetans of his time period, a correct cognition, for there is indeed a conch shell. But the conceptual judgment is not considered an instance of knowledge, for it imparts no new information over and above that contained in the perceptual awareness. Once again, the perceptual experience wherein a person apprehends a conch shell can very well be an episode of knowledge, but the conceptual judgment that there is a conch shell, which immediately follows the perceptual experience, is not regarded to be an episode of knowledge.

Now, obviously, this way of applying the term "knowledge" departs from how these cases would standardly be understood within the analytic tradition of epistemology. These differences in understanding are largely tied to two critical areas where the relevant traditions of epistemology diverge, both of which were discussed at the beginning of this book. First, whereas the contemporary analytic tradition of epistemology emphasizes a *dispositional* interpretation of knowledge, the Buddhist tradition—like their non-Buddhist counterparts in ancient India—favor an *episodic* interpretation of knowledge. On the first interpretation, knowledge is a *state* of a person—one that can persist for long periods of time. On the second, Buddhist interpretation, knowing is an *event* that occurs at some particular moment within a larger stream of mental episodes/events.

The second key difference, related to this first one, is that the Buddhist tradition of epistemology highlights much more clearly the connection between a cognition and the *source* or *means* by which a cognition arises in order to explain what makes it an episode of knowledge than does the analytic tradition.

Much (but certainly not all) of twentieth-century analytic epistemology has prioritized an understanding of knowledge in which the source or origin of a person's belief matters very little in assessments of knowledge. Instead, what has been much more highly prioritized is the justification or support that a belief has (typically, support from other beliefs), largely independent of the origins that gave rise to the belief.

The case of postknowledge cognition, then, is one that shows more about differences in how these two broad traditions of epistemological discourse operate and less about any substantial, philosophical disagreement over how the question of what is required for knowledge over and above having a true belief or true cognition. While this Tibetan category of conceptual postknowledge cognitions can be, roughly speaking, classified under the heading of "true beliefs that are not knowledge," the reasons why these cognitions do not suffice for knowledge are not so much tied to epistemic considerations—for example, they are not disqualified for reasons pertinent to questions about the *reliability* of or *warrant* for beliefs/cognition—but are rather tied to peculiarities of the Buddhist understanding of the term *pramāṇa*. Having said that, there is a completely separate category of conceptual cognitions formalized by eleventh- and twelfth-century Tibetan Buddhist philosophers that is much more relevantly connected to contemporary epistemological discussions of the distinction between knowledge and mere true belief; and that is the category of cognitive episodes called "factive assessment."

6.3.2. Factive Assessment

Consider the following scenario, introduced in chapter 2: A person is trekking through the Himalayas up and over a series of mountain passes. He looks toward another mountain pass in the distance and catches a glimpse of something funneling up into the air. It is actually a swarm of flies that have congregated above a fire where meat is being grilled. The grilling meat has produced no smoke, but the swarming flies are mistakenly believed, by the trekker, to be a cloud of smoke. Unable to see any fire, and operating under the mistaken belief that there is smoke on the mountain pass, the trekker forms the (inference-like) judgment that there is a fire on the mountain pass. This judgment is correct, for there is a fire on the mountain pass. But the judgment is derived from the mistaken belief that there is smoke on the mountain pass. Should we say that the trekker knows that there is a fire on the distant mountain pass?

Here, according to Indian and Tibetan Buddhist epistemologists, we have a case where a person forms a correct, conceptual cognition—the judgment that there is a fire on the mountain pass—but one that, nevertheless, falls short of what should be required for knowledge. The judgment that there is a fire on the mountain pass is an ignorant one.

This sort of case is classified by twelfth-century Tibetan epistemologists as an instance of *factive assessment*.[14] Broadly speaking, these are inference-like judgments that hit their marks—that is, they are correct cognitions—but they do not do so in a way that comports with what is required for knowledge. More will be said later about how this insufficiency is described by Tibetan authors, but let us start by saying more about the various different subtypes of factive assessment that are delineated within eleventh- and twelfth-century Tibetan epistemology treatises.

The simplest form of factive assessment is one we can term "factive assessment lacking evidence." These are cases where a person forms a correct judgment but does so without relying on any evidence in order to support that judgment.[15] A standard example given in this context is that of a person who simply forms the belief that there is water in an old well, but does so without having any evidence to back up that belief. This judgment happens to be correct, but the person had no basis for believing there is water in the well, and so these Tibetan epistemologists claim that the judgment in question is not an instance of knowledge but merely an episode of factive assessment.

Of more interest to us are cases like the earlier-mentioned scenario of swarming bugs inducing a person to judge that there is a fire on the mountain pass. This is the second form of factive assessment, which is termed "factive assessment having incorrect evidence." These judgments are formed in reliance on an appeal to "evidence," but the evidence cited is mistaken. On an alternate formulation, the evidence may be accurate, but the person relies on the mistaken belief that the evidence entails the property to be proven when it does not. Taking some liberties, and using terms more familiar within contemporary analytic epistemology, we can represent these two versions of factive assessment having incorrect evidence in the following ways:

(FA_{M1}) S takes *e* as evidence, and knowing that *e* entails *p*, judges that *p*. *e* is false but *p* is true.

(FA_{M2}) S takes *e* as evidence, and believing that *e* entails *p*, judges that *p*. *e* and *p* are both true, but *e* does not entail *p*.

Presented in this way, it is not surprising that Tibetan epistemologists regard the resultant judgments in both these cases to be instances of ignorant awareness, and not instances of knowledge. Though the resulting judgments are correct, those judgments are reached through faulty reliance on the purported evidence.

The third form of factive assessment is called "factive assessment having true but uncertain evidence." As the name suggests, these are cases where a person relies on correct evidence, but where the person either does not possess *knowledge* of the truth of the evidence or does not possess knowledge that the evidence entails that which is to be proven. For example, suppose there is a fire burning on a distant mountain pass, and that there is smoke rising from the fire. A trekker, from a distance, spots something rising into the air above the mountain pass and believes it to be smoke but is uncertain about that. (This belief that there is smoke on the mountain pass may, itself, just be an instance of "factive assessment.") Nevertheless, even though the trekker does not know that there is smoke on the mountain pass, as a result of believing that there is smoke present there, she draws the inference-like conclusion that there must be fire on the mountain pass. That resultant judgment turns out to be correct, but Buddhist epistemologists would agree that it is not an instance of knowledge, for her judgment was formed through a reliance on evidence about which she was (correct but) ignorant.

Just as in the case of the second form of factive assessment, we can formalize this third type (and its two different formulations) in the following ways:

(FA_{U1}) S takes *e* as evidence, and knowing that *e* entails *p*, judges that *p*. *e* is true, *p* is true, but S does not know that *e* is true.

(FA_{U2}) S takes *e* as evidence, and believing that *e* entails *p*, judges that *p*. *e* is true, *p* is true, but S does not know that *e* entails *p*.

Looking at these formalized versions of factive assessment having incorrect evidence and factive assessment having true but uncertain evidence, we can identify the following characteristics of Tibetan Buddhist views of inferential knowledge. First of all, it is apparent (from the union of FA_M and FA_U)

that these Tibetan epistemologists maintain that inferential knowledge—that is, knowledge by way of evidential reasoning—has both a factual requirement and an epistemic requirement. Or, put differently, it has an objective requirement and a subjective requirement. A person cannot gain inferential knowledge unless the evidential appeal is actually correct and the evidence entails that which is to be proven (this is the objective/factual component), and the person drawing the inference actually has knowledge of the evidence and knows that the evidence entails that which is to be proven (this is the subjective/epistemic component). If either of these components is not met, then even if the inference-like judgment turns out to be correct, it will merely be an episode of ignorant awareness, not an instance of knowledge.

6.3.3. Is All Factive Assessment Ignorant?

Let's take a step back and reflect on the consequences of the Tibetan appeal to factive assessment. One might think that the scope of this form of cognition shows the Tibetan Buddhist account of inferential knowledge to be too narrow. Is it really the case that a person cannot gain inferential knowledge from evidence about which one is mistaken? Is it really the case that a person cannot gain inferential knowledge from correct evidence about which one is correct but uncertain?

Consider, for example, a scenario in which I *wrongly* believe that the man walking down my street with the aid of a cane is eighty years old. (Let's assume that he is actually eighty-two.) Because I believe he is eighty years old, and because I know that eighteen is the minimum voting age for in my state, I "infer" that the old man walking down my street is old enough to vote. Is it really fair to say that I am ignorant of this fact—that I don't know the man is old enough to vote? True enough, I am mistaken about the man's age, I believe him to be eighty years old, though he is actually eighty-two. But does the fact that I am wrong about his age mean that I cannot inferentially know that he is old enough to vote? Yes, one possible response is that I *can* know that he is old enough to vote, but *not through the evidence* that the man is eighty years old. But why is that? Why must inference always proceed through correct evidence in order to gain knowledge? In the example given, my belief of the man's age is, one might say, *close enough to the truth*, such that its falsity doesn't infect the quality of my subsequent judgment. And, yet, Buddhist epistemologists are adamant that one cannot achieve inferential knowledge from a false evidential basis.

We could modify the earlier example in such a way as to make it an instance of factive assessment having true but uncertain evidence. Suppose that I correctly judge the man walking down the street to be eighty-two years, but that I don't actually know him to be eighty-two years old. Does that really mean that I cannot inferentially know that the man is old enough to vote? After all, my belief that the man walking down the street is old enough to vote is an incredibly safe one—it is highly unlikely to be false. Does inferential knowledge really require me to know every single thing that I use as evidential support for my inferences? If it does, that looks like it will severely limit a person's potential range of knowledge.

Careful readers will recognize that the concern addressed here is the same as that raised at the end of chapter 4, where the topic of epistemic closure principles was discussed. Buddhist epistemologists are committed to the position that a person can inferentially know *p* (via evidence *e*) only if he or she knows *e* and knows that *e* entails *p*.[16] The Tibetan category of factive assessment is essentially formalizing the class of cognitions that arrive at a correct inference-like judgment, but do so without the epistemic counterclosure requirement being satisfied.

This topic also runs parallel to concerns raised in chapter 5 regarding the status of testimonial knowledge. Just as Buddhist epistemologists maintain that a person cannot come to know a proposition *p* via an inference from *e* unless one also has knowledge of *e*, so, too, these same epistemologists maintain that a hearer cannot acquire knowledge from testimony unless the source or speaker of that testimony has knowledge. These assumptions undergird standard Buddhist interpretations of testimonial and inferential knowledge. What I want to emphasize, however, is that it is not at all obvious that these assumptions are correct or even necessary for an adequate theory of inferential knowledge.

3.d. Is Factive Assessment a Type of Cognition?

One final, related matter worth discussing is the question of whether this Tibetan category of factive assessment is really a genuine type of cognition at all. Factive assessment is said to be a form of cognition in which a person forms a correct, inference-like judgment, but one that falls short of knowledge. Yet whether a cognition is correct or incorrect is a matter that is determined (in many cases) by what the world is like external to and independent of the cognition itself. As such, one might think that a correct judgment—classified as an episode of factive assessment—is no different, qua cognition, from an incorrect judgment.

It is obviously the case that some judgments are true and others false, and it is helpful to distinguish these two sorts of cases. But it does not follow that 'true judgment' is a distinct form of *cognition* from that of 'false judgment.' Prima facie, whether the cognition is correct or incorrect should have no bearing on what kind of cognitive episode a person is having. (This might be seen more clearly by considering the parallel case in the analytic tradition of epistemology: belief is a type of mental state, and some beliefs are true and others false; but 'true belief' is not a distinct mental state from 'false belief'; the mental state is simply that of belief.) It is, thus, rather peculiar that Tibetan epistemologists in the eleventh and twelfth centuries put forward factive assessment as a separate form of cognition that is distinct from episodes of false conceptual cognition.

To elaborate on this point, consider again a case where a person walking along a mountain trail looks up to the far-off mountain pass and sees smoke rising into the air. Having seen smoke, she thus deduces—under the mistaken belief that 'wherever there is smoke there is incense burning'—that there is incense burning on the mountain pass. Now, consider two opposing scenarios: in scenario α there really is incense burning on the far-off mountain pass; in scenario β there is no incense—all that is burning is a campfire. According to Chaba and other Tibetan epistemologists of his time period, the person would be having a different form of cognition in scenario α than she would be having in β. The correct cognition in α is an episode of factive assessment, and the incorrect cognition in β is an episode of mistaken cognition. But to think that the person's cognitive episodes in these two scenarios are different is incredibly peculiar. Holding such a view requires an extreme form of externalism about mental episodes—one in which the kind of mental episode a person is having is dependent on the truth status of a state of affairs external to the mental episode itself.

Even within the Tibetan tradition itself, there was clearly some debate about the legitimacy of factive assessment as a distinct form of cognition. The critically important thirteenth-century Tibetan scholar Sakya Paṇḍita, for example, disagrees vehemently with earlier thinkers like Chaba (and his followers) who designate factive assessment as a specific form of cognition.

On Sakya Paṇḍita's view, there is not, nor could there be, any such category of cognition as factive assessment. After all, this purported form of cognition is one that, by definition, involves a correct judgment. Whenever a person factively assesses that *p*, it must be the case that *p* is true—and this is just to say that factive assessment is, as defined, a *factive* cognitive episode. But given that it is a factive cognitive episode, it isn't clear why it would fail to deliver knowledge. Sakya Paṇḍita argues that factive assessment should stand or fall alongside inferential knowledge itself. On the assumption that factive assessment is a genuine form of cognition, it should either be a third *pramāṇa*, alongside perceptual and inferential cognition, or, if not, inferential cognition likewise shouldn't qualify as knowledge.[17]

The historical origins of this form of cognition, factive assessment, are not fully clear. Though numerous example cases falling within this category are discussed within Indian Buddhist treatises, the specification of factive assessment as a distinct form of cognition appears to be a Tibetan invention. Moreover, though the twelfth-century Tibetan epistemologist, Chaba—whose sevenfold typology of cognition played an important role in popularizing factive assessment as a distinct category of cognition—accepted the position that factive assessment is a kind of factive mental episode, it is not fully clear whether all of his immediate epistemological predecessors (including his teachers) endorsed this same view. Chaba and many of his followers explicitly criticize an alternative definition of factive assessment that is much broader in scope and that, notably, does not require the judgment to be true or correct.[18] This alternative definition affirms that factive assessment is a kind of cognition that reaches a decisive judgment about some state of affairs but does so without relying on experience or (correct) evidential reasoning. In saying that it does not rely on experience, the intention is to distinguish factive assessment from the aforementioned category of postknowledge cognition. In saying that it does not rely on (correct) evidence, the intention is to distinguish factive assessment from genuine inferential knowledge. But what is explicitly missing from this alternative definition is any explicit claim that factive assessment must be a *correct* cognition. Instead, the insinuation is that it is a form of conceptual cognition that results in a determinate judgment on some matter, but is such that it could include both correct conceptual judgments and mistaken conceptual cognitions.

Little else is known about this alternative definition, for it appears to have passed into obscurity, but what little we know suggests that the form of cognition translated here as "factive assessment" may *not* have always been understood to be a factive mental episode at all. And as I've pointed out earlier, there are some philosophical difficulties that arise from interpreting this form of cognition as one that necessarily takes a true state of affairs as its contents. In particular, as Sakya Paṇḍita points out, if this form of cognition is correct by necessity, then it isn't clear why we should deny it the status of being an instance of knowledge. After all, it is a cognitive judgment that, on Chaba's definition, must be correct/true, and in this way it would appear to have a law-like relation to the truth. However, as can be seen from some of the examples of cognitions that get classified as instances of factive assessment, this form of cognition is intended to capture a set of inference-like judgments that do not have a law-like connection to the truth—judgments that are just accidentally correct. One can thus understand why Sakya Paṇḍita concludes that those examples labeled by Chaba and his followers as "factive assessments" do not designate a genuine type of cognition. The definition of factive assessment is, in Sakya Paṇḍita's view, philosophically incoherent.

Further Reading

For a more detailed presentation of Chaba Chokyi Senge's account of perception, and of the difference between perception and perceptual knowledge, see Hugon, P. (2011). Phya pa Chos kyi seng ge's views on perception. In H. Krasser, H. Lasic, E. Franco, & B. Kellner (Eds.), *Religion and logic in Buddhist philosophical analysis: Proceedings of the fourth international Dharmakīrti conference*. Vienna: Verlag der Österreichischen Akademie der Wissenschaften.

For a more extensive discussion of factive assessment within Tibetan Buddhist epistemology, see Stoltz, J. (2007). Gettier and factivity in Indo-Tibetan epistemology. *The Philosophical Quarterly*, *57*, 394–415.

For a much more detailed overview of those forms of cognition that Tibetan Buddhist epistemologists claim are not instances of knowledge, see chapter IV of Hugon, P., & Stoltz, J. (2019). *The roar of a Tibetan lion: Phya pa Chos kyi seng ge's theory of mind in philosophical and historical perspective*. Vienna: Austrian Academy of Sciences Press.

7
Skepticism

Up to this point in the book, it has largely been taken for granted that knowledge is obtainable—that some cognitions can satisfy the requirements associated with episodes of knowledge. The belief that humans can and do have knowledge is widely accepted by philosophers, both in the European tradition of philosophy and in the Indian (and Buddhist) epistemological tradition(s). Not everyone shares this perspective, however. There are a number of philosophers throughout history who have argued that knowledge is fundamentally beyond our reach. They are skeptics about the possibility of knowledge. And to be clear, by and large, these skeptical philosophers are not quacks. Instead, they are rigorous thinkers who believe that when we reflect deeply on what knowledge is and what is required for it, we see that it is something that unfortunately cannot be attained by humans.

"The problem of skepticism" is as much a problem in the Buddhist tradition of epistemology as it is in classical European philosophy and in contemporary analytic epistemology. That said, the precise ways in which concerns about skepticism arise in these traditions are distinct, as are the conceptual frameworks within which epistemologists seek to make sense of the challenge of skepticism. As such, it will be helpful to examine how Buddhist philosophers made sense of and responded to the threat of skepticism. This chapter will explore the skeptical arguments put forward by the most prominent Buddhist critic of *pramāṇa*-based epistemology in India, the (circa) second-century philosopher, Nāgārjuna. We will see how his attacks on the Indian tradition of epistemology proceed, and we will then reflect on the lessons to be learned from Nāgārjuna's criticisms of Indian epistemology.

7.1. Skepticism and Skeptical Scenarios

Though it is not the only way by which to motivate skepticism about knowledge, one of the most common avenues proceeds by describing a so-called *skeptical scenario*—a situation that is intended to be indistinguishable from

Illuminating the Mind. Jonathan Stoltz, Oxford University Press (2021). © Oxford University Press.
DOI: 10.1093/oso/9780190907532.003.0007

our ordinary, run-of-the-mill experiences of reality, but in which our beliefs are somehow or other systematically mistaken.[1] Especially since the time of Descartes in the first half of the seventeenth century, it has been standard for skeptics to appeal to a variety of skeptical scenarios in order to ground their arguments against the possibility of knowledge. In his *Meditations on First Philosophy*, Descartes asks his readers to entertain skeptical scenarios such as the possibility that we are dreaming or the possibility that we are being deceived by an all-powerful, evil demon—one who can ensure that our beliefs, though appearing to be true, are systematically false. The concern is that even if in point of fact we are *not* in one of these skeptical scenarios, and even if our experiences of the external world are veridical and our beliefs true, the mere epistemic *possibility* that we could be in one of these skeptical scenarios—that is, our inability to rule out the possibility that we might be in a skeptical scenario right now—is enough to show that we cannot have any knowledge of the external world. Standardly presented, as long as it is indeed impossible to distinguish wakefulness from dreaming, the mere possibility that we could be dreaming is sufficient to prevent us from having knowledge of the external world, even in a situation in which we are in fact awake and experiencing the external world as it really is.

Perhaps, contrary to Descartes's own assertion, it is possible to distinguish wakeful experiences from experiences in one's dreams. This would not deter the skeptic. All he or she needs is the mere possibility of there being *some scenario* in which a person's experiences would be indistinguishable from those experiences a person would have were he or she to be veridically experiencing things in the external world. As such, instead of appealing to a scenario involving dreaming, the skeptic can call upon some other, even more elaborate experience. For instance, the skeptical scenario could be one in which you not dreaming, but are, instead, floating in a tank of fluid somewhere near Alpha Centauri and receiving electrode stimulations to your brain that give rise to sensory experiences that are fundamentally indistinguishable from those of the sort you would have were you to be on Earth experiencing the world as usual.

As I have already said, using skeptical scenarios so as to motivate one's arguments against the possibility of knowledge is widespread within modern and contemporary Western epistemology. Appeals to such scenarios are not essential to skeptical arguments about knowledge, however, and they are not generally operative in the most prominent skeptical arguments found in the Buddhist tradition of philosophy. Yet, it is well worth noting that one can find Buddhist thinkers on occasion appealing to examples that are akin to Cartesian skeptical scenarios. The seventh-century Buddhist philosopher Candrakīrti, for example, offers an example of a scenario that I shall term "the land of the crazy."[2] Imagine that nearly everyone in a certain land—everyone, that is, except for the king of that land—becomes afflicted with a peculiar form of mental illness as a result of drinking "crazy water" that arrived in the form of a rain shower. The king has not consumed any of this crazy water himself, and his reasoning remains sound. But because all the king's subjects have drunk the water, they adopt beliefs that are systematically in error. Yet, because these persons' beliefs are in mutual accord, they all believe the king to be insane. After all, the king is the one and only person whose beliefs differ from the consensus. Recognizing this, the king decides that it is best that he too drink the crazy water so that his beliefs will be systematically false just like everyone else's.

This story is meant to show that universal agreement does not guarantee truth. Nor does such universal agreement serve to warrant our beliefs. Though everyone in the land of the crazy agrees in their beliefs, they are all systematically mistaken. Candrakīrti likens this to what people would believe about beauty (or physical wellness) in a situation where everyone suffers from the same bodily deformation (or disease). If everyone had a goiter in one's neck, all would agree that to have such a condition is to be beautiful—and that those without a goiter are unattractive. More generally, a condition would not be regarded as a failing or imperfection if nearly everyone were afflicted with it. With respect to the status of one's beliefs, let us suppose that everyone has systematically erroneous beliefs such as in the land of the crazy. We would not be in a position to notice that our beliefs are mistaken and would continue to believe ourselves to be holding true beliefs.

Though it appears that Candrakīrti's main intention is to call into question the idea that consensus can be used as a guide to truth, his "land of the crazy" example could also be used as a skeptical scenario to demonstrate the impossibility of knowledge. Much like Descartes' evil demon example, if we cannot distinguish between a situation in which our beliefs are reliably correct and a situation in which our beliefs are systematically erroneous, then we are not in a position to have knowledge—even if we do happen to have beliefs that are, as a matter of fact, reliably correct. Candrakīrti does not explicitly use the land of the crazy example for precisely these skeptical purposes. Proponents of Cartesian skepticism, after all, are concerned about the impact that these skeptical scenarios have on our knowledge of the world *even on the assumption that we are not actually in such a scenario.* Candrakīrti, by contrast, appears to be principally concerned with what we should conclude about knowledge and belief *in these hypothetical scenarios themselves.* In other words, Candrakīrti is interested in what we should say about beliefs and knowledge for people who are in these scenarios, whereas the Cartesian skeptic is interested in what these scenarios tell us about the beliefs of people who are not, in fact, in such a scenario but who cannot rule out the possibility that they might be.

Be this as it may, the most common lines of argumentation used by Indian Buddhist skeptics about knowledge acquisition are not ones that rely on skeptical scenarios like the earlier described case. Instead, the most prominent criticisms of knowledge in the Buddhist tradition are ones that seek to undercut the foundational assumptions that are at the heart of the Indian tradition of epistemology. Those assumptions include, most critically, the very idea that humans can make use of "instruments of knowledge" (*pramāṇas*) in order to gain knowledge of truths about the world. In this respect, these criticisms are aimed at showing not that knowledge is unobtainable, but rather that the whole project of *pramāṇa*-based epistemology is fundamentally untenable. It is this attack on the legitimacy of *pramāṇa*-based epistemology to which we must now turn.

7.2. Knowledge and Instruments of Knowledge

Much of this book has proceeded under the assumption that the term *pramāṇa* refers to a special kind of cognitive episode—an episode of knowledge. The sixth-century Buddhist epistemologist Dignāga famously maintained that there is no meaningful distinction to be made between an instrument of knowledge, on the one hand, and the cognition that is its result, on the other. In this way, Buddhist epistemologists from the time of Dignāga onward focus much of their attention on exploring the natures of episodes of cognition and the relations that these cognitions bear to the objects that are cognized.

As traditionally understood within other schools of Indian philosophy, however, a *pramāṇa* is a means or instrument by which a person comes to have an episode of knowledge. Instruments of knowledge are used to establish the existence of objects or of certain states of affairs. Given this kind of account, in addition to positing the cognition that is an episode of knowing (*pramā*), one can isolate two items critical for knowledge: the epistemic instrument (*pramāṇa*) and the epistemic object (*prameya*). Items such as perception, inference, and testimony were put forward by Indian philosophers as basic instruments of knowledge. It is by virtue of an epistemic instrument that a person gains knowledge of an epistemic object. Expressed differently, we can say that epistemic instruments are used to *establish* the existence of epistemic objects. Just as a telescope might be used to establish the existence of a far-off planet, or a pregnancy test kit might be used to establish the existence of a pregnancy, so too a *pramāṇa* is used to establish the existence of an object or state of affairs.

The general claim that *instruments* can be used to establish the existence of *objects* is, at first glance, unquestionable. In particular, there is much intuitive support for the idea that an instrument may be, practically speaking, indispensable for establishing some objects' existences. For example, one might think that—at least practically speaking—it would not have been possible to establish the existence of the moons of Saturn were it not for telescopes. The invention of the telescope was, for all intents and purposes, a necessary condition for establishing the existence of Saturn's moon Titan. Likewise, the invention of the microscope may have been a necessary condition for establishing the existence of bacteria. It is, of course, conceivable that another instrument could have been invented that would allow humans to establish the existences of bacteria and the moons of Saturn, but that is not really the issue. What is important here is just to point out how familiar and intuitively plausible it is to maintain that *instruments* are used to establish the existence of *objects*.

The earlier examples of a telescope and a microscope are ones that we might consider *indirect* or *second-order* instruments of knowledge. What is at issue in the Indian tradition of epistemology is not the status of these sorts of instruments, but rather the status of direct/first-order instruments of knowledge, which are the true *pramāṇas*. There are disagreements within ancient Indian philosophy about what sorts of instruments constitute genuine, irreducible *pramāṇas*, but there is very little dispute about this theoretical framework—one in which instruments of knowledge (*pramāṇas*) provide humans with a means by which to establish (and thus have knowledge of) the existence of objects and states of affairs.

This interpretive framework in which epistemic instruments serve to establish the existence of objects does not go entirely uncontested, however. There is, it could be argued, a fundamental paradox at the heart of the traditional Indian account of knowledge involving its appeal to epistemic instruments. To see this, but before getting into the specific arguments, allow me to briefly set the stage. Let us assume that epistemic instruments are used to establish the existence of objects. Expressed more carefully, let us assume that for any knowable object or state of affairs, *x*, there must be some epistemic instrument, *y*, by which the existence of *x* is to be established. Once this point is granted, it can then be asked: Since epistemic instruments are also, themselves, objects, how is it that we can come to establish the existence of these epistemic instruments? *By what epistemic instruments* can we come to establish the existence of epistemic instruments?

Consider again the sample case of using a telescope to establish the existence of the moon Titan. Here, a telescope is the instrument that serves to establish the existence of an object, but it is also undoubtedly true that a telescope is an object. How, then, do we establish the existence of such a telescope? Obviously, we do have good grounds for concluding that telescopes exist, but their existence is established by instruments other than telescopes themselves. Yes, it is possible that a person might use one telescope to establish the existence of another, far-off telescope. For example, a telescope atop one skyscraper in New York City might be used to establish the existence of a separate telescope on the top of a different, distant building in the city. That's all well and good, but could a single telescope be used to establish its own existence? It seems not.

This question may sound contrived—and it is. But consider this related example. Let us suppose that we wish to measure the lengths of various objects. I might, for example, use a ruler to measure the length of an envelope or to measure the length of a pencil. Here, the instrument of measurement is the ruler, and the objects measured are an envelope and a pencil. But the ruler is itself an object—one that, no doubt, has a measurable length. It seems that I cannot use the ruler to measure itself. So how can I determine how long the ruler is? Obviously, if a ruler can be used to determine the lengths of various objects, it is important to know whether the ruler is an accurate instrument of measurement. How can I determine the ruler's accuracy? One would be hard-pressed to argue that its accuracy could be established by self-measurement. But even if I were to rely on another ruler, or some other measuring device (a tape measure, perhaps), the further question can be asked: How do I know that the latter measurement device is accurate? We are threatened with a potentially vicious regress.

7.3. Nāgārjuna and the Epistemic Regress Problem

It is concerns of the sort just described that the (second- or possibly third-century) Buddhist philosopher Nāgārjuna seeks to employ against Indian appeals to *pramāṇas*. Nāgārjuna is an incredibly important figure in the Buddhist tradition. His most famous text, *The Fundamental Verses on the Middle Way* (*Mūlamadhyamakakārikā*), works through a wide array of metaphysical concerns about the nature of existence.[3] With respect to the topic of epistemology, however, we must look to a separate text that is purportedly authored by Nāgārjuna, *The Dispeller of Disputes* (*Vigrahavyāvartanī*).[4] This short text grapples aggressively with a series of philosophical quandaries about the nature of epistemic instruments and their relation to epistemic objects. Failing to find satisfactory answers to his questions about epistemic instruments, Nāgārjuna ultimately concludes that the *pramāṇa*-based epistemological program cannot secure knowledge.

It must be kept in mind that Nāgārjuna was writing in the late second (or perhaps early third) century, hundreds of years before the time of Dignāga and Dharmakīrti. First of all, this means that the very notion of "*pramāṇa*" that is under attack in Nāgārjuna's writing is one that principally refers to the *means* or *instruments* of knowledge, not to the episodes of knowledge themselves. He is, therefore, criticizing just *pramāṇa*-based theories of knowledge and not necessarily the very possibility of knowledge in general. It is only in the time of Dignāga several centuries later that the concept of *pramāṇa* comes to be merged with those episodes of cognition that result from the use of such an instrument. Second, one must additionally be cognizant of the fact that Nāgārjuna's intended audience is likely a mix of Buddhist and non-Buddhist philosophers in India. While his criticisms of epistemic instruments are to a large extent aimed at non-Buddhist proponents of *pramāṇa*, such as proponents of the Nyāya School of logic, those criticisms also apply to his fellow Buddhist philosophers, some of whom may have been inclined to endorse the (possibly widespread) theoretical framework that includes appeals to epistemic instruments. It is this entire theoretical framework that Nāgārjuna seeks to undermine.

7.3.1. Establishing Epistemic Instruments

Let us now examine Nāgārjuna's various lines of argumentation in greater detail. As discussed in the preceding section, the Indian tradition of epistemology proceeds from the general assumption that epistemic instruments are used to establish the existence of epistemic objects. To take an example, a person might use her power of (visual) perception so as to establish the existence of a white conch shell. But once this initial assumption is granted, the question can then be asked: how do we establish the existence of these very epistemic instruments? As Nāgārjuna ponders:[5]

> If you think that epistemic objects of some kind are established through the epistemic instruments, just as a measuring instrument establishes what is to be measured, then where does the establishment of the four epistemic instruments, perception, inference, likeness, and testimony, come from?

Nāgārjuna then proceeds to walk through and reject a number of potential answers to this question.

Before examining these possible answers and Nāgārjuna's criticisms of them, let us first pause to reflect on what is meant by "establishment of the four epistemic instruments." One plausible reading is that the expression has a meaning parallel to that associated with establishing ordinary epistemic objects. And if that's the case, it would seem that "establishment of the four epistemic instruments" simply means *knowing these four instruments to exist.* On a second, and stronger, reading, "establishment of the four epistemic instruments" refers to *recognizing, of these four instruments, that they are genuine pramāṇas.* These two interpretations are importantly different.

To see more clearly what the difference is between these two interpretations, consider a somewhat parallel case in which a doctor uses a scale to weigh a baby. Here, a scale is put forward as the instrument of measurement, and yet it might reasonably be held that in order for me to gain knowledge of the baby's weight, I need first to "establish the scale." But this could mean at least two different things. "Establishing the scale" might mean *verifying that a scale was used*—that is, that there really exists a scale that was used by the doctor. On a different reading, "establishing the scale" means *verifying that the scale used is an accurate instrument* for measuring the weights of objects. The second reading requires a higher threshold to be met than does the first. Clearly, a person can verify that a scale was used without also verifying that the scale is a trustworthy instrument.

In a parallel fashion, a person can plausibly come to know of an epistemic instrument's existence without knowing *that* it is an epistemic instrument and without knowing *that* the item can be used to gain knowledge of objects. This is certainly true of the Buddhist account of knowledge coming from Dignāga. On that account, because perceptual cognitions are nonconceptual, a given perception provides knowledge of some particular object but does so without imparting the knowledge *that* the object perceived is such and such.

So, again, what does Nāgārjuna mean by "establishment of the four epistemic instruments"? The answer is not fully clear from Nāgārjuna's text. What is clear, however, is that we should not assume that he has the latter, and stronger, of the earlier two readings in mind. The lines of reasoning that Nāgārjuna pursues are focused almost entirely on formal criticisms of epistemic instruments—that is, criticisms involving the *structure* of epistemic support. He does not, for example, argue against any specific definitions of *pramāṇas*, nor does he seek to show that there are specific properties—along the lines of "nondeceptiveness" or "revealing truth"—that fail to be realized in the traditionally accepted epistemic instruments. Instead, he raises broad structural inconsistencies in the very idea of something being an epistemic instrument. For this reason, I believe that it is safest to conclude that "establishment of the four epistemic instruments" refers *not* to recognizing that these four instruments meet the defining conditions for *pramāṇas*, but only to knowing that these instruments exist.

When understood in this way, there are four possible answers to the question of how epistemic instruments can be established:

Epistemic instruments are either . . .

(E_o) established by other epistemic instruments, or

(E_s) self-established, or

($E_\sim$) established, but not by *any* epistemic instruments, or

(~E) not established.

The middle portions of Nāgārjuna's *Dispeller of Disputes* contain a sequence of arguments aiming to show that all four of these answers are untenable.

7.3.2. Do Epistemic Instruments Need To Be Established?

To begin, let us first note the clear parallels between the possible ways in which epistemic instruments could be established and the standard responses to what is frequently called the "epistemic regress problem" in Anglo-American epistemology.[6] In that tradition of epistemology, it is commonly maintained that beliefs serve to justify other beliefs. Defenders of foundationalism then affirm the view that for a special subset of one's beliefs—which we can call *basic beliefs*—these beliefs are *not* justified by other beliefs. With respect to the epistemic status of these basic beliefs, it could be held that they are self-justifying, or that they are justified by something that is not a belief, or that they are not justified at all (but also not in need of justification, and yet somehow still capable of justifying other beliefs). With respect to these last two options, the more common view is that basic beliefs are indeed justified, but that their justification is rooted in something that is not a belief—such as one's immediate experiences. Yet it could also be argued that basic beliefs are capable of conferring justification on other beliefs without themselves being justified or even in need of justification.

Similar to these questions about the justificatory status of basic beliefs, Nāgārjuna is asking about the status of epistemic instruments. Setting aside for the time being (E_s) epistemic instruments being self-established and (E_o) epistemic instruments being established by other epistemic instruments, what can we say about these third and fourth possibilities?

With respect to ($E_{\sim}$), what would it be like for an epistemic instrument to be established to exist, but not by way of any epistemic instrument? One possibility that Nāgārjuna entertains is that epistemic instruments might be established by (or established via an appeal to) *epistemic objects*.[7] This proposal, however, appears to lead to a vicious circle—one in which it is both the case that epistemic instruments are established by epistemic objects (A establishes B) and in which epistemic objects are established by epistemic instruments (B establishes A). Understandably, Nāgārjuna is of the view that such a circularity would leave both the epistemic instruments and epistemic objects unestablished.

This is not the only difficulty with position ($E_{\sim}$). Nāgārjuna recognizes a much more basic problem with asserting that epistemic instruments are established independent of any epistemic instrument. The problem is that defenders of *pramāṇa*-based epistemology are understood to support the view that *all objects* must be established by epistemic instruments. But since epistemic instruments are themselves objects, it follows that those epistemic instruments could only be established to exist by virtue of epistemic instruments. Thus, to adopt ($E_{\sim}$) is to renege on a core assumption of how *pramāṇa*-based epistemology is supposed to work.

Although Nāgārjuna spends a significant portion of his treatise arguing against ($E_{\sim}$), he spends much less space arguing against (~E). Again, that fourth position is to affirm that epistemic instruments are "not established." This may sound like precisely the view that Nāgārjuna is seeking to promote, but there is an interpretation of (~E) that, if true, would be consistent with the possibility of human knowledge via epistemic instruments. Just as it could be maintained, at least in theory, that basic beliefs are capable of conferring justification on other beliefs without being justified themselves, so, too, it could be held that epistemic instruments can be used to establish the existence of other objects without needing to be established themselves. On such a view, the mere existence of epistemic instruments is what is needed for human knowledge, even without humans needing to possess any knowledge or awareness that there are such epistemic instruments. In this way, by adopting (~E) one could maintain that everything known or knowable must be established by some epistemic instrument, but that the existence of these epistemic instruments is not something that is known or perhaps even knowable.

Such a stance toward epistemic instruments may not sound very plausible, and as I have said, Nāgārjuna only addresses this position briefly. His criticism, found in verse 33 of *The Dispeller of Disputes*, is that anyone adopting this fourth response has abandoned the core thesis of *pramāṇa*-based epistemology—namely, that all objects must be established to exist via epistemic instruments. Yet those who endorse the *pramāṇa*-based approach to epistemology offer no account of why epistemic instruments are to be treated differently from other objects.

Having said that, and stepping away from Nāgārjuna's response, position (~E) is not entirely outlandish. It amounts to accepting a version of *strong externalism* about epistemic instruments. That is, this fourth position effectively denies that a person needs to have any knowledge of, or awareness of, the existence of epistemic instruments in order to gain knowledge by means of said epistemic instruments. As long as these epistemic instruments actually exist and are employed for the production of human cognitions—whether or not a person recognizes this—that person can obtain knowledge of objects and states of affairs. Such a view has as much or as little plausibility as does strong externalism in analytic epistemology, wherein it is affirmed that knowledge depends on there being reliable belief-forming processes and/or cognitive faculties that are functioning properly, regardless of whether a person has knowledge or awareness of the existence and functioning of those processes and/or faculties.

Consider, for example, the case of animal knowledge. Suppose that an eagle uses its power of vision to spy a rabbit running through a grass field. Even those who wish to reject the idea that animals like eagles have conceptual capacities may be strongly inclined to the view that animals can and do have a form of perceptual knowledge. In this case, the eagle visually perceives the rabbit. But this perceptual knowledge can be exemplified even if the eagle fails to recognize that it has a visual sense faculty. Even supposing that eagles fundamentally lack the higher-order knowledge that they have a visual sense faculty, that should not prevent these birds from possessing perceptual knowledge. By parallel reasoning, one might argue that, in the case of humans, a *pramāṇa* can be used to successfully establish the existence of some object without that *pramāṇa* needing to be established.

This sort of strong externalism appears to go entirely unrecognized by Nāgārjuna. His reasoning presupposes that epistemic instruments need to be established—and the central question for him is that of what could serve to establish the existence of epistemic instruments. From the perspective of *pramāṇa*-based epistemology, the most sensible answer is that it is epistemic instruments themselves that establish the existence of epistemic instruments. But this admits of two distinct possibilities. First, it may be thought that (E_o) one epistemic instrument serves to establish the existence of *another* epistemic instrument. A second possibility is that (E_s) epistemic instruments are *self-established*. It is these two responses on which we should devote the most attention. Let us now turn to his arguments concerning those two positions.

7.3.3. Establishment from Other Epistemic Instruments

The first proposal that Nāgārjuna entertains in response to the question of how epistemic instruments are to be established is that they are established by other epistemic instruments.[8] Nāgārjuna's reply is swift and dismissive: if this were the case there would be a vicious, infinite regress.

Nāgārjuna's criticism has a lot of intuitive force behind it. After all, if it is claimed that *every single* epistemic instrument must be established by a *separate* epistemic instrument, then one can always ask of that latter instrument "And what establishes that epistemic instrument?" Expressed more fully, suppose that the object *o* has its existence established by way of the epistemic instrument P_0. The question then becomes that of what establishes the existence of P_0; and the answer, given this proposal, is that there is some other epistemic instrument P_1 that serves to establish P_0. It is then appropriate to ask what establishes P_1; and the answer must be that there is some other epistemic instrument P_2 that serves to establish P_1. Nāgārjuna is obviously right that this process could, theoretically at least, continue on ad infinitum. To speak more precisely, according to this first proposal, one must accept the following principle:

(OE) For every epistemic instrument P_i, there is some instrument P_j, with $P_i \neq P_j$, such that P_j establishes P_i.

Given (OE), there can never be a firm end to the process of establishing epistemic instruments. The process could go on ad infinitum.

Nāgārjuna is convinced that this renders untenable the position that each and every epistemic instrument is established by other epistemic instruments. There are, however, some well-known replies to philosophical charges of a vicious infinite regress. First, it could be responded that while such a regress could *theoretically* continue on ad infinitum, as a *practical* matter the process of asking what establishes the existence of one's epistemic instruments would eventually end. In other words, the reply is that regresses are not necessarily vicious because, practically speaking, they would not be infinite. This rejoinder admits that an ultimate foundation for epistemic instruments may be impossible to secure, but it denies that such a foundation is needed in order for ordinary epistemic instruments to be established.

A second and even more common response is the one that is put forward by the epistemic coherentist. In reply to Nāgārjuna's reasoning, it could be stated that the establishment of one epistemic instrument by another epistemic instrument does not necessarily result in an infinite regress because, instead of being linear, the process of establishing epistemic instruments may be circular in structure. More formally, it is consistent with (OE) to have the following structure: epistemic instrument P_0 is established by epistemic instrument P_1, which is in turn established by epistemic instrument P_2, which is itself established by epistemic instrument P_0. In such a scenario, each epistemic instrument is "established" by some other epistemic instrument, and yet there is no infinite regress.

It does not appear that Nāgārjuna directly addresses this specific form of circular establishment. He does take up, as mentioned earlier, the possibility that epistemic instruments might be established by epistemic objects and vice versa; and this form of circular establishment could be considered a version of coherentism. But that is quite different from the view just described where multiple epistemic instruments mutually support each other. Now, this sort of mutual dependence—where epistemic instrument P_0 is established by instrument P_1, which is established by P_2, which is established by P_0—would still be problematic for Nāgārjuna, since it is, after all, a process of establishment that never terminates and thus fails to genuinely establish any of these instruments at all.

7.3.4. Self-Establishing Epistemic Instruments

Within his discussion of epistemic instruments in his *Dispeller of Disputes*, Nāgārjuna dedicates the largest amount of space to attacking the thesis of self-established epistemic instruments.[9] The thesis of self-establishment, (E_s), stands in accord with the thesis of other-establishment, (E_o), in two important respects. First, they both agree that the existence of each and every epistemic instrument is something that *does* need to be established—which is in contrast to the position adopted by proponents of (~E). Second, they agree that the only things that can serve to establish epistemic instruments are epistemic instruments—which is in contrast to the position adopted by proponents of ($E_{\sim}$). The core difference between (E_o) and (E_s) is that proponents of the latter position contend that epistemic instruments have the power to establish themselves, which is something not accepted by proponents of (E_o). In essence, position (E_s) rejects the reference to *inequality* ($P_i \neq P_j$) found in principle (OE):

> (OE) For every epistemic instrument P_i, there is some instrument P_j, with $P_i \neq P_j$, such that P_j establishes P_i.

While eliminating the inequality clause ($P_i \neq P_j$) from (OE) does not thereby entail that *all* epistemic instruments must be self-established, proponents of (E_s) do push for this stronger principle, which we can call (SE):

> (SE) For every epistemic instrument P_i, P_i establishes P_i.

One thing that should be immediately clear is that the thesis of self-established epistemic instruments bypasses all concerns about a vicious epistemic regress. On the self-establishment view, *pramāṇas*—that is, epistemic instruments—are to play the role of the *unmoved movers* of epistemology.[10] They are held to be capable of rendering other objects known/established, but not themselves in need of being established by anything outside themselves. In this way, epistemic instruments serve two roles simultaneously: they establish epistemic objects, and they establish themselves.

This assertion that epistemic instruments can both establish the existence of other objects and establish their own existence is not as crazy as it may seem. Consider the parallel situation in contemporary analytic epistemology concerning self-justified beliefs. Proponents of foundationalism commonly maintain that there are certain beliefs, often called *basic beliefs*, that have the dual capacity to justify themselves and justify other beliefs. Examples of the sorts of beliefs that might qualify as basic beliefs include those falling into the categories of incorrigible beliefs and self-presenting beliefs. Incorrigible beliefs are those such that, necessarily, if the belief is held, it is guaranteed to be true; where the prime example is a person's belief that he or she exists. Just by holding the belief that I exist, it is guaranteed to be true that I do exist. Given this incorrigibility, many philosophers take a person's belief in one's own existence to be self-justifying. Yet my belief that I exist can also serve to justify other beliefs that I hold, such as my belief that there are some things in the world that currently exist.

None of this is to say that these claims about self-justifying beliefs go uncontested within contemporary epistemology. There is significant disagreement concerning the plausibility of the foundationalist's arguments concerning epistemically basic, and self-justifying, beliefs. What is important for our purposes is not the soundness of these arguments, but just the fact that these appeals to self-justifying beliefs are so (epistemologically) commonplace. In fact, given the available evidence from within the Indian tradition, the claim that epistemic instruments can be self-established was clearly a commonplace reply to concerns of the sort that Nāgārjuna is entertaining.[11]

The focus of Nāgārjuna's criticism of the thesis of self-established epistemic instruments, (E_s), involves an attack on an analogy that had likely been used to help support that thesis. The analogy in question is that of comparing an epistemic instrument to a lamp or fire. An illuminated lamp is an example of an instrument par excellence. Lamps are used in order to see other objects. And just as lamps serve to illuminate objects, so, too, epistemic instruments serve to establish the existence of objects. In these respects, epistemic instruments are analogous to fires/lamps. But lamps do not merely illuminate other objects, they also illuminate themselves. And so it may be argued, by analogy, that epistemic instruments likewise have the capacity not only to establish other objects but also to establish their own existence. As Nāgārjuna's putative interlocutor states, "As fire illuminates itself as well as others, so the epistemic instruments prove themselves and others."[12]

Nāgārjuna devotes six verses to attacking the viability of the lamp/fire analogy. His aim is to show that the analogy is problematic, and hence that the self-establishment of epistemic instruments cannot be secured by way of this analogy. In particular, he objects to the claim that lamps can rightly be said to illuminate themselves. There is no need, however, to walk through the details of Nāgārjuna's criticisms. Instead, our chief concern should be with the broader implications flowing from Nāgārjuna's attack on the self-establishment thesis.

First, it is critical to be attentive to the fact that Nāgārjuna's principal line of criticism against the self-establishment of epistemic instruments proceeds by way of an analogy. As will be discussed next, this appeal to the lamp analogy is not Nāgārjuna's only criticism of the self-establishment thesis, but it is his most fully developed line of argumentation. With respect to the analogy in question, Nāgārjuna's criticism is not that the analogy between epistemic instruments and lamps is inherently flawed. That is, he does not argue that epistemic instruments cannot be likened or compared to fires or lamps. Rather, Nāgārjuna's reasoning takes for granted—or at least assumes for the sake of argument—that epistemic instruments are analogous to lamps. What he believes is mistaken is the assertion that lamps are genuinely self-illuminating. It is this point that he spends the most space criticizing. Left unstated by Nāgārjuna is the inference from the claim that lamps do not illuminate themselves to the conclusion that, by analogy, epistemic instruments fail to establish themselves.

Though most of the space that Nāgārjuna dedicates to criticizing the self-establishment thesis is grounded in the lamp/fire analogy, he does put forward a subsequent argument against self-established epistemic instruments—one that does not make use of that analogy. That argument proceeds, essentially, as a reduction to absurdity. It begins with the assumption that

(A) Epistemic instruments are self-established.

Nāgārjuna then affirms the premise that

(B) If epistemic instruments are self-established, then they are established independent of all (other) epistemic objects.

But given these two claims, it follows that

(C) Epistemic instruments are established independent of all epistemic objects.

Nāgārjuna takes this latter point to imply that

(C′) Epistemic instruments are not the instruments of anything.

In other words, provided that the existence of any given *pramāṇa* is secured entirely independent of all objects (save the *pramāṇa* itself), what makes something a *pramāṇa* is something that is independent of its relationship to epistemic objects. This, in Nāgārjuna's view, is absurd, and so we should reject the initial assumption (A). The truth of the matter is that epistemic instruments are *not* established independent of epistemic objects.

Compared to his earlier analogical argument concerning fire, this latter line of argumentation has the potential to be a more powerful refutation of the self-establishment thesis. It is, after all, a more direct attack on that thesis; one that proceeds by exposing an inherent flaw in the very idea of self-established epistemic instruments. That being said, I must admit that, in contrast to several other scholars, I do not find Nāgārjuna's line of reasoning to be philosophically persuasive.[13] In my estimation, the argument proceeds by conflating a *pramāṇa*'s *epistemic* status with its *ontological* status (and likely also its *semantic* status).

The thesis of self-established epistemic instruments is supposed to be a claim about the epistemic status of *pramāṇas*. It affirms (SE), that for any epistemic instrument P_i, P_i is established by P_i. Contrary to what Nāgārjuna maintains, that epistemic thesis is consistent with the *ontological* claim that the truth of that very state of affairs—viz., that P_i is established by P_i—depends on other objects. To see why, consider the parallel case of *self-justified beliefs* in Anglo-European epistemology. It is frequently held that the belief 'I exist' is self-justifying. Let us use the shorthand B_s to represent some person S's belief that 'I exist.' This belief is, as mentioned earlier, an example of an *incorrigible* belief. But by granting that B_s justifies itself, it does not follow that this state of affairs—viz., that B_s is self-justified—is true independent of all other objects. In particular, the truth of the statement 'B_s is self-justified' *ontologically depends* on the existence of person S. In short, the epistemic status of B_s depends on the ontological status of S. More generally, a self-justified belief can ontologically depend on an object or state of affairs distinct from that belief.

Likewise, just because (epistemologically speaking) an epistemic instrument establishes itself, it does not necessarily follow that (ontologically speaking) that very fact is true independent of all epistemic objects. Let us suppose that an epistemic instrument, P_i, is self-established. What *establishes* P_i's existence is, by hypothesis, P_i itself. But what *makes it true* that P_i has the property of being an epistemic instrument might very well be some object or state of affairs distinct from P_i. In this respect, self-established epistemic instruments can ontologically depend on epistemic objects.

Now, the claim that epistemic instruments depend on epistemic objects is something that Nāgārjuna thinks his opponents ought to accept; and he may very well be right about that. But he takes that claim to be incompatible with the separate thesis that epistemic instruments are self-established. It is this assumption of incompatibility that I believe to be mistaken. And, as such, I do not believe that he has entirely succeeded in demonstrating the absurdity of self-established epistemic instruments.

7.4. The Structure of Knowledge

Taking a step back from the specific arguments supplied by Nāgārjuna, and regardless of whether those arguments are fully successful or not, there are several broad observations that can be made from this examination of Nāgārjuna's criticisms of *pramāṇa*-based epistemology. Even though Nāgārjuna likely did not intend to put forward his own positive account of the nature of knowledge, his criticisms reflect a number of his own presuppositions about both the nature of knowledge and the conditions necessary for gaining knowledge. First and foremost, the line of criticism that he puts forward strongly suggests that Nāgārjuna had a predilection for (what we now think of as) a *foundationalist* approach toward the acquisition of knowledge. This is not to say, of course, that Nāgārjuna actively *supported* a foundationalist account of knowledge. Owing to his skepticism about the whole *pramāṇa*-based approach, he was not in a position to endorse any account of how knowledge is attained. Yet Nāgārjuna's various lines of argumentation suggest that, counterfactually speaking, if knowledge could be established via epistemic instruments, then that knowledge would need a foundation. In other words, his reasoning suggests that if an object *were* to be known via some epistemic instrument, then (a) that epistemic instrument must itself be established, and (b) the process of establishing epistemic instruments is something that must be finite and terminate with some epistemic instrument whose establishment does not depend on any other epistemic instrument.

It must be emphasized again that Nāgārjuna does not positively endorse a foundationalist account of knowledge, for he does not believe that any proper foundation can be established. Nevertheless, his reasoning throughout this portion of *The Dispeller of Disputes* takes advantage of the standard foundationalist presupposition that knowledge needs to have a foundation so as to demonstrate for readers the insufficiencies of *pramāṇa*-based epistemology. This carries with it the consequence that Nāgārjuna would reject any *infinitist* "solution" to the epistemic regress problem. That is, he would unequivocally reject the view that epistemic instruments can be established by other epistemic instruments, which are in turn established by other epistemic instruments, and so on, ad infinitum.

Prior to the nineteenth century, at which point in time important advances were made by mathematicians like Georg Cantor, the idea that there could be such a thing as an actual or completed infinity was a difficult pill for most Western philosophers to swallow.[14] In this way, an infinitist solution to the epistemic regress problem was not considered a viable path for defending the justification of beliefs. Given this, we should not be entirely surprised that Nāgārjuna likewise rejects a version of infinitism. Even among contemporary philosophers, proponents of an infinitist solution to the epistemic regress problem are few in number. The most vocal proponent of the infinitist solution is Peter Klein.[15] He has, over the course of many years and many published works, argued that infinitism provides the only viable solution to the epistemic regress problem. In particular, he believes that infinitism is superior to both coherentism, which suffers from a question-begging form of circularity, and foundationalism, which requires an arbitrary stopping point to regresses of reason-giving.

As noted earlier, there is no evidence of Nāgārjuna fully distinguishing between an infinitist response to the epistemic regress problem and a coherentist response. Both positions would be deemed insufficient by Nāgārjuna for the single reason that they fail to bring an end to the regress of establishing epistemic instruments via other epistemic instruments; and if there is no end to the process of establishing epistemic instruments, then, according to Nāgārjuna, those instruments have not been established at all.

The only response that Nāgārjuna entertains that is in the neighborhood of coherentism is contained within his discussion of position ($E_{\sim}$), wherein it is supposed for the sake of argument that epistemic instruments are not established via any epistemic instruments but are instead established by their respective epistemic objects. Such a position would resemble coherentism, insofar as it is linked to a kind of mutual support—with epistemic instruments both establishing and being established by epistemic objects. Yet to endorse the idea that an epistemic instrument (which is itself an object) could be established by something that is not itself an epistemic instrument is to give up on the fundamental tenet of *pramāṇa*-based epistemology that all objects must be established by epistemic instruments.

Nāgārjuna appears to be fully aware that epistemic regresses—in which it is granted that each epistemic instrument needs to be established by some other epistemic instrument—are problematic. It is thus not surprising that he dedicates the most space to addressing (E_s) the self-establishment thesis. By granting that epistemic instruments are self-established, epistemic regresses never arise. But there is a different way to avoid the epistemic regress problem, and that is by rejecting the assumption that epistemic instruments need to be established in the first place. It could be argued that epistemic instruments are capable of establishing the existence of objects and states of affairs without those instruments needing to be established themselves. As I mentioned earlier, this is essentially to adopt a version of strong externalism about knowledge. On such an account, in order to have knowledge of objects and states of affairs, a person's cognitions must be generated by way of legitimate epistemic instruments, but there is no further requirement that these epistemic instruments be verified or established by the cognizer.

Although Nāgārjuna does raise one objection to the proposal that epistemic instruments don't need to be established—viz., that adopting such a proposal would be tantamount to giving up on the general principle that *all objects* must be established by epistemic instruments—it may still be accurate to say that Nāgārjuna was in no position to recognize, let alone endorse, a strong externalist account of knowledge. To see why this is the case, I shall make use of John Greco's distinction between the "Project of Vindication" and "Project of Explanation" in epistemology.[16] On Greco's account, the project of vindication in epistemology aims to prove that humans can indeed have knowledge; its goal is to show that knowledge is possible. The project of explanation, by contrast, is simply to explain what knowledge is, typically on the assumption that we possess knowledge.

Proponents of *pramāṇa*-based epistemology in India are primarily engaged in the project of explanation. They want to explain what knowledge is, what instruments can be used to attain knowledge, and how those instruments work. Nāgārjuna, however, is concerned not with disputing any particular definition of knowledge, nor any account of perception or inference. Rather, he is obsessed with probing the question of whether the entire project of epistemology, as conceived by *pramāṇa* theorists, is tenable at all. He believes that it is the epistemologist's job to prove that knowledge can be attained and to do so by establishing the existence of epistemic instruments. Nāgārjuna is, as one can see from this chapter, quite skeptical that the project of vindication can be accomplished. But regardless of whether *pramāṇa*-based epistemology can ultimately be vindicated, it could be argued that his deeper aim is to show his readers that the project of vindication is something that should be taken seriously.

Nāgārjuna does not engage at all in the project of explanation. He is not concerned with elucidating what a *pramāṇa* is or with what the necessary and/or sufficient conditions for knowledge are. Because of this, the whole idea that knowledge—or its nature—can be *explained* by appealing to epistemic instruments is something that would not at all have been on Nāgārjuna's radar. Likewise, the idea that a person could have knowledge—knowledge generated via some epistemic instrument—without being required to prove or establish that the person's cognition was generated by a veritable epistemic instrument is something that would not have made sense to Nāgārjuna given his preoccupation with the project of vindication.

In contrast to Nāgārjuna, Buddhist epistemologists in the tradition of Dignāga and Dharmakīrti were much more attentive to the project of explanation than they were to the project of vindication. Though these Buddhist epistemologists and their followers were clearly interested in showing that perception and inference are the only *pramāṇas*, their main focus is on explicating these two instruments—largely under the assumption that humans do possess (quite a bit of) knowledge. The fact that Dignāga, writing in the early sixth century, devotes no explicit attention to addressing skeptical concerns of the sort raised by Nāgārjuna may strike some readers as surprising. It is possible that Dignāga was unfamiliar with the writing of Nāgārjuna, or that Nāgārjuna's views were known by Dignāga but held to be insignificant.[17] But the distinction between the project of vindication and project of explanation is relevant here as well. Because these two philosophers were engaged in two completely different epistemological endeavors—and because Dignāga was consumed with the project of explanation, not the project of vindication—there was no reason for him to respond to Nāgārjuna's skeptical criticisms.

Further Reading

For three different treatments of Nāgārjuna's criticisms of *pramāṇa*-based epistemology, see Bhattacharya, K. (1971). The dialectical method of Nāgārjuna. *Journal of Indian Philosophy*, *1*, 217–261.

Siderits, M. (1980). The Madhyamaka critique of epistemology I. *Journal of Indian Philosophy*, *8*, 307–335.

Westerhoff, J. (2010). *The dispeller of disputes: Nāgārjuna's Vigrahavyāvartanī*. Oxford: Oxford University Press.

8

Sensitivity and Safety

In chapter 2, a concern was raised about Dharmakīrti's definition of knowledge episodes vis-à-vis the issue of epistemic luck. Dharmakīrti, writing in the seventh century, defined a *pramāṇa*, an episode of knowledge, as a "nondeceptive cognition." A nondeceptive cognition must be correct (or true), but it would seem that *merely* being correct/true is not, by itself, sufficient for knowledge. After all, a correct cognition could be merely *accidentally* correct, or correct only as a result of *luck*, and in such a circumstance one might think it reasonable to deny to that cognition the status of knowledge. Indeed, at least as early as the time of Dharmottara in the eighth century, if not earlier, there is a clear recognition that merely having a correct or true cognition ought not to be viewed as sufficient for knowledge. To use a traditional example given by Buddhist thinkers, if a person, in the complete absence of evidence, were to form the belief that there is a treasure buried under her house, that person should not be deemed to have an episode of knowledge—even if there does happen to be a treasure buried there. The person's belief, if true, could lead to pragmatic success, but this success does not, in a case like this, seem to be sufficient for concluding that such a person has genuine knowledge.

The central project in this chapter is to show how Buddhist epistemologists in the centuries following Dharmakīrti sought to refine their accounts of *pramāṇa* so as to ensure that instances of "epistemic luck" would not quality as episodes of knowledge.[1] In particular, I will examine two possible paths for restricting what counts as knowledge that are developed by post-Dharmakīrtian Buddhist epistemologists. The first approach primarily impacts conceptual judgments and uses a principle of *cognitive sensitivity* to restrict knowledge to a proper subset of true (conceptual) cognitions. The second approach is tied to the status of perceptual (and, hence, nonconceptual) cognitions and uses an appeal to *perceptual discrimination* to restrict knowledge to a proper subset of true (perceptual) cognitions.

Illuminating the Mind. Jonathan Stoltz, Oxford University Press (2021). © Oxford University Press.
DOI: 10.1093/oso/9780190907532.003.0008

8.1. Knowledge, Perception, and Inference

In order to show more clearly why the status of accidentally correct cognitions is of such importance to Buddhist epistemologists, it will be helpful to reframe the problem of epistemic luck in the following way. In the writing of Dharmakīrti, but even more so in the epistemological treatises composed in the centuries immediately following Dharmakīrti, there are three definitions that are the most crucial for Buddhist accounts of knowledge. One of these three key definitions, not surprisingly, is the definition of *pramāṇa*—an episode of knowledge. The other two definitions of critical import are those of *perception* and *inference*.

The standard Buddhist view, promoted by Dignāga and Dharmakīrti, and accepted by nearly all of their (Buddhist) successors, is that perception and inference are the only two *pramāṇas*. But this very position—that perception and inference are the only *pramāṇas*—is not something that can be just baldly asserted. Instead, if the definitions of the three relevant terms—*pramāṇa*, *perception*, and *inference*—are at all adequate, both of the following two claims should be not just true but also capable of being proven or established to be true:

(1) All episodes of perception and all episodes of inferential cognition are instances of knowledge.
    [(P or I) entails K]
(2) All instances of knowledge are either episodes of perception or inferential cognition.
    [K entails (P or I)]

Establishing the truth of these two claims is far from trivial, however.

Neither of these two propositions appears to be a straightforward analytic truth. After all, the definition of *pramāṇa*, as expressed by Dharmakīrti, refers either to the property of being nondeceptive or to revealing a state of affairs not already known. But the accounts of (and definitions of) perception and inference put forward by Buddhist epistemologists do not typically make any explicit appeal to either of these same concepts. Given this, Buddhist epistemologists in the centuries following Dharmakīrti recognized that an argument needs to be provided in order to establish (1) that all episodes of perception and inference are instances of nondeceptive cognition. The converse claim, (2) that all instances of knowledge are either episodes of perception or inference, is even more difficult to establish. It is not prima facie obvious that every episode of cognition satisfying the definition of *pramāṇa*—call this class of cognitions K—must fall within the scope of those cognitions satisfying the definition of perception (class P) or the scope of those cognitions satisfying the definition of inference (class I). After all, many non-Buddhist philosophers in India did maintain that there are more knowledge sources than just perception and inference. The possibility that there could be cognitions that satisfy the definition of *pramāṇa*, but that do not meet the defining conditions of perception and/or inference, is not something that can be ruled out with the wave of a hand.

Consider, for example, the case described earlier of a homeowner who forms the belief that there is a treasure buried under her house, but who has no evidence whatsoever in support of this belief. And suppose that there does just happen to be a treasure buried beneath the house; and so the person's judgment is correct. It should immediately be clear that this judgment that there is treasure under the house does not meet the requirements for being an instance of perceptual knowledge. In addition, since the judgment is not formed in reliance on any evidence, it cannot satisfy the "three characteristics" associated with successful inferential reasoning. In short, this cognition, though true, is neither an instance of perceptual knowledge nor inferential knowledge. On the other hand, the cognition is correct/true: the person judges that there is a treasure under the house and she is right about that. Why, then, is this *not* a cognition that "reveals a state of affairs not already known"? Why is this *not* an instance of "nondeceptive cognition"? In other words, why does this example not fulfill Dharmakīrti's defining conditions for being a *pramāṇa*?

There is, we all might agree, a strong *intuition* that the homeowner's belief fails to be an instance of knowledge, and there is little question that Buddhist epistemologists, by and large, would have shared that intuition. But what is missing is a clear account of the reason(s) why the person's judgment fails to fall within the scope of Dharmakīrti's definition(s) of *pramāṇa*. The person has a correct cognition; a cognition that would lead to pragmatic success (were she to dig up the ground below her house). In what respect, then, is this a "deceptive" cognition? What is needed is a perspicuous way in which to capture the necessary and sufficient conditions for being an episode of knowledge, one that succeeds in limiting such knowledge episodes to all and only those cognitions that are either instances of perception or instances of inference.

As I said at the beginning of this chapter, one way of understanding this problem is as a puzzle of how to deal with cases of epistemic luck. It seems that merely forming a true judgment is not enough for knowledge, especially if that judgment's truth is somehow or other only accidental to it. If that's right, we are in need of an interpretation of Dharmakīrti's definitions that shows why these cases of lucky, true cognition should be excluded from the category of *pramāṇa*. In chapter 2, I described three different formulations of such an interpretation. Buddhist studies scholar Georges Dreyfus argues that Dharmakīrti's definitions imply that in order for a cognition to be "nondeceptive" it must not just be correct/true, but *normatively true*. Helmut Krasser translates the key notion of "nondeceptiveness" (*avisaṃvādi*) as "reliable," thus implying that a cognition must be reliably true in order to be an episode of knowledge. A third and I believe more accurate way to express this point is to say that the nondeceptiveness of a cognition requires a *law-like connection to the truth*. Expressed slightly differently, we might say that a nondeceptive cognition is one that *invariably tracks the truth*. Let us examine in more detail how such an account plays out within the Buddhist tradition of epistemology.

8.2. Tracking and Sensitivity

Human cognition is fallible. Though our cognitions are perhaps frequently true, they do not always hit upon the truth. There is broad agreement among Buddhist epistemologists that false judgments or erroneous cognitions cannot be episodes of knowledge. We have seen that it is much less clear what to say about those cognitions that are in fact true, but that are such that their truth is, somehow or other, only accidental to it.[2] The philosopher Dharmottara, for example, writing in the eighth century, is particularly fond of entertaining examples of accidentally correct cognitions. In doing so, his goal is surely not to dispute Dharmakīrti's earlier definition(s) of knowledge episodes, but rather, it appears, to arrive at a clearer understanding of the boundaries of knowledge.

We might think of Dharmottara as adopting something along the lines of what Roderick Chisholm has called a *particularist* approach toward epistemology, an approach that begins by appealing to various examples (of knowledge and ignorance) around which one's formal theory is to be constructed. Dharmottara, in trying to make sense of the concept of a *pramāṇa*, puts forward various examples of situations—cognitive judgments—where it appears obvious that a person does not have knowledge but where it may not be easy to specify why the situation fails to meet Dharmakīrti's definition of *pramāṇa*. Recall that Dharmottara himself is inclined to emphasize the connection between knowledge and pragmatic success. Episodes of knowledge allow us to achieve our ends—that is, to obtain the objects/goals that we seek. But pragmatic success may likewise be found in accidentally true beliefs. Consider this example given by Dharmottara: A person, who is inside a house, forms the belief, without any solid evidence at all, that there is water in a nearby well. The person hasn't seen water in the well, nor does she have any reasons or evidence to support her belief that there is water in the well. Yet she believes there is water in the well; and let's suppose that belief happens to be correct.

Surely this belief, though true, should not be considered an instance of knowledge. However, in such a scenario, the belief would be pragmatically successful, for were the person to go to the well, she would obtain what she wants—namely, water. By working through examples like this one, Dharmottara is seeking a clearer understanding of what the general conditions are for having an episode of knowledge.[3]

As alluded to already, it is fairly obvious that such a belief about there being water in a well is not going to meet the definition associated with perceptual knowledge nor satisfy the definition of inferential knowledge. It is less clear that (or why) it fails to satisfy the general definition of *pramāṇa*—namely, that of being a nondeceptive cognition. What is needed is an explanation of why accidentally true beliefs fail to be nondeceptive. To be sketched in the following pages is one explanation—one that is developed partly in response to examples like those raised by Dharmottara, and which may very well have been implicit in the accounts of various Indian epistemologists, but which is made explicit by Tibetan Buddhist epistemologists at least as early as the twelfth century.

The key insight is to focus on the ontological relation between a cognition and its content—that is, the object or state of affairs that the cognition is about—and to show that the relation between a cognition and its content is fundamentally different in an episode of knowledge from what that relation is like in a case of accidentally true cognition. In particular, the account appeals to the concept of an *invariable dependence* existing between a cognition and its truth/correctness. It is affirmed that, in cases where a person has an episode of knowledge, the cognition must ontologically depend on the existence of the object or state of affairs associated with the content of the cognitive episode.

More explicitly, the claim is that an episode of knowledge—and, thus, an episode of "nondeceptive cognition"—is one where there is an invariable dependence of the cognition C(*p*) on the state of affairs *p*. In particular, it is affirmed that the following (counterfactual) conditional must hold:

(S_s) If state of affairs *p* had been false, cognition C(*p*) would not have occurred.

Of course, with respect to nonconceptual cognitions, such as in sensory experiences, it would be more appropriate to speak, not of a state of affairs' truth or falsity, but of an object's (real) existence or nonexistence. In such a case, the invariable connection could be more naturally expressed as:

(S_o) If object *o* had not existed, cognition C(*o*) would not have occurred.

An episode of knowledge is one where the cognition is not merely correct/true, but *invariably* correct/true in the sense of satisfying the counterfactual conditional (S_s) or (S_o)—though, for simplicity, I shall restrict my discussion to just the former formulation, (S_s).

As has previously been noted in chapter 2, these counterfactual conditionals capture what is now generally termed a *sensitivity* requirement for knowledge. It is claimed that a cognition must be *sensitive to the truth* if it is to be an episode of knowledge. Just as we might say that a smoke detector is "sensitive to smoke" provided that it beeps only when there is smoke, and that a bomb-sniffing dog is "sensitive to the presence of explosives" provided that (in the appropriate contexts) it sits down and barks only when there are explosives nearby, so, too, we can speak of a cognition being sensitive to the truth (or sensitive to the way things really are) provided that the cognition would arise only when it is true/correct.[4]

The claim I am making here is a strong one: that there are Buddhist epistemologists in the twelfth century who explicitly appeal to a version of the principle of sensitivity in order to capture the law-like connection to the truth that must be exhibited in cases of knowledge, but which is absent in cases of merely accidental true cognition. In just a moment, I will discuss the way in which this sensitivity constraint on knowledge comes to be made explicit in early Tibetan Buddhist epistemology. Before doing so, however, let us look more carefully at the Indian precursor of this appeal to sensitivity, so that we can see why a sensitivity condition may have been primed to take hold within the Buddhist tradition of epistemology.

8.2.1. The Origins of Invariable Dependence

As discussed in chapter 4, one of the most important contributions made by Dharmakīrti was his articulation of a metaphysical basis for the existence of a universal entailment (*vyāpti*) between the 'evidencing property' and the 'property to be inferred' in cases of inferential reasoning. When discussing this relation between the two relevant properties involved in inferential judgments—the evidencing property and the property to be proven—Dharmakīrti describes this relation as one in which there is an *invariable dependence* (*avinābhāva*) of the evidencing property (*hetu*) on the property to be inferred (*sādhyadharma*). What this invariable dependence avows is that if the one item didn't exist, then the other item couldn't exist either. In particular, the evidencing property entails the property to be inferred provided that

> (A) If the property to be inferred didn't exist, then the evidencing property couldn't exist either.

It is this conditional that is being referenced when Dharmakīrti and his followers appeal to the notion of *invariable dependence* (*avinābhāva*). In instances of inferential reasoning, the evidence entails the property to be inferred in the sense that were 'the property to be inferred' not to exist, 'the evidencing property' couldn't exist either.

To be clear, when Dharmakīrti appeals to the concept of invariable dependence, he does so almost always within the context of discussing inferential reasoning and while aiming to address the relationship that must exist between the two properties that figure into inferential reasoning. On the standard Dharmakīrtian account, in order for evidential reasoning to be warranted—and thus result in an episode of knowledge—it is essential for that evidence to invariably depend on the property to be inferred. Yet this appeal to invariable dependence of the evidence on the property to be inferred additionally serves to *guarantee* the truth of inferential cognitions. In other words, this appeal to invariable dependence serves to rule out accidentally correct inference-like cognitions.

Having said all that, early in the first chapter of his *Ascertainment of Knowledge*, there is one place where Dharmakīrti defends the view that this talk of invariable dependence applies not just to inference but can be extended to *perception* as well.[5] This may sound odd. After all, perceptual cognitions do not rely on evidence, nor on any conceptual reasoning at all. Perceptions are thus, in very important respects, quite unlike instances of inferential reasoning. Yet Dharmakīrti affirms that the concept of invariable dependence can be applied ("by analogy" or owing to "similarities") to perceptual cognitions. In such cases, the idea appears to be that this extension of the term is permissible insofar as there is, in perception, an invariable dependence between the object and the cognition. As he puts it, "because one affirms the existence of an object from the existence of the cognition [of that object], it can be said that the cognition depends on that [object]."[6]

It is not fully clear how much weight Dharmakīrti believes should be placed on this extension of the concept of invariable dependence (*avinābhāva*) to perceptual cognitions. As has already been noted, in the numerous other places where the concept of invariable dependence is referenced in his *Ascertainment of Knowledge*, it is always within the context of inferential reasoning and the relation between the evidencing property and the property to be proven. Yet there is this one place where Dharmakīrti does link the concept of invariable dependence to the status of perception. It is also notable that, when he affirms this extension of invariable dependence to perception, Dharmakīrti explicitly draws a link between that notion and the idea of "nondeceptiveness." In other words, it is suggested that the concept of invariable dependence is connected to the general defining condition for a knowledge episode.

8.2.2. Co-opting Invariable Dependence

It would take a tremendous amount of philological sleuthing to figure out the full story of how the concept of invariable dependence (*avinābhāva*) is employed by Buddhist epistemologists in centuries following Dharmakīrti. While such an investigation is well beyond the scope of this book, what is clear is that by the time we reach the twelfth century, a range of Tibetan Buddhist epistemologists employ the concept of invariable dependence within their discussions of the definition of *pramāṇa*; and when they do so, they construe this invariable dependence as a relationship existing between a cognitive episode and the truth/correctness of the object or state of affairs that is apprehended in the cognitive episode. This position is held, in particular, by Chaba Chokyi Senge (1109–1169) and many of his intellectual descendants.[7] (This is not to say that they do not *also* discuss invariable dependence when addressing inferential knowledge and the relation between one's evidencing property and the property to be inferred. The concept of invariable dependence is centrally addressed in those discussions as well.)

A cognition can qualify as an episode of knowledge, according to these Tibetan epistemologists, only if that cognition invariably depends on the truth of the state of affairs in question. That is, there must be an invariable dependence between the cognition and the object/state of affairs that is the content of that cognition. And, as noted earlier, this invariable dependence is captured by an appeal to a counterfactual conditional. In order to have knowledge, a person's cognition must (in addition to several other things) satisfy the following counterfactual conditional:

> (S_s) If state of affairs p had been false, cognition $C(p)$ would not have occurred.

Tibetan epistemologists in the twelfth and thirteenth centuries speak of this counterfactual conditional as capturing the cognitive episode's "mode of apprehension." In contemporary terminology, this same conditional, when satisfied, indicates that the cognition is *sensitive to the truth*. Putting these two points together, we can say that an episode of knowledge requires the cognition to have the right mode of apprehension—and this can happen only if the cognition is sensitive to the truth.

The most common Tibetan examples that are put forward in order to show why this sensitivity condition is required for episodes of knowledge involve cases of accidentally true, inference-like judgments. Examples of this sort include the case of the person who believes that there is a treasure buried under her house and the case of the person who, while sitting inside one's house, believes there to be water in a nearby well, but who forms this belief without any supporting evidence. In both of these cases, the judgments are correct—given the setup of the stories—but they fail the sensitivity requirement, for even if the relevant states of affairs had been false, the two people still would have believed them to be true. Counterfactually speaking, even if, in the first example, there were no treasure buried under the person's house, she still would have believed there was. After all, her belief was not really linked, causally or evidentially, to the actual existence of the treasure. Likewise, since the second person had no real evidence to support her belief that there is water in the nearby well, her cognition was not sensitive to the presence or absence of the water.

It is clear that the sensitivity requirement could be extended to instances of visual (and more broadly sensory) cognition as well. On the standard *Sautrāntika* model experience, in successful cases of perceptual knowledge, the person's cognition of an object is causally linked to the object itself. For example, when I visually perceive a white conch shell, it is the conch shell itself that is causally responsible for my cognition as of a white conch shell. Provided that this is the case, the sensitivity requirement should be satisfied—for if the conch shell didn't exist, the person would not have had a cognition as of a white conch shell.

This stands in sharp contrast to what we would say in a case of "veridical illusion." Imagine that a person looks toward a table and has a visual experience as of a silver cup; and let us suppose that there is, in fact, a silver cup on the table. The actual silver cup, however, is hidden behind a small opaque screen, but an image of a silver cup is being projected onto the screen. In such a scenario, the person's visual experience as of a silver cup is, in a sense, veridical—for there is a real silver cup there—but that real silver cup is not causally linked to the person's experience as of a silver cup. As a result, even if the (real) silver cup had not been on the table, the person still would have had a cognition as of a silver cup—and so the cognition is not sensitive to the truth. Thus, we should not classify this visual experience as an instance of perceptual knowledge of a silver cup.

Admittedly, this case could be more easily understood were we to describe it in terms of a perceptual *judgment*. After a person has a particular visual sensory experience, that person is likely to form a judgment or concept-laden belief from that experience. In particular, given the setup of the scenario, the person is likely to judge that there is a silver cup on the table. This belief that there is a silver cup on the table is true, but the belief is certainly not sensitive to the truth because, all other things being equal, even if there had been no silver cup on the table, the person still would have believed there was (due to the image projected onto the screen). As a result, this belief, though in fact veridical, could not be an instance of knowledge. The key point, again, is that a cognition's truth or correctness is not a sufficient condition for knowledge.

In order for a cognition to be an episode of knowledge, that cognition must be sensitive to the truth in the sense that, counterfactually speaking, had the object/state of affairs not existed, the cognition of that object/state of affairs would not have arisen.

8.2.3. The Significance of Sensitivity

Tibetan Buddhist epistemologists' appeals to the principle of sensitivity are, as I have already stated, principally geared toward alleviating concerns about the epistemic status of accidentally true cognitions. Even a person who relies on faulty evidence can end up with beliefs that happen to be true. Given that these cognitions are true/correct, it may appear that they are nondeceptive, or that they reveal a previously unknown states of affairs. The sensitivity requirement provides a clear criterion for excluding accidentally true cognitions from the realm of knowledge.

The fact that Buddhist epistemologists in twelfth-century Tibet appeal to the principle of sensitivity is remarkable in a number of ways—for reasons that go well beyond the fact that this appeal occurs over eight hundred years before analytic philosophers like Robert Nozick took up the cause of promoting a sensitivity requirement for knowledge. First and foremost, this appeal to the principle of sensitivity indicates an awareness of the importance of *modal* considerations when making sense of knowledge. In particular, whether a person is having an episode of knowledge depends not just on what the world is *actually* like—for example, that the person's cognition is, in fact, true—but also on the other *possible* ways the world could have been. The fact that Tibetan Buddhist epistemologists were attentive to modal notions like possibility and necessity is not entirely surprising, especially given the fact that Dharmakīrti, centuries earlier, focused so much on concepts like universal entailment and invariable dependence.

Even if Buddhist philosophers' attention to modal considerations is not altogether unsurprising, the fact that these modal considerations are specifically linked to *counterfactual* possibilities is incredibly important. In the typical cases that philosophers like Dharmottara are concerned with, the person's cognition turns out to be, as a matter of fact, correct. For example, a person might, without any solid evidence at all, form the true belief that there is water in a nearby well. The reason why this belief, though true, nevertheless fails to be an instance of knowledge is—according to the sensitivity requirement—because of counterfactual considerations involving what would have happened had things been different from the way they actually are. There is, in fact, water in the well, but even if, counterfactually speaking, there had been no water in the well, the person still would have believed that there was.

There is, however, one important difference between how this appeal to counterfactual scenarios is understood in the Buddhist tradition of epistemology and how it is understood in contemporary, analytic formulations of sensitivity that are tied to people like Robert Nozick. Nozick's treatment of counterfactual conditionals is guided, in part, by the semantic interpretation of these conditionals that was put forward by David Lewis in his 1973 book *Counterfactuals*. On Lewis's account, the truth conditions of a counterfactual conditional (e.g., "If A had been the case, B would have been the case") are determined by considering a set of possible worlds/situations that are *similar* to the actual world, but where the if-clause, A, is true rather than false. Practically speaking, this has the consequence that the truth conditions for a counterfactual conditional do not depend on remote counterfactual possibilities. For example, consider the counterfactual conditional,

> (M) If this matchstick had been struck against the matchbox, it would have ignited.

Suppose that the matchstick is not in fact struck. In order to assess whether (M) should be considered true or false, we are to consider what would have happened in situations similar to the actual one, but where the matchstick was struck. Remote possibilities—such as a situation in which the matchstick is struck against the matchbox by someone swimming under water—are irrelevant when assessing the truth status of (M). More carefully, these remote possibilities are irrelevant as long as one is adopting an analysis of counterfactual conditionals similar to that which is supported by David Lewis.[8]

There is no indication that Buddhist epistemologists understood the counterfactual conditionals associated with their principle of sensitivity, conditionals (S_s) and (S_o), to be similarly affected by considerations of 'close' versus 'remote' possibilities. On the other hand, the only way in which the sensitivity requirement has a chance of being satisfied within the Buddhist model is if the counterfactual conditionals in question are interpreted as containing some sort of ceteris paribus clause. Here, a ceteris paribus clause refers to a restriction along the lines of "All else being equal . . . " or "Holding everything else constant . . . ". In other words, the conditional "If state of affairs p had been false, cognition $C(p)$ would not have occurred," must be interpreted as meaning "*Everything else being equal*, if state of affairs p had been false, cognition $C(p)$ would not have occurred."

That this restriction is needed can be seen by considering a generic case of visual perception. Suppose that I visually perceive a (real) silver cup on a table. According to this Buddhist account of knowledge, my cognition of a silver cup qualifies as an instance of perceptual knowledge only if it satisfies the counterfactual conditional, "If there were no silver cup, I would not have had a cognition as of a silver cup." Intuitively, this sensitivity requirement should be satisfied in an ordinary case of visual perception, but not be satisfied in a case of veridical illusion, such as was described earlier. Yet, in any case of genuine perception, the scenario could have been altered in such a way that (a) the real object is removed, but (b) some sort of mechanism is introduced that leads to an illusion as of that object. For example, with respect to a person perceiving a silver cup on the table, it is possible to describe a counterfactual situation in which (a) there is no silver cup on the table but (b) some scientists have produced a holographic projection as of a silver cup. In such a counterfactual scenario, the person would have had a cognition as of a silver cup. So in order for the sensitivity requirement on knowledge to be satisfied, outlandish possibilities of this sort need to be precluded. A ceteris paribus clause would serve to do just that. The counterfactual conditional, "If there were no silver cup, the person would not have had a cognition as of a silver cup," is true provided that we are considering situations *just like the actual case*—in which there is a silver cup on the table—*except that* there is no silver cup on the table. If everything else were the same except that there is no silver cup, the person would not have had a cognition as of a silver cup.

Admittedly, though Tibetan Buddhist epistemologists in the twelfth and thirteenth centuries explicitly appeal to this sensitivity requirement, and frame it as an invariable dependence of one's cognition on the object cognized, it is nowhere stated that the relevant counterfactual conditional is to be interpreted with a ceteris paribus clause. Yet, if knowledge (via perception or inference) is to be possible at all, something along the lines of such a ceteris paribus clause needs to be granted.

8.3. Safety and Knowledge

As it has been framed here, the sensitivity requirement, (S_s) or (S_o), effectively ensures that accidentally true/correct cognitions will not qualify as instances of knowledge. This appeal to a sensitivity requirement does not appear to have been made explicit in Buddhist interpretations of *pramāṇa* until sometime around the twelfth century or so. But the position that a cognition should count as episodes of knowledge only if it is nonaccidentally correct is something that was already implicit in Buddhist accounts of perception and inference coming from Dharmakīrti in the early seventh century. That said, the fact that a group of Tibetan Buddhist epistemologists hit upon a *sensitivity* requirement as the most suitable means by which to limit knowledge to nonaccidentally correct cognitions may, itself, have just been an accident. After all, there could plausibly have been several other ways by which to prevent accidentally true cognitions from qualifying as instances of knowledge.

Instead of appealing to a principle of sensitivity to solve the problem of accidentally true cognitions, many contemporary epistemologists now argue in favor of a *safety* requirement for knowledge. This requirement is, formally at least, the contrapositive of the sensitivity requirement. The sensitivity thesis states that

(Sens) If *p* had been false, S would not believe *p*.

The safety requirement, by contrast, demands that

(Safe) If S were to believe *p*, *p* would be true.

The idea behind the appeal to (Safe) is that knowledge does not just require having a true belief, but requires having a true belief that *could not easily have been false*.

Though (Sens) and (Safe) are formally contrapositives of each other, contraposition fails as a logical principle for counterfactual conditionals (at least under the now standard logical analysis of counterfactuals put forward by David Lewis). As such, the truth conditions of (Sens) and (Safe) are not identical. Yet either of these conditions, when called upon as a requirement for knowledge, has the capacity to rule out accidentally true beliefs from the realm of knowledge. On one plausible interpretation, an "accidentally true belief" is one that, though true, could easily have been false. The safety requirement thus serves to exclude from the domain of knowledge those beliefs that could easily have been false.

While Tibetan Buddhist epistemologists do appeal to the notion of invariable dependence (*avinābhāva*) and the principle of sensitivity, there does not appear to be any invocation of the principle of safety in the Buddhist tradition of epistemology. Whether this is or is not an important observation is less than fully clear. On the one hand, the now widely accepted logical difference between (Sens) and (Safe) is rooted in an understanding of counterfactual conditionals—one grounded in David Lewis's semantics for counterfactual conditionals—that would not have been recognized in the historical Buddhist tradition of epistemology or logic. As such, the absence of any reference to (Safe) in Buddhist epistemology may just reflect the fact that they treated the relevant conditionals—(Sens) and (Safe)—as logically equivalent to each other. On the other hand, it might be thought that the formulation in (Safe) more straightforwardly captures the actual relation (between a cognition and its truth/correctness) that must exist in order for a cognition to have the status of *pramāṇa*. After all, an episode of knowledge is, on the Buddhist account, a cognition that is not merely true/correct, but rather a cognition that bears a law-like connection to the truth.

Yet, when expressing the relation between a cognition and its truth, Buddhist epistemologists generally describe the relation in negative terms: in order to be an episode of knowledge, the cognition in question is one such that if the object/state of affairs *hadn't* existed, the cognition would *not* have occurred. In fact, this attention to alternative possibilities is something that shows up not only in Tibetan Buddhist epistemologists' appeal to a sensitivity requirement on knowledge but also in another, tangentially related, area of concern. Specifically, in addition to being sensitive to the truth, an episode of knowledge should be one where the cognizer can *discriminate* between what is and what is not the case.

8.4. Discrimination and Alternatives

8.4.1. Discrimination and Sensitivity

There is a fairly straightforward connection between the epistemic thesis of sensitivity and claims about the power of discrimination. To be able to *discriminate* between (or *distinguish*) a pine tree and a fir tree is, loosely speaking, to be able to tell the difference between these two kinds of trees; and this ability to tell the difference can be thought of as a version of sensitivity—one which can be expressed in terms of counterfactual conditionals. For example, a person who can distinguish pine trees from fir trees is someone who, when observing an actual pine tree,

(3) Believes that it is a pine tree, but
(4) If it had been a fir tree (instead of a pine), would not have believed that it was a pine tree.

Perhaps more intuitively, a person who fails condition (4) here—that is, someone who still would have believed it to be a pine tree even if it had been a fir tree—is someone who simply cannot adequately distinguish pine trees from fir trees.

Even if there is a connection between the power of discrimination and the thesis of sensitivity, they are not necessarily equivalent to each other. In particular, a person's beliefs or cognitions may be sensitive to the presence/absence of an object without having the power to distinguish between some contrary alternatives to that object. And insofar as a commitment to the thesis of sensitivity is effectively a way to exclude accidentally true cognitions from the realm of knowledge, it follows that not all *nonaccidentally* true cognitions are ones where there is a capacity to discriminate between the actual state of affairs and contrary alternatives.

Consider, for example, a case where a person has a perceptual experience as of a piece of silver (under water), but where the person cannot distinguish silver from mother-of-pearl. Let us suppose that the presence of a real silver coin is causally responsible for the person's cognition as of a piece of silver. In light of the causal link between the actual silver coin and the person's cognition, there is good reason to think that the person's cognition is sensitive to the truth; for, all else being equal, if there had been no piece of silver, the person would not have had a cognition as of a piece of silver. But whereas the thesis of sensitivity is asking what would happen *were the piece of silver not to exist at all*, the appeal to a power of discrimination is considering a different kind of counterfactual hypothesis. It could be asking what would happen *were the piece of silver to be replaced by a mother-of-pearl shell*. These two counterfactual scenarios are different:

(5) If there had been no piece of silver at all, the person would not have had a cognition as of a piece of silver.
(6) If the piece of silver had been replaced by a mother-of-pearl shell, the person would not have had a cognition as of a piece of silver.

The first counterfactual, (5), is what must be satisfied in order for the cognition to be sensitive to the existence of silver, but the latter, (6), is the counterfactual that must be satisfied in order for a person to have the power to distinguish between silver and mother-of-pearl. It is possible for (5) to be true even while (6) is false.

8.4.2. Discrimination and Perception

Insofar as the conditions that need to be met in order to satisfy the principle of sensitivity are different from the conditions that need to be met in order to discriminate between an object and relevant alternatives of that object, it is sensible to ask which of these sets of conditions is actually necessary for knowledge. Does knowledge merely require that one's beliefs/cognitions are sensitive to the truth, or does knowledge further require one's beliefs/cognitions to suitably discriminate between the actual state of affairs and various contrary alternatives?

Here it would be instructive to think about this question in the twentieth-century context. Alvin Goldman (1967) proposed a causal theory of knowledge in response to Gettier's criticisms of the "justified true belief" analysis of knowledge. Goldman initially argued that the Gettier problem could be bypassed by affirming that what was needed for knowledge is a true belief that is causally produced in the right way (and, in particular, causally related to the fact that is believed). The exact details of Goldman's causal account do not concern us. What matters, instead, is that less than ten years after developing his causal theory of knowledge Goldman rejected that account, noting that it failed other intuitions we have about knowledge. The now famous "red barn" case is meant to demonstrate this point. Imagine a person driving through farm country. In the fields along the side of the road there are many objects that appear to be red barns. Let us suppose, however, that the area the person is driving through consists mostly of papier-mâché barn-façades, and that only a small proportion of the objects that look like barns are actually real ones. Further assume that, while driving along the road, the person cannot readily distinguish a real barn from a mere papier-mâché façade. When the driver, call him "Henry," looks out the window and catches a glimpse of one of these objects, he forms the belief that it is a red barn. And in this particular case, let's suppose that he is right—the object Henry is seeing is a real, red barn, not a mere façade. Here, the causal theory of knowledge would imply that Henry knows there is a barn in the field—for the causal process proceeded correctly, insofar as an actual red barn was causally responsible for the driver's belief that there is a red barn in the field.

Goldman believes this conclusion to be counterintuitive. While the causal requirements for knowledge were met, Henry *cannot discriminate* between a real barn and a mere papier-mâché barn façade. Given this inability to distinguish a real barn from a fake one, and given that most of the items in the area that appear to be barns are actually just façades, Henry's belief that there is a (real) barn in the field could very easily have been false. In light of this inability to distinguish a real barn from a mere barn façade, Goldman contends that we should, intuitively, deny that Henry has knowledge and conclude instead that the causal theory of knowledge is inadequate. As he puts it, "My old causal analysis cannot handle the problem either. Henry's belief that the object is a barn is caused by the presence of the barn; indeed, the causal process is a perceptual one. Nonetheless, we are not prepared to say . . . that Henry knows."[9] The broader point is that knowledge seems to require not just getting a true belief that is caused in the right way, but also that the person possesses the power to discriminate between the truth and relevant contrary alternatives.

Let us now think about how this might apply within the Buddhist epistemological context. Dignāga, Dharmakīrti, and most of their Indian followers endorse a broadly causal theory of perception. Moreover, they support the position that perception is a *pramāṇa*—that all perceptual cognitions are episodes of knowledge. Does that mean that this Buddhist account could fall prey to objections similar to those raised by Alvin Goldman? To be clear, Goldman is concerned with propositional beliefs—such as the belief *that there is a red barn*—whereas Buddhist accounts of perception and perceptual knowledge are emphatically nonpropositional. Nevertheless, we can still ask whether merely having a veridical perceptual experience of an object is sufficient for concluding that the perceptual experience is an instance of knowledge. Is it possible that a person could, for example, actually perceive a silver coin in water, and yet not have that perceptual experience qualify as knowledge?

Among Indian Buddhist epistemologists from the time of Dignāga onward, the available evidence would suggest that what is needed for perceptual knowledge is a merely having a veridical (nonconceptual) experience. There is no indication that an ability to distinguish between the actual object and various contrary alternatives is deemed to be necessary for knowledge. This is not particularly surprising, given that the power to discriminate between alternatives may very well require conceptual resources, and yet Buddhist epistemologists agree that perceptual cognitions are devoid of conceptuality.

Over time, however, we come to find changes in the views of Buddhist epistemologists on these matters. As has been described in chapter 6 (section 6.2), Tibetan Buddhist epistemologists in the twelfth century parted ways with the views of their Indian predecessors and adopted a position much more similar to that of Alvin Goldman. According to Tibetan proponents of this view, having an episode of perception does not automatically imply that one is having an episode of knowledge. All perceptions are, by definition, nonconceptual, and they must apprehend their objects nonerroneously. But these Tibetan Buddhist thinkers contend that only a proper subset of cognitions satisfying those requirements are instances of knowledge. The subtype of perception that is a *pramāṇa* can be called "perceptual knowledge." But there are other forms of perceptual awareness—episodes in which a person nonerroneously, and nonconceptually, apprehends a real object—that do not constitute knowledge. A more detailed examination of these perceptual cognitions has already been carried out in chapter 6 when discussing various forms of "ignorant cognition." Given its relevant connection to the thesis of sensitivity, however, let us look briefly, once again, at how Tibetan epistemologists in the twelfth century understood the link between perceptual knowledge and the power to discriminate between real objects and contrary alternatives.

8.4.3. Discrimination and Countering Superimpositions

Consider once again a case like that described earlier of a person perceiving silver under water, but where now the person has a *veridical* visual experience as of a mother-of-pearl shell (under water). On the standard Indian Buddhist model, such a veridical visual experience would qualify as an episode of perceptual knowledge. Among various Tibetan epistemologists in the late twelfth and early thirteenth centuries, it would be agreed that this visual experience is an instance of perception, but they would deny that this automatically implies that it is an episode of knowledge. Whether it is or is not an instance of knowledge depends on (among other things) whether the cognition in question is capable of "countering" or "eliminating" *superimpositions*. Here, a superimposition is a quality or feature that does not actually exist but is superimposed by the cognizer's mind on one's experience of reality. For example, in a situation where a person is afflicted with jaundice, the quality of being yellow might be superimposed on that person's experience of a (white) conch shell.

As the notion is understood within Buddhist contexts, a superimposition is necessarily erroneous—it is something that does not actually exist. But even when someone has a veridical sensory experience, it does not necessarily follow that his or her cognition can counter the capacity to produce superimpositions. Depending on a person's circumstances—such as when one is observing an object from a distance—it is possible for a veridical cognition of a mother-of-pearl shell to be compatible with the generation of a superimposed property such as 'silver.' Likewise, in such circumstances it is possible that, immediately after having a veridical visual cognition of a mother-of-pearl shell, the cognizer could form the judgment *that there is a piece of silver*.

Recognizing these sorts of possibilities, Tibetan epistemologists in the twelfth century uphold the view that while perception merely requires having a veridical, nonconceptual awareness, perceptual *knowledge* requires more. A perceptual experience is not a *pramāṇa* unless it additionally counters the capacity to produce superimpositions.[10] Expressed differently,

> (ELIM) A cognition qualifies as an instance of perceptual knowledge only if that cognition counters the capacity to produce all actual and potential superimpositions.

Importantly, this power to counter/eliminate superimpositions can be seen as linked to the issue of perceptual discrimination and the view that knowledge requires discriminatory powers. To see this more clearly, suppose that two contrary objects or qualities, x and y, are visually indistinguishable. In such a situation, it is quite plausible to maintain that a person's perceptual cognition of x would be incapable of countering or eliminating the superimposition y. For example, if in a given context (such as when viewed under water) a silver coin is indistinguishable from a mother-of-pearl shell, then even if a person has a veridical perceptual experience as of mother-of-pearl, that sensory cognition would not be able to eliminate the potential superimposition 'silver.' Likewise, if a person, due to poor lighting conditions, cannot distinguish a blue statue from a green statue, then even if that person has a veridical visual experience as of a green statue, his or her perceptual cognition would not be able to eliminate the potential superimposition 'blue.' In short, indistinguishability implies that one cannot counter superimpositions from arising. And that is just to say that

> (DIST) A cognition can counter the capacity to produce superimpositions only if one can distinguish what is actually the case from contrary alternatives.

From (ELIM) and (DIST) it follows that in all instances of perceptual knowledge there must be the ability to distinguish what is actually the case from all those alternatives that are directly contrary to the item perceived. In order to have perceptual knowledge of blue, for example, one must be able to distinguish blue from nonblue. In order to have perceptual knowledge of a mother-of-pearl shell, one must be able to distinguish a mother-of-pearl shell from silver.

To be clear, this assumes—as Tibetan Buddhist epistemologists in the twelfth and thirteenth centuries did—that (ELIM) is true. It also assumes, rather controversially, that this power to counter or eliminate superimpositions is something that can indeed occur within cognitions that are devoid of conceptuality. As was already mentioned in chapter 6, this is something that would have been denied by most Buddhist epistemologists in India. What it is important to be attentive to at present is the connection between the thesis of sensitivity and the restriction of perceptual knowledge to a proper subset of veridical, nonconceptual cognitions. Just as a requirement involving *sensitivity* (in the form of *invariable dependence*) is put forward by some Buddhist epistemologists so as to restrict knowledge to a proper subset of true conceptual judgments, so, too, a parallel requirement involving *discriminatory power* (in the form of *countering superimpositions*) is put forward by those same epistemologists so as to restrict knowledge to a proper subset of veridical nonconceptual cognitions. These restrictions on knowledge are far from universally accepted by post-Dharmakīrtian Buddhist epistemologists, but they do serve to exemplify the trend toward restricting knowledge to just cognitions that are nonaccidentally true or that have a law-like connection to the truth.

Further Reading

For a clear introduction to the topic of anti-luck epistemology and its connection to the thesis of sensitivity, see Pritchard, D. (2008). Sensitivity, safety, and anti-luck epistemology. In Greco, J. (Ed.), *The Oxford handbook of skepticism*. Oxford: Oxford University Press.

For an example of anti-luck epistemology in the (non-Buddhist) Indian tradition of philosophy, see §2 of Das, N. (2018). Śrīharṣa. In E. Zalta (Ed.), *The Stanford encyclopedia of philosophy* (Winter 2018 edition), https://plato.stanford.edu/archives/spr2018/entries/sriharsa/.

For a slightly more detailed account of sensitivity and discriminatory power in the Tibetan Buddhist tradition of epistemology, see chapter I of Hugon, P., & Stoltz, J. (2019). *The roar of a Tibetan lion: Phya pa Chos kyi seng ge's theory of mind in philosophical and historical perspective*. Vienna: Austrian Academy of Sciences Press.

9
Internalism and Externalism

Earlier in this book, while explicating Dharmakīrti's definition of *pramāṇa*, I characterized an episode of knowledge within classical Buddhist epistemology as being *a novel, truth-tracking cognition*. This chapter probes the Buddhist account of knowledge in greater depth and explores a few of the critical epistemological consequences stemming from this Buddhist conception of knowledge episodes. In particular, at its heart, this chapter grapples with the debate between internalism and externalism in epistemology and argues that there are multiple grounds for concluding that the classical Buddhist account of knowledge episodes is best understood as being in accord with an externalist account of epistemic warrant. That topic will then lead to a subsequent discussion of the classical Indian debate between "intrinsic" versus "extrinsic" determination of a cognition's knowledge status, and how that debate plays out in the Buddhist tradition of epistemology in the centuries after Dharmakīrti.

9.1. The Etiology of Cognition

In chapter 2, it was shown that the Buddhist account of nondeceptive cognition cannot be assimilated to the notion of a justified belief, nor to a reliable belief—at least under the standard assumption that justification and reliability are fallible. Instead, it was affirmed that nondeceptiveness should be understood as indicating that a cognition invariably "tracks the truth." Yet, to the extent that this is the case, and given that a cognition's being nondeceptive logically entails its being correct/true, more should be said about what this tracking of the truth consists in. When a person has an episode of knowledge, where does the guarantee of correctness come from?

In the preceding chapter, it was shown that the truth-tracking feature of *pramāṇas* can be explicated by reference to those cognitions satisfying a *sensitivity* constraint on episodes knowledge. This invocation of sensitivity did not become explicit until, it appears, sometime around the twelfth

Illuminating the Mind. Jonathan Stoltz, Oxford University Press (2021). © Oxford University Press.
DOI: 10.1093/oso/9780190907532.003.0009

century in Tibet, and yet I have claimed that a truth-tracking understanding of *pramāṇas* might be viewed as implicit in earlier, Indian Buddhist epistemological accounts as well. Why should we think that Indian Buddhist epistemologists upheld the position that episodes of knowledge must invariably track the truth? The answer comes not from their explications of the term *pramāṇa*, but instead from their discussions of the two *pramāṇas* endorsed by Buddhist epistemologists: perception and inference. Both of these two types of knowledge episodes are ones that, given how those cognitive episodes arise, invariably track the truth.

Let us begin with the truth-tracking nature of perception. When a person has a sensory cognition, what does it mean to say that the cognition tracks the truth? One possible interpretation, one that could be adopted by a direct realist, would be to hold that a sensory cognition tracks the truth provided that the cognition directly encounters or experiences a real, external object and does so in such a way that the cognition could not arise in the absence of the object. Dharmakīrti does not adopt a direct realist understanding of perceptual experience, however, and neither do the vast majority of the Buddhist epistemologists that follow him. Instead, the most common (but not universally adopted) portrayal of perceptual experience in the Buddhist epistemological tradition is a version of representationalism. On this representationalist model, an external object leaves a mark or stamp on cognition. This mark or stamp is ordinarily understood to be generated through a causal process that integrally involves the (potentially external) object itself. In this way, a nondeceptive sensory cognition is one that does not merely correspond with its object as it exists in reality; it is a cognition that invariably tracks its object insofar as the cognition and its representational mark are causally generated by the real object itself. When, for example, I perceive a clay pot, there is a causal process that links the real clay pot to my cognition of that pot. In other words, the invariable truth-tracking exhibited in episodes of perceptual knowledge is grounded in the etiology of sensory experience.

The status of inferential knowledge episodes will need to be explained differently. In episodes of inferential judgment, the judged state of affairs is not directly causally responsible for the inferential judgment itself. For example, when a person infers that clay pots are impermanent, this state of affairs does not directly cause the person's inferential cognition. And yet in the post-Dharmakīrtian tradition of Buddhist epistemology, when a person inferentially knows that clay pots are impermanent, the episode of inferential cognition is one that must be invariably connected to a true state of affairs. This can be shown by focusing in on the necessary conditions for inferential knowledge, which were discussed in chapter 4.

For any inferential judgment C(*p*) with respect to the state of affairs *p*, the fact that the cognition C(*p*) is invariably connected to a true or correct state of affairs *p* is grounded in the logical structure of inferential cognitions. In particular, Buddhist epistemologists standardly maintain that the inferential judgment C(*p*) could occur only if the cognitive agent in question antecedently knows two facts that themselves logically guarantee the truth of the state of affairs *p*. As we saw in chapter 4, the judgment C(*p*) qualifies as an instance of inferential knowledge only if the cognizer (1) knows that *e* and (2) knows that *e* entails *p*.[1] But these two conditions are ones that jointly guarantee the truth of *p*. In this way, the logical structure of inferential cognitions are, in the post-Dharmakīrtian tradition of Buddhist epistemology, invariably truth-tracking. Yet, insofar as these two conditions on inferential knowledge, (1) and (2), are themselves momentary episodes of cognition that are temporally prior to the judgment C(*p*), the causal structure of inferential cognitions is relevant to truth-tracking as well. The causal process that produces the inferential cognition C(*p*) likewise guarantees that the resulting cognition C(*p*) could only arise in circumstances where *p* is true.

Taken together, what it is important to recognize is that, in the Buddhist tradition of epistemology that flows from Dignāga and Dharmakīrti, episodes of knowledge are not merely true cognitions. They are cognitions that invariably track the truth; and they do this, in part, by virtue of the causal processes that generate these episodes of cognition. Expressed differently, the point is that a cognition's being true or correct is not sufficient for establishing its nondeceptiveness. Even being "reliably correct" is not enough to make a cognition nondeceptive—at least on the standard assumption that reliability is a matter of being probabilistically truth conducive. Instead, what is needed for nondeceptiveness is a cognition that invariably tracks the truth—a cognition that is produced in such a way that it has a law-like connection to the truth.

Thus understood, the Buddhist account shares much in common with other causal theories of knowledge. In contemporary analytic epistemology, causal theories of knowledge are frequently taken to be wed to an *externalist* conception of justification or warrant. Inasmuch as this is the case, one might expect that the Buddhist theory of knowledge episodes that is associated with Dignāga, Dharmakīrti and their followers will likewise support an externalist understanding of what warrants a cognition. This, I will argue, is fundamentally correct. But by examining the issue in fine detail we will be better positioned to appreciate several related matters of importance regarding the Buddhist account of knowledge.

9.2. Analyzing Knowledge and Internalism

9.2.1. The Distinction between Internalism and Externalism

Before we can address the question of whether the classical Buddhist theory of knowledge is best understood as endorsing epistemic internalism or externalism, a first step is to clarify how we should understand the contrast between "internalism" and "externalism" in epistemology, and then to explore whether or how those notions can meaningfully be applied within the Buddhist tradition of epistemology. These initial steps are important especially insofar as Buddhist philosophers do not make use of the same linguistic or conceptual framework as we find in contemporary analytic debates over internalism and externalism.

As was mentioned in chapter 2, the most entrenched accounts of knowledge within contemporary philosophy are *analytic accounts* that seek to break down the concept of knowledge into a set of individually necessary and jointly sufficient conditions for someone knowing something. Most of these analytic accounts assume that a person S has knowledge if and only if:

(A1) S is in a mental state, B,
(A2) B satisfies a truth or correctness condition, T, and
(A3) B (or S) meets some additional condition, X.

In so doing, knowledge is analyzed as B + T + X.

Regardless of what the additional condition or conditions for knowledge are over and above having a true belief, we can ask of each and every of these ingredients whether the satisfaction of that condition is determined exclusively by factors *internal* to the cognitive agent or whether the condition's satisfaction depends on factors that could be *external* to the subject. (At this moment, details of what is meant by "internal to . . . " and "external to . . . " shall be left unspecified.) On the assumption that condition B is the mental state of 'believing *p*' and condition T is the truth of the proposition *p*, a plausible view might be to defend internalism with respect to B and externalism with respect to T. More specifically, if *p* were the proposition that *all swans are white*, satisfaction of the truth condition would—on the assumption of external realism—depend on factors external to the cognitive agent. As such, we should be inclined toward an externalist account of the truth condition. However, given that belief is a fundamental kind of mental state, it is standardly argued that the belief that all swans are white is something fully determined by factors internal to the believer's mind; and to hold this position would be to accept an internalist account of the belief condition. (Yet, if externalism about mental content is true—that is, if the content of one's mental states is sometimes determined by factors in the external world—then even the satisfaction of condition B might depend on factors external to the cognitive agent.[2])

Having said this, in epistemological contexts, philosophers are not really concerned with the status of internalism/externalism with regard to B and T. Instead, the central debates over the past fifty years have been focused entirely on the question of whether the additional necessary condition for knowledge, X, is determined by factors internal to or external to the cognitive subject, with the most famous example being the debate over internalism/externalism with respect to *justification*. For those philosophers who defend the standard analysis of knowledge—where knowledge is analyzed as justified true belief—or some extension of the standard analysis, the central question is whether justification is or is not determined by factors wholly internal to the cognitive agent's mind. Internalist interpretations of justification were largely the norm throughout the history of Western epistemology, but externalist accounts of justification have become much more prominent over the past forty years.

Hybrid views are possible as well. Some philosophers now argue that internalism is the correct account of justification, but that there is a fourth condition required for knowledge—some property of de-Gettierization—a condition whose satisfaction is claimed to depend on factors external to the cognizer.[3] In this way, it is possible to preserve *justificatory internalism* while admitting that, overall, one must be an *externalist* about the conditions needed for knowledge over and above holding a true belief. In light of this, and because there can be widely divergent views on what the analytic components of knowledge are aside from belief and truth, one way to generalize the question of internalism versus externalism in epistemology is to reframe the issue by making use of Alvin Plantinga's concept of *epistemic warrant*.

Plantinga simply defines warrant as whatever is needed for knowledge over and above true belief.[4] By understanding warrant in this way, it is easy to identify a very clear contrast between epistemic internalism and externalism. Internalists with respect to warrant maintain that the condition or conditions necessary for knowledge (aside from holding a true belief) are determined entirely by factors internal to the cognizer's mind, whereas externalists disagree and argue instead that what helps to warrant beliefs can be factors external to the cognizer. Yet Plantinga takes for granted an understanding of knowledge that, in chapter 2, was labeled a *Platonic analysis*, which differs from what is found in the Buddhist tradition of epistemology.

Nevertheless, to sum up, the central issue of the debate between internalism and externalism in epistemology is that of whether the condition or conditions necessary to transform a true belief into knowledge are conditions that obtain entirely by virtue of factors internal to the cognitive agent's mind (internalism), or whether these necessary conditions for knowledge (over and above true belief) could depend on facts in the world external to the cognitive agent's mind (externalism). Let us now take this formulation of the topic and investigate whether the post-Dharmakīrtian Buddhist interpretation of knowledge episodes should be considered a version of epistemic internalism or externalism.

9.2.2. Warranted Cognitive Episodes

We have already seen in both chapters 1 and 2, that the Buddhist tradition of epistemology does not make use of a concept closely approximating that of justification. Nor, as explained in those chapters, does the Buddhist account of knowledge essentially involve an appeal to propositional (or dispositional) beliefs. Instead, the mental basis for knowledge is a momentary cognitive awareness—an awareness of an object or state of affairs. It was additionally noted that, while Dharmakīrti frequently adopts an external realist understanding of reality, he sometimes shifts toward adopting a version of idealism when addressing a select few topics. Yet, since the vast majority of Dharmakīrti's epistemological accounts proceed from the perspective of external realism, and since the whole debate between internalism and externalism in epistemology would largely crumble under the assumption of full-blown idealism, in this chapter we will operate under the assumption of external realism and will assume that what makes (at least some) cognitions correct or true are objects or states of affairs that are external to a cognitive agent's mind. Keeping these points in mind, let us see whether it is possible to extend the idea of epistemic warrant to the Buddhist theory of knowledge.

As a first approximation, we could define "warrant for an episode of cognition" as whatever is necessary for having an episode of knowledge over and above having a true/correct cognition. There is one immediate difficulty with this formulation of warrant, however. As detailed in chapter 2, on the post-Dharmakīrtian account of *pramāṇa*, what it is to be an episode of knowledge is *not* analyzed in terms of there being (1) a cognition that (2) is true/correct and which (3) meets some additional condition X. For Buddhist epistemologists, having an episode of knowledge does indeed entail that one's cognition is true/correct, but this does not mean that episodes of knowledge are to be analyzed as true cognitions meeting some further condition. (In general, just because some item logically entails the possession of some property *P* does not mean that the item should be analyzed in terms of property *P*. For example, what it is to be a cat surely entails the property of 'being spatially extended,' but this does not mean that the nature of a cat should be defined by reference to the property 'spatially extended.')

What all this means is that the standard understanding of warrant that derives from Plantinga is inoperable in the Buddhist context. In fact, Plantinga's conception of warrant cannot be deployed in any analysis of knowledge for which (mere) truth is not an independent condition for knowledge. We can, of course, adopt a modified understanding of "warrant for an episode of cognition." On such a modified understanding, warrant is *whatever is necessary for an episode of knowledge over and above having a cognition.*[5] In this way, a particular cognitive episode C(*p*) that apprehends the object/state of affairs *p* qualifies as an episode of knowledge if and only if C(*p*) has the property of being warranted. When understood in this way, it is possible to make a few immediate observations about this extension of the concept of warrant to the classical Buddhist theory of knowledge.

First, given the biconditional formulation earlier, whenever a person has a warranted cognition, that cognition is thereby an episode of knowledge. Moreover, since knowledge entails truth or correctness, this definition of *warrant* is one that entails the truth or correctness of the cognition—that is, warrant entails truth. Both of these entailments—that warrant entails knowledge and that it entails truth—are far from standard in contemporary analytic treatments of warrant and represent radical departures from Plantinga's own understanding of warrant. While a few contemporary philosophers do argue that warrant entails truth, this claim is tenuous and not at all widely accepted by contemporary epistemologists.[6] Nevertheless, it must be emphasized that on this modified understanding of warrant, whatever warrants a cognition will be sufficient for ensuring the truth or correctness of the cognition.

If we add the further assumption of external realism with respect to the objects of cognition, then the truth or correctness of a cognition is something that can, in those cases involving knowledge of the external world, only be determined by factors external to the mind. For example, if I were to have a sensory cognition as of a white shell, the question of whether that cognition is veridical would depend on whether there is a real white shell external to my mind. As such, it follows that on this modified understanding of warrant, the question of whether a cognition is warranted will in many cases depend on factors external to the cognizer's mind, thus implying that Buddhist epistemologists in the Dharmakīrtian tradition are committed to externalism with respect to warrant. In short, it appears that the classical Buddhist account of knowledge episodes is one that must be paired with an externalist account of warrant.

Yet, as described, externalism has been established on the cheap. After all, this attribution of externalism follows simply from how the term "warrant" has been interpreted in the Buddhist context, and from the consequence that whatever warrants a cognition also entails the truth of that cognition. This stands in contrast to the debate over internalism and externalism in contemporary epistemology, which is standardly fought between parties who assume precisely the opposite view—that warrant is a property that is logically *independent* of the truth of one's belief.

As such, the fact that Buddhist characterizations of *pramāṇa* stemming from Dharmakīrti imply externalism with respect to warrant—at least as the notion of warrant has been defined here—is *not* a particularly revelatory detail. Thankfully, there are other, more substantive points that can be made about the post-Dharmakīrtian Buddhist account of knowledge episodes and its relation to the debate between internalism and externalism. For much of the remaining portions of this chapter, I shall look at a series of interrelated points concerning meta-judgments about episodes of knowledge in the Buddhist tradition of epistemology and how those meta-judgments relate to the topic of internalism versus externalism in epistemology.

9.2.3. Access Internalism

Internalists with respect to warrant maintain that what warrants a belief or cognition are factors wholly internal to the cognitive agent's mind. How this phrase, "internal to the . . . mind," is to be understood, however, is subject to various interpretations. The most common way to interpret this phrase involves making an appeal to factors that a person has access to through a process of cognitive reflection or introspection. This is commonly referred to as *access internalism*. According to that view, in order for a person's belief that *p* to be justified, the factors that contribute to one's justification must be ones that the person could become aware of through reflection. Ordinarily, these justificatory factors are taken to be other beliefs that the person holds and that he or she can introspectively access.

Given this understanding, it is commonly maintained that access internalists should be open to defending the thesis that when a belief is justified, the believer is in the position to know that his or her belief is justified. That is, whether or not one is justified is something that is transparent to the cognitive agent. Even more so, the adoption of access internalism is often associated with the claim that when a person has knowledge, that person is in the position to know that he or she knows—that is, *'knowing p' implies 'knowing that one knows p'* (sometimes called the 'KK thesis').

The evidence is clear, however, that the classical Buddhist account of knowledge stemming from Dharmakīrti supports neither access internalism nor the KK thesis. In particular, and depending on the exact specification of the KK thesis, Buddhist epistemologists have clear grounds for maintaining that when a person has an episode of knowledge, it does not follow that the person knows he or she is having an episode of knowledge. This can be seen most clearly in reference to instances of perceptual knowledge. As readers saw in chapter 3, for Dignāga and Dharmakīrti (and their Buddhist followers), episodes of perceptual knowledge are held to be *nonconceptual* cognitions. In an instance of perceptual knowledge of, let us say, a white conch shell, the perceiver has a nonerroneous sensory experience of a white conch shell. But, according to Dignāga and Dharmakīrti, the perceiver does not in that very episode of sense perception conceive of the object as being a white conch shell. Likewise, since the judgment *that this cognition is an episode of perceptual knowledge* is itself a conceptual judgment, it follows on the Buddhist account that such a judgment cannot occur within an episode of sense perception. In short, when a person has a perceptual cognition of a white conch shell, there is no simultaneous knowledge that one is having an episode of perceptual knowledge.

What Buddhist epistemologists from at least the time of Dignāga onward do believe, however, is that all episodes of cognition have a reflexive dimension whereby there is an awareness of one's cognitive episode itself. This awareness is actually a species of perceptual cognition—a form of perceptual knowledge—one that I have called a *reflexive perception* (*svasaṃvedana*).[7] According to Dignāga and all later Buddhist epistemologists, reflexive perception pervades all cognition. When, for example, a person deduces that there is a fire on the far-off mountain pass, that inferential judgment (that there is fire on the mountain pass) is accompanied by a reflexive awareness of the inferential judgment itself. Likewise, when a person perceives a white conch shell, that sensory cognition is accompanied by a reflexive awareness of the sensory cognition.

Insofar as all episodes of cognition have this reflexive dimension, it might be thought that this reflexivity can be used to ground something along the lines of the KK thesis. But this is not at all what Buddhist epistemologists traditionally believed. When a person has a visual cognition of a conch shell, that person is also, by virtue of reflexive perception, aware of his or her cognition itself. Nevertheless, this reflexive perception, qua (inner) awareness, does not provide the person with knowledge that his or her visual cognition is an instance of knowledge (as opposed to being, for example, a hallucinatory experience). The person perceives his or her cognition but does not necessarily know whether that cognition is an episode of knowledge. In particular, Buddhist epistemologists are clear that reflexive perception is incapable of determining whether a given cognition is or is not veridical. A person may, for example, have a visual experience as of a piece of silver, but reflexive perception does not provide the person with information by which to determine whether the visual experience is a veridical perception as opposed to an illusory experience. As such, reflexive perception does not serve to ground anything like the contemporary internalist thesis that knowledge implies knowing that one knows.[8]

A different approach toward grounding something akin to access internalism in the Buddhist tradition of epistemology would be to call upon not reflexive perception, but instances of rational reflection or introspective awareness that are posterior to the cognition in question. Suppose that I have an episode of warranted perceptual cognition in which I apprehend a white conch shell. Let us also suppose that my reflexive perception of that sense perception is incapable of determining that the sense cognition has warrant. Nevertheless, it might still be thought that through a subsequent process of introspection I can come to recognize that my earlier episode of cognition apprehending the white conch shell was warranted, and hence was an episode of knowledge. If warrant can be introspectively (albeit subsequently) recognized, then that would suggest that the Buddhist model of warrant is compatible with a form of access internalism.

Whether Buddhist epistemologists believed that something like a process of introspection can determine whether one's (preceding) cognitions did or did not have the status of warrant is a delicate topic. There are, I believe, plausible grounds for concluding that warrant is not something that can always be established merely through a process of introspection. For example, it is doubtful that a person necessarily can, through introspection, readily determine whether he or she has just had an episode of veridical perception as opposed to an episode of illusion. Likewise, it is questionable whether a person can, through a process of introspection, be certain about whether his or her inference-like judgment that there is a fire on the mountain pass is an actual instance of inferential knowledge or merely an instance of false cognition.

Yet, on this very issue, there is a line of argumentation within the writings of post-Dharmakīrtian Buddhist epistemologists that could be viewed as supporting a thesis in the broad neighborhood of access internalism. That line of argumentation relates to the broader topic in Indian epistemology of *intrinsic versus extrinsic determination* of knowledge-hood.

9.3. Intrinsic versus Extrinsic Determination of Knowledge Status

9.3.1. The Mīmāṃsaka and Buddhist Accounts

The question of whether the validity or "knowledge-hood" (*prāmāṇya*) of a cognition is *intrinsic* (*svataḥ*) or *extrinsic* (*parataḥ*) to that cognition is a key topic of discussion within the Mīmāṃsā tradition of Indian philosophy.[9] The issue was prominent within the writing of Kumārila Bhatta, a proponent of the Mīmāṃsā tradition of hermeneutics who likely flourished sometime around the end of the seventh century. Kumārila defends the position that all cognitions have the status of intrinsic knowledge-hood—for if such a view is not accepted, he thinks it would lead to an infinite regress where determining the knowledge-hood of any cognition would depend on its having been verified from some other cognition, ad infinitum. Moreover, given the importance of scriptural authority in the Mīmāṃsā tradition, it is only the thesis of intrinsic knowledge-hood that can adequately establish the epistemic authority of Indian religious scriptures (such as the Vedas). Unfortunately, precisely how Kumārila's claims about intrinsic versus extrinsic knowledge-hood were to be understood has been a matter of considerable historical dispute. Substantially different interpretations of Kumārila's position were put forward by later writers in the Mīmāṃsā tradition.[10] In addition, one can find widely divergent presentations of this topic within contemporary scholarship, which reflects not just disagreement or uncertainty about how the core notions of "intrinsic knowledge-hood" and "extrinsic knowledge-hood" are to be understood but also disagreement about how this topic relates to themes that are relevant to contemporary Western epistemology.

All parties in India agree that the notion of *prāmāṇya*—here translated as a cognition's "knowledge-hood," but often characterized by scholars as a cognition's "validity"—refers to *the quality or qualities through which a cognition comes to have the status of being an episode of knowledge*. What is less clear is whether philosophers in ancient India, much less contemporary scholars, all share the same understanding of how the terms *intrinsic* (*svataḥ*) and *extrinsic* (*parataḥ*) are to be applied. The twentieth-century Indian philosopher B. K. Matilal, for example, identifies the key question in this debate as that of "Whether or not whatever exposes/reveals a knowledge-event as an awareness, exposes it also (by the same token) as a piece of knowledge?"[11] Defenders of the thesis of intrinsic knowledge-hood are then identified as those who maintain that when an episode of cognition is revealed to a person, its status as an episode of knowledge is also revealed. Other recent scholars, however, have put forward accounts of intrinsic knowledge-hood that are, in many ways, quite different from the account of Matilal.[12]

Whether Matilal has pinned down the "correct" understanding of the intrinsic/extrinsic dichotomy, or even the understanding that was operative in the writing of Kumārila, is a matter up for debate. Fortunately, we needn't concern ourselves with what Kumārila's actual account was. What is important for our purposes are the subsequent Buddhist claims relating to intrinsic and extrinsic knowledge-hood. Kumārila, as already noted, defends the view that in all cases a cognition's knowledge-hood is *intrinsic* to it. He also maintains that, among his opponents, Buddhist epistemologists are committed to the opposite view, the thesis of *extrinsic* knowledge-hood. That is,

Buddhists are claimed by him to hold the view that a cognition's status as an episode of knowledge is established not from the cognition itself, but only through other (subsequent) cognitions. The two most foundational thinkers in the Buddhist tradition of epistemology, Dignāga and Dharmakīrti, do not themselves address this issue in their writings, for the topic did not come into prominence until the time of Kumārila, who certainly postdated Dignāga and likely Dharmakīrti as well.[13] Discussions of intrinsic and extrinsic knowledge-hood do, however, become a fixture in later Buddhist epistemological treatises beginning in the eighth century.

What is remarkable is that, contrary to Kumārila's assertions, nearly all Buddhist epistemologists from the eighth century onward adopt a position on this matter that is almost diametrically opposite to that which Kumārila ascribes to Buddhists. There is a widespread agreement by post-Dharmakīrtian Buddhist epistemologists that most instances of knowledge are such that the cognition's knowledge status is determined *intrinsically*, not extrinsically. So what are we to make of this? What can explain this mismatch between Kumārila's claims about the Buddhists and the views that are actually propounded by later Buddhist epistemologists? One possibility is that this disagreement about whether Buddhists affirm intrinsic or extrinsic knowledge-hood could be the result of very different perspectives on what those labels mean and on what the possible range of views is on this issue. As the eighth-century Buddhist philosopher Śāntarakṣita points out, all that Buddhists reject is the thesis that cognitions can *universally* have their knowledge status determined intrinsically.[14] But in rejecting universal intrinsic knowledge-hood, it doesn't follow that they think all or even most cognitions must have their status as episodes of knowledge determined extrinsically.

A second possible explanation for why Kumārila attributes to Buddhists a position that they themselves widely reject could be that the relevant parties understand the whole project of determining knowledge-hood in substantially different ways. To see this possibility more clearly, consider the case of Śaṅkaranandana. This Buddhist figure, who lived in the tenth or eleventh century, is purported to have defended the view that all cognitions must be extrinsically validated. Śaṅkaranandana's views on this topic were certainly a minority position in the Buddhist tradition, however. But the fact that his views were so different from those held by other—earlier and later—Buddhist epistemologists strongly suggests that he simply interpreted the intrinsic/extrinsic distinction in a completely different way than did these other Buddhist epistemologists.

The far more widespread position adopted by Buddhist thinkers was to affirm that all inferential episodes of knowledge have their knowledge-hood determined intrinsically, as do many (but not all) instances of perceptual knowledge. This sort of view was held by, for example, Śāntarakṣita, Kamalaśīla, and Dharmottara, all of whom flourished in the eighth century. Most later Buddhist epistemologists, both in India and in Tibet, adopted (slightly modified) versions of the positions held by these eighth-century scholars.[15] So the predominant position among Buddhist epistemologists was to claim that most episodes of knowledge have their knowledge status determined intrinsically, and not extrinsically, as is reported by Kumārila.

How then, finally, did these Buddhist thinkers interpret the thesis that knowledge-hood is determined intrinsically? In short, intrinsic versus extrinsic knowledge-hood is taken by post-Dharmakīrtian Buddhist epistemologists to be a claim about the *causal genesis* of (a set of) determinate judgments—determinate judgments about some episode of knowledge.

Let us look at the Buddhist account more fully. There is widespread agreement among Buddhist epistemologists that perceptual cognitions are nonconceptual and thus are not determinate judgments (for such determinations can occur only in conceptual thought). Nevertheless, perceptual cognitions can and often do induce a person to form a subsequent conceptual cognition. For example, having had a visual sensation of a clay pot, I may form the subsequent determinate judgment that there is a clay pot. I might also, however, form a determinate cognition not about the content of my visual experience, but about the nature of that experience. That is, I may form the determinate judgment that I am having (or have had) a cognition as of a clay pot. In this way, my ordinary perceptual cognition can give rise to certain kinds of *meta-determinations*.

Buddhist epistemologists agree that any given cognition, $C(p)$, has the power to generate the determinate judgment that one is having (or has had) a cognition as of p. But what about other kinds of determinate judgments, such as the determinate judgment that this cognition was an instance of knowledge, or the determinate judgment that this cognition was nondeceptive, or the determinate judgment that this cognition tracked the truth? How are those determinations made? Those are the main kinds of questions Buddhist epistemologists are concerned with under the heading of intrinsic versus extrinsic determination of knowledge-hood.

At its foundation, as understood by Buddhist epistemologists, the issue involves the relationship between two mental episodes: (1) a given cognition—one that is an instance of knowledge—and (2) the cognitive agent's meta-judgment that the defining characteristics of knowledge have been satisfied with respect to that first cognition. As the thirteenth-century Tibetan scholar Sakya Paṇḍita explains the matter:[16]

> If a determinate cognition is capable of being produced immediately by the power of the perception itself, it is *intrinsically determined.* And if a determinate cognition is incapable of being produced immediately by the power of the perception, but that there must instead be a determination through a subsequent episode of knowledge, then it is *extrinsically determined.*

Note that the determination of the cognition's knowledge status (i.e., whether it satisfies the conditions necessary for being an episode of knowledge) is held to be temporally subsequent to the cognition in question. So, here, "intrinsic" does not mean that a cognition has its knowledge-hood determined *within* itself, but instead just that the cognition can causally produce or generate a subsequent determination of knowledge-hood *from* itself. Second, note that though the quote is explicitly expressed in terms of a perceptual cognition, the analogous point holds for inferential cognitions as well. So, for example, one might be concerned about the relationship between a given episode of inferential knowledge (call this episode C(*p*)) and the subsequent determination that C(*p*) is a 'nondeceptive' cognition. The standard view among Buddhist epistemologists is to claim that an episode of inferential cognition, C(*p*), has its knowledge-hood determined intrinsically, since the determinate judgment that C(*p*) is nondeceptive is something that arises (or could arise) directly from the earlier cognitive episode C(*p*) without the need for any separate supporting cognition.

To make these points clearer, let us look at some examples of the difference between two forms of perception: one form that these Buddhist philosophers call *trained perception* (*abhyāsavat pratyakṣam*), which is said to have its knowledge-hood determined intrinsically, and a second form that is *untrained perception*—spoken of by Tibetans as "first perception" (Tib: *mngon sum dang po ba*)—which is claimed to have its knowledge-hood only determined extrinsically. Here, an untrained or "first" perception refers to an episode of (veridical) perceptual cognition of an object the likes of which one has not encountered before. So, to take a common example found in the Buddhist literature on this topic, consider a case where a person has a visual experience as of a red glow in the far-off distance. Let us assume that the person's perceptual capacities are functioning perfectly well, and that the cognition of the red glow is nondeceptive. In this way, it is an instance of perceptual knowledge. Yet, if this visual experience is unfamiliar to the person, she may very well be consumed with doubt as to whether her experience was or was not a veridical experience of a fire. In such an untrained case of visual experience, though the cognition is in fact an instance of perceptual knowledge, that perceptual cognition is nonetheless incapable of generating (by itself) any subsequent determinate judgment that the cognition was nondeceptive. Expressed differently, the determination that one's cognition of the red glow was veridical is something that could only be generated through a separate cognition (such as might arise by getting much closer to the red glow and perceiving it again). In cases like this where, due to the novelty of one's experience, the perceiver may be consumed with doubt, the cognition's knowledge status is said to be determined extrinsically.

In instances of trained perception, by contrast, these doubts are not present, and the occurrence of the perceptual cognition has the power immediately to produce a determinate cognition. For example, suppose that I look toward a table and have a perceptual experience of a clay pot. Owing to my familiarity with such experiences, my perception may induce me immediately to form the determinate judgment that there is a clay pot on the table. More importantly, my perception of the clay pot can also give rise to my determinate judgment that my cognition of a clay pot meets the requisite conditions for being an episode of perceptual knowledge. To the extent that this is the case, my trained perceptual cognition is said to have its knowledge-hood determined intrinsically.

9.3.2. Determination and Warrant

Let us turn now to the question of whether or how this Buddhist account of intrinsic versus extrinsic determination relates to the topic of internalism and externalism with respect to epistemic warrant. The standard Buddhist position in the post-Dharmakīrtian period is to affirm that, in most cases, episodes of knowledge have an intrinsic determination of their knowledge-hood. And to say this is to say that for a given episode of knowledge, C(*p*), that cognitive episode has the power to generate, from itself, the subsequent determination that C(*p*) meets the criteria necessary for knowledge. For example, upon visually perceiving a white conch shell, a person can be induced to form the subsequent determinate judgment that one's preceding cognition as of a white conch shell was nondeceptive.

At first glance, this might make it sound as though the Buddhist account aligns with the view of internalism with respect to warrant. Yet I will argue that this gets the issue precisely backwards. I believe that the Buddhist support for intrinsic determination of knowledge episodes is really evidence that they would be inclined toward an *externalist* theory of warrant. Let us examine why this is so.

The first step is to draw a contrast between two episodes of cognition being *causally* related and two episodes of cognition being *epistemically* related. The issue of intrinsic versus extrinsic determination involves a relationship between the following two kinds of cognitions:

C(*p*)	the cognitive episode of knowing object/state of affairs *p*
D(C(*p*))	the cognitive determination that C(*p*) satisfies the defining conditions for knowledge

As understood by Buddhist epistemologists in the post-Dharmakīrtian tradition, the thesis of intrinsic determination of knowledge-hood is essentially a claim about the causal relationship between C(*p*) and D(C(*p*)). In particular, the thesis of "intrinsic determination" affirms that D(C(*p*)) can be causally generated directly from the preceding cognition C(*p*). But this emphatically does not mean that D(C(*p*)) serves any role in epistemically warranting the cognition C(*p*). The determinate cognition D(C(*p*)) does not, and cannot, provide any *epistemic* support for the *earlier* cognition C(*p*). What the appeal to "intrinsic determination" is capturing, instead, is the idea that episodes of knowledge can be causally sufficient for the production of the subsequent determination that the episode of cognition satisfies the necessary conditions for perceptual or inferential knowledge.

A second reason to believe that the relationship between C(*p*) and D(C(*p*)) is causal rather than epistemic has to do with the possibility of incorrect determinations, and of determinations for cognitions that are not instances of knowledge. Though the Buddhist thinkers addressing this topic are concerned principally with the question of which episodes of knowledge can generate which determinate judgments, this does not preclude the possibility that erroneous cognitive episodes can likewise generate determinate judgments regarding their own epistemic status. In fact, Tibetan Buddhist epistemologists extend the concepts of intrinsic and extrinsic determination to the various forms of cognition that are not instances of knowledge. So, for example, were I to have an illusory visual experience as of a yellow conch shell, there can still be an examination of how it is determined that the defining characteristics of that illusory visual experience are satisfied. Not surprisingly, in a case of sensory illusion, Tibetan epistemologists maintain that the determination that it is a false cognition is something that can only be extrinsically determined. That is, it is only through a subsequent perception that one can come to recognize that the earlier illusory experience was a false cognition.

It could also be the case that an episode of visual illusion induces a person to form the (mistaken) determinate judgment that one's visual awareness was veridical. This judgment would be erroneous, of course, but such a mistaken judgment is certainly not out of the question. Now, in neither of the aforementioned two cases—the case where there is a determination that one has had a false cognition and the case where there is a (mistaken) determination that one's cognition was veridical—is the determinate judgment playing any sort of role in warranting the illusory visual experience. That simply is not the role that these determinations of a cognition's epistemic status are designed to play.

Having said that, the claim that many episodes of knowledge do have the causal power to generate subsequent meta-judgments about their own knowledge status is an important assertion. What it indicates is that these Buddhist epistemologists in the centuries after Dharmakīrti are open to the idea that many cognitions have something along the lines of *a presumption of warrant*—which is a view that is more closely associated with the Mīmāṃsā tradition of Indian philosophy from which this entire debate about intrinsic versus extrinsic determination of knowledge-hood originated. Yet, to the extent that Buddhist epistemologists accept some version of this presumptive warrant thesis, it implicitly supports the conclusion that they would embrace an externalist conception of epistemic warrant. For, if this presumption of warrant were not granted, people would need to go through separate, deliberative processes so as to (extrinsically) determine the knowledge status of their cognitions. In point of fact, however, ordinary humans do not regularly engage in these separate determination processes, nor do we have to do so, according to the Buddhist account. In fact, just as was mentioned in relation to Kumārila Bhatta earlier, the central reason why Śāntarakṣita and other Buddhist epistemologists (aside from Śaṅkaranandana) reject the thesis of extrinsic determination of knowledge-hood is precisely because they believe it would lead to a vicious regress in which no episodes of knowledge could ever be determined to fulfill the necessary conditions for knowledge.

Whether a given cognition C(*p*) is an episode of knowledge depends on whether the cognition satisfies the conditions necessary for knowledge. But the question of whether those necessary conditions *actually* obtain is very different from the question of whether a person can *determine* (either from that very cognition C(*p*) or from a separate cognition) that C(*p*) meets the required conditions for knowledge. The Buddhist endorsement of intrinsic determination of knowledge-hood reflects their view that an *independent determination* that the cognition C(*p*) possesses the requisite characteristics for knowledge is not needed. In other words, the crux of their view is that in order to have an episode of knowledge a person need not verify (through an independent determination) that the cognition in question meets the requirements for knowledge.

9.4. Factive Mental Episodes and Externalism

Three separate grounds have now been given as (either direct or indirect) support for the conclusion that classical Buddhist epistemological thought accords with an externalist understanding of epistemic warrant. First, these epistemologists promote a causal theory of knowledge in which a cognition's status as a *pramāṇa* is rooted in the etiology of the cognition. Second, they support an account in which whatever warrants a cognition logically guarantees the truth or correctness of the cognition. Finally, Buddhist epistemologists in the generations after Dharmakīrti support the thesis that the knowledge-hood of (most) episodes of knowledge is something that is determined intrinsically, and thus does not require any sort of independent verification. In the last segment of this chapter I shall draw upon one additional observation concerning the classical Buddhist account of knowledge, and I will argue that it gives us grounds for concluding that this account of knowledge requires a completely different form of externalism—not just externalism about epistemic warrant, but externalism about one's cognitive episodes themselves.

At the end of chapter 2 it was argued that the Buddhist conception of knowledge episodes coming from Dharmakīrti is similar in structure to the "factive mental state" theory that has been proposed by Timothy Williamson. On that view, knowledge is a special kind of mental state, one different from (mere) belief. The Buddhist epistemological tradition is concerned with momentary episodes as opposed to dispositional states, but that tradition supports a stance analogous to Williamson. When a person has an episode of knowledge, he or she is having a cognitive episode different in kind from those cognitions that are not *pramāṇas*. In particular, episodes of knowledge are cognitions such that when they occur, they are guaranteed to be true or correct. Episodes of knowledge are, to modify the language of Williamson, *factive cognitions*.[17]

What I now wish to show is that the thesis that episodes of knowledge are factive cognitions requires a strong form of externalism about one's cognitive episodes. Here, let us define *internalism* with respect to cognitive episodes as the claim that the constitutive nature of a person's cognition—including what kind of cognition he or she is having—is fixed entirely by factors internal to one's mind. *Externalism* with respect to cognitive episodes, by contrast, is the thesis that the nature of a person's cognition can sometimes constitutively depend on factors in the world external to that person's mind.[18]

Even if elements in the external world play a causal role in the production of a given sensory experience, it is possible, and indeed quite common, to defend internalism with respect to cognitive episodes. For example, suppose that a person has a visual experience as of a yellow conch shell. The cognitive episode that a person has in such a case might be caused by a real, external object—a genuine yellow conch shell. Yet this does not necessarily mean that the type of cognition that the person has in such a case is fixed by or dependent on that external object. Proponents of a representationalist theory of perceptual experience, for example, often maintain that what is constitutive of a person's cognitions are the *representational contents* of those experiences, and not the external objects that are the causes of those experiences. To make this clearer, consider two different situations:

(Case α) a situation in which a person has a veridical visual experience as of a yellow conch shell—an experience that is causally connected to an actual yellow conch shell in the external world, and

(Case β) a situation in which that same person has an illusory experience as of a yellow conch shell—an experience that is brought about as a result of (let us suppose) the person having jaundice and visually encountering what is actually a white conch shell.

A representationalist about perceptual experience will be inclined to maintain that these two situations can result in the exact same mental state, or the exact same cognitive episode. In other words, the cognitive episode in α could be the same as the cognitive episode in β. But provided that this is the case, it follows that the person's cognition, even in the veridical case α, does not constitutively depend on the external object that was its cause. It depends, instead, merely on the representational content of the experience, which is the same in the two situations.

As has already been shown in chapter 3, Indian Buddhist epistemologists from the time of Dignāga onward defend a broadly representationalist theory of perceptual experience. Yet, to the extent that episodes of knowledge are factive cognitions, those episodes of cognition are regarded to be fundamentally different in kind from those cognitions that are mistaken or erroneous. This carries the implication that in the earlier two situations, α and β—both of which are situations in which the person has a visual experience as of a yellow conch shell, and both of which might accurately be described as representing a yellow conch shell—*the cognitive episodes occurring in the two situations must be different.* The cognitive episode in α is an instance of (perceptual) knowledge, whereas the cognition in β is not. They are two fundamentally different types of cognition. It is in this way that Buddhist epistemologists adopt a view consistent with Timothy Williamson's proclamation that "Knowing is a state of mind." For Buddhist epistemologists, episodes of knowledge are cognitions different in kind from other cognitions, including erroneous cognitions.[19]

Finally, to the extent that having an episode of knowledge can constitutively depend on the existence of an object or state of affairs external to the knower, it likewise follows that the Buddhist account of knowledge must affirm externalism with respect to cognitive episodes. (This assumes, of course, the acceptance of an external realist ontology, which is the standard position adopted by Dharmakīrti and his successors in most contexts.) This means that, on the assumption of external realism, what kind of cognition a person is having when she has a visual experience as of a yellow conch shell can constitutively depend on whether there is or is not a real yellow conch shell in the external world. More to the point, when a person has an episode of perceptual knowledge (of a yellow conch shell), the cognitive episode stands in a constitutive relation to a real yellow conch shell—one that is external to the perceiver's mind. The fact that the cognizer bears this relation to the external object is constitutive of the cognition that occurs in the sense that were that relation not to obtain, that same type of cognition could not occur. As such, the Buddhist account necessitates a version of externalism with respect to cognitive episodes.

Further Reading

For a clear, introductory account of Indian views about the 'determination of knowledge-hood,' see Matilal, B. K. (2002). Knowledge, truth and pramātva. In J. Ganeri (Ed.), *Mind, language and world: The collected essays of Bimal Krishna Matilal*. New Delhi: Oxford University Press.

For a much more extensive presentation of the Mīmāṃsā tradition's account of the "determination of knowledge-hood," see chapters 3 and 4 of Arnold, D. (2005). *Buddhists, Brahmins, and belief: Epistemology in South Asian philosophy of religion*. New York: Columbia University Press.

For an overview of topic of "determination of knowledge-hood" within the Buddhist tradition of epistemology, see Krasser, H. (2003). On the ascertainment of validity in the Buddhist epistemological tradition. *Journal of Indian Philosophy*, *31*, 161–184.

10
Experimental and Cross-Cultural Epistemology

Over the course of the previous nine chapters, I have provided a summary of many of the most important themes in Buddhist epistemology. For some readers, those chapters may have constituted their first exposure to Buddhist accounts of knowledge—including their theories of perception, inference, and the like—and thus may have served to open their eyes to a different tradition of epistemological inquiry. For some other readers, including those who are coming at these topics with a pre-existing background in Buddhist philosophy, the preceding chapters may have served to reorient the way they think about the relationship between Buddhist epistemology and contemporary Anglo-American epistemology. It is also possible that those chapters have done little more than exacerbate readers' existing mistrusts of the project of putting contemporary analytic philosophy in conversation with Buddhist epistemology. Yet, even with respect to persons falling into this last camp, I believe that this conversation between philosophical traditions is an important one to have. For, though many scholars of Buddhism may regard their principal scholarly duty to be one of providing historical exegesis, it is critical to keep in mind that philosophy consists of much more than just explicating historical texts. Philosophical investigation is, at its core, the ongoing pursuit for a deeper and more complete understanding of the nature of reality. In this way, exposure to historical ideas in the Buddhist epistemological tradition can and should play a valuable role in helping contemporary philosophers advance toward a more complete understanding of knowledge, its scope, and its limits.

My underlying goal in this final chapter is to make the case that there is real value in contemporary philosophers learning about and grappling with the arguments made by philosophers from the Buddhist tradition of epistemology. Before making that case directly, however, I shall begin this chapter by looking at the recent growth of "experimental philosophy" as well as the increased attention that is being paid to philosophical intuitions in

Illuminating the Mind. Jonathan Stoltz, Oxford University Press (2021). © Oxford University Press.
DOI: 10.1093/oso/9780190907532.003.0010

contemporary epistemology. In particular, I will take up the questions of whether there is any value in identifying shared, cross-cultural intuitions about knowledge, and whether developing a deeper understanding of the Buddhist tradition of epistemology can play a role in shaping philosophers' "intuitions" about knowledge. In the third section of this chapter, I will step away from those discussions of intuitions about knowledge and will move on to directly appraising the value of Buddhist epistemology for contemporary philosophers.

10.1. Philosophical Intuitions and Experimental Epistemology

For many compelling reasons, René Descartes is often thought of as the father of modern philosophy. He ushered in, as philosophical lore commonly has it, the "epistemological turn" in European philosophy. Even though the epistemological turn in Indian philosophy occurred much, much earlier in time—more than a thousand years before the time of Descartes—this should not prevent us from recognizing Descartes as an incredibly important philosophical figure. His systematic investigations of knowledge, in his *Meditations on First Philosophy* and elsewhere, have played an important role in the development of epistemology over the past four hundred years. Yet his methodical approach to the study of knowledge has largely been supplanted by a quite different approach toward the theory of knowledge. Descartes endorsed what Roderick Chisholm has famously termed "methodism" in epistemology. That is, Descartes prioritized the project of determining the conditions necessary for knowledge, and only afterward proceeded to identify what items are and are not knowable given those conditions. In contemporary analytic epistemology, by contrast, the vast majority of philosophers are "particularists" about knowledge. They begin with a series of examples of knowledge (and examples of the absence of knowledge) and then use those examples so as to determine, in light of those examples, what a fully adequate set of conditions for knowledge must look like.

This inclination toward particularism in contemporary epistemology has been coupled with a pronounced emphasis on *epistemological thought experiments*. Such thought experiments begin with a description of a hypothetical scenario and ask, almost invariably, whether the person at the heart of the scenario does or does not have knowledge of some specific proposition.

Edmund Gettier did not initiate this movement toward epistemological thought experiments, but his 1963 article on the "justified true belief" analysis of knowledge certainly popularized philosophers' reliance on these sorts of thought experiments. As Timothy Williamson notes, "The canonical example in the literature on philosophical thought experiments is Edmund Gettier's use of them to refute the traditional analysis of knowledge as justified true belief."[1] In the years since the publication of Gettier's article, the use of such thought experiments has become more and more prominent within epistemology.

Linked to this growing emphasis on thought experiments is a related appeal to so-called *intuitive judgments* about whether a person does or does not possess knowledge in a given thought experiment.[2] Given their attachment to epistemological particularism, contemporary analytic epistemologists generally agree that philosophers' intuitive assessments of these thought experiments are to *precede* the articulation of a full set of necessary conditions for the possession of knowledge. It is philosophers' intuitive judgments about knowledge that are to guide them toward a set of general principles of knowledge.

So, for example, consider the way in which thought experiments are used by Laurence BonJour in one of his more famous articles criticizing externalism in epistemology.[3] He details four "cases," each of which involves a person who, as a matter of fact, has the power of clairvoyance and forms a correct belief about the U.S. President's whereabouts through the use of that clairvoyant power. In each of the four cases, however, the person has no positive reasons for thinking that he or she has the power of clairvoyance—and in three of the four cases the person has reasons *against* believing that he or she has clairvoyant powers. In all four of these cases, BonJour thinks it is "intuitively clear" that the person does not possess knowledge. Those intuitive assessments are then used to support BonJour's theoretical assessment that forming a true belief through a reliable belief-forming process is *insufficient* for knowledge—and also that any adequate account of knowledge demands an appeal to *responsible* belief formation. In short, thought experiments and intuitive judgments about knowledge are precursors to a fully articulated theory of knowledge.

Though appeals to philosophers' intuitive judgments are still very widespread in contemporary epistemology, this reliance on intuitions about thought experiments has not gone entirely unchallenged. Concerns about the pervasiveness of thought experiments and "armchair philosophy" have increased, and there are some worries about philosophers' overreliance on their own philosophical intuitions. Partly due to these sorts of concerns, numerous philosophers—sometimes teaming up with social scientists—have tackled philosophical intuitions from a different perspective: by conducting empirical studies of people's intuitive judgments about philosophical thought experiments. In this way, there has been a turn toward *experimental philosophy*; and this turn toward empirical studies of intuitions has been most pronounced in the field of epistemology.[4]

Simplifying immensely, scholars engaging in research on experimental philosophy believe that there is positive value in examining the intuitions and beliefs held by philosophers and nonphilosophers on a variety of philosophical questions. With respect to questions of epistemology, the work done by experimental philosophers provides a mechanism by which to determine whether it is defensible for philosophers to appeal to their intuitions when making judgments about various (epistemological) thought experiments. Experimental data on intuitions about knowledge give rise to a series of important questions: If philosophers (either individually or en masse) take it to be intuitively obvious that the person described in a given scenario does not possess knowledge, how much weight should be put on these intuitive judgments? What should philosophers do if their own intuitions about knowledge do not match up with the beliefs held by nonphilosophers entertaining the same thought experiments? Finally, and most importantly for our purposes, what would we learn if we were to find that intuitions about knowledge are *not* shared across all cultures? What would we learn if we were to find that these intuitions are, by and large, universal?

10.2. Cross-Cultural Intuitions about Knowledge

Among the earliest research findings within the literature on experimental philosophy was the observation that persons of South Asian ancestry had intuitions about knowledge that were substantially different from those held by persons of European ancestry. While acknowledging the tentative nature of their findings, Weinberg, Nichols, and Stich (2001) made the remarkable claim that "If these results are robust, then it seems that what counts as knowledge on the banks of the Ganges does not count as knowledge on the banks of the Mississippi!"[5]

Although the article just cited ushered in a new emphasis on measuring folk intuitions about knowledge, the specific findings pertaining to differences between persons of "Western" ancestry and "South Asian" ancestry have not held up very well to subsequent scrutiny. Various scholars have criticized that 2001 article on a variety of methodological grounds. In particular, the article relied on rather weak sampling techniques, and the specific conditions under which the questions were asked may have led to unreliable results. Subsequent experimental studies have largely failed to replicate the results reached in the original article by Weinberg, Nichols, and Stich. The cumulative experimental evidence now looks like it points to the opposite conclusion—that there are *not* fundamentally different intuitions about knowledge between persons for European ancestry and persons of South Asian ancestry.[6] Yet, even if the totality of the experimental evidence indicates that persons from South Asian and European ancestry do share similar intuitions about knowledge, we should not take that as a reason to conclude that philosophers have nothing to gain from examining the intuitions of those who have different cultural, historical, or philosophical backgrounds from their own. It would be wrong to conclude, even provided that there are shared folk intuitions about knowledge and its absence, that cross-cultural investigations of knowledge should cease to be carried out.

The fact, if indeed it is a fact, that persons of South and East Asian ancestry share many of the same intuitions about knowledge and about Gettier cases as do persons of "Western" descent is, I would maintain, an important result in its own right; and I believe that there is much value in probing the depths of this shared intuition. Yet, in addition to focusing their attentions on folk intuitions, philosophers would be well served to examine different traditions' *philosophical theorizing* about the nature of knowledge. In particular, I will argue that we can benefit from attending to the important ways in which epistemologists in the Buddhist tradition made use of hypothetical scenarios (i.e., epistemological thought experiments) of their own so as to support their theories about the nature of knowledge episodes.

10.2.1. Philosophical Intuitions and the Language of Knowledge

When experimental philosophers investigate folk intuitions about knowledge, they do so under the belief that the ways in which ordinary persons speak about knowledge provides useful information not just to linguists and lexicographers—revealing how words are used—but also to philosophers—by helping to reveal what (people think) knowledge really is. Whether the work done by experimental philosophers on knowledge attributions actually does provide us with helpful information about the *nature* of knowledge—over and above the linguistic information it provides about how people speak about knowledge—is a matter of controversy. I myself am inclined to believe that there *is* an informative connection between folk attributions of knowledge and the theoretical investigations of knowledge undertaken by philosophers, at least when we look at the English language and the analytic tradition of epistemology. Yet we must be careful not to overgeneralize on these findings, for reasons that I will now note.

As we have seen in previous chapters, the most common way by which contemporary philosophers attempt to make sense of knowledge proceeds by identifying a set of necessary and sufficient conditions for the propositional form "S knows that *p*." In chapter 2, for example, I discussed "the standard analysis" of knowledge, which maintains, as expressed by Gettier:[7]

(a) S knows that P IFF (i) P is true,
(ii) S believes that P, and
(iii) S is justified in believing that P.

Though there is significant and ongoing disagreement about what the actual necessary conditions are for knowledge, there has been comparatively little disagreement with Gettier's framing of the problem as one of identifying the necessary and sufficient conditions for the truth of sentences having the form 'S knows that *p*.' Even if very few philosophers now accept the justified true belief model of knowledge, nearly all analytic philosophers continue to endorse Gettier's project of seeking necessary and sufficient conditions for statements of the form 'S knows that *p*.'

Be that as it may, it is critical to observe just how important of a role this particular framing of the problem plays in philosophers' investigations of knowledge. Though there could conceivably be myriad ways in which to grapple with the question of what knowledge is, there is no question that for the past fifty years the central way of approaching that question has been to seek out the conditions under which sentences of the form 'S knows that *p*' are deemed to be true. This particular approach is manifest in a wide number of instances, such as when philosophers ponder the truth conditions for statements like "Bob knows that Jill drives an American car" and "Smith knows that the man who will get the job has ten coins in his pocket."

Given this recent history, it is not surprising that when experimental philosophers seek to identify folk intuitions about knowledge, they frequently do so by asking people to respond to statements like that of whether some person knows some proposition to be true. To take an example from Weinberg, Nichols, and Stich (2001), the authors provide a short description of a scenario and then ask,[8]

(1) Does Bob really know that Jill drives an American car, or does he only believe it?

Though this is certainly a valuable question to ask, I believe it is important that we be attentive to the ways in which experimental philosophers' research projects—including the very questions they ask in surveys—have been both guided by and artificially constrained by the standard ways in which analytic epistemologists talk about knowledge. Though it is not surprising that experimental philosophers (either intentionally or not) frame their survey questions about knowledge so that they closely parallel the precise ways that analytic epistemologists theorize about knowledge, the ways in which these questions are framed may very well reflect cultural biases about what knowledge is and how one should speak about knowledge.

It is, therefore, important to take a step back from these experimental studies of knowledge by contemporary philosophers and be more attentive to the possible ways in which these studies could be operating from a limited conceptual framework; and this is where attentiveness to other epistemological systems, including traditional Buddhist epistemology (and Indian epistemology more generally), can prove helpful. Given what has already been said about Buddhist epistemology in the previous nine chapters, it is possible to expose some of the key methodological assumptions that are made within the studies employed by experimental epistemologists, as well as the limitations that result from those assumptions.

Consider the statement that "Bob knows that Jill drives an American car." There is no fundamental difficulty representing such a statement in Indian languages like Hindi or Bengali. After all, inasmuch as Hindi and Bengali are members of the Indo-European family of languages, those two languages' words for the verb "know"—*jānnā* and *jānā*, respectively—are linguistically connected to the English word "know." And just as the word "know" is incredibly common in ordinary English speech, so is the Hindi word *jānnā*.[9] Nor would it be fundamentally difficult to render this English sentence in a language like Sanskrit. Yet, in attempting to render this sentence in philosophical Sanskrit, two concerns arise.

The first concern is simply that Buddhist theorizing about knowledge does not typically involve *propositional* attributions of knowledge of the sort that we find in contemporary analytic epistemology. Instead, the paradigmatic examples of knowledge in Buddhist epistemology are instances of knowing some object. While it is possible to represent propositional cases of knowledge using Buddhist terminological conventions, those propositional cases would not come close to approximating the range of ways in which Buddhist epistemologists formulate their attributions of knowledge. Thus, given that experimental epistemologists have largely restricted their surveys to cases of propositional knowledge, they are only capable of capturing an artificially restricted range of intuitions about the nature of knowledge.

A second concern is linguistic, but reflective of a much deeper issue pertaining to the way in which experimental philosophers seek to identify intuitions about knowledge. The Sanskrit term *jñāna* and its root *jñā-* are linguistically related to the contemporary Hindi and Bengali verbs for "know" and are also related to the Greek root *gno-*. But as we have seen in chapter 1, the term *jñāna* does not come close to capturing the philosophical concept of knowledge in Indian epistemology. Instead, *jñāna* captures a much broader concept, one that contemporary scholars of Indian epistemology often translate into English as "cognition" or "awareness."[10] The verbs that are much more commonly featured in Buddhist articulations of propositional knowledge are the Sanskrit (and Tibetan) analogs for verbs like "establish," and "determine," or even "cognize." Yet, in order for sentences with these verbs to securely mark out genuine instances of knowledge, such sentences are commonly supplemented with the instrumental clause "with a *pramāṇa*." So, for example, to accurately represent the English statement "Bob knows that Jill drives an American car" in standard Buddhist epistemological terminology, one could say something along the lines of:

(2) Bob established, with a *pramāṇa*, that Jill drives an American car.

As this example shows, attributions of knowledge in Indian and Buddhist philosophy are not necessarily, or even commonly, linked to any precise Sanskrit equivalent for the verb "know." But, to the extent that this is the case, it elicits a concern with the way in which experimental epistemologists have focused almost exclusively on sentences of the form 'S knows that *p*' in order to make sense of knowledge attributions. To focus on sentences of that form is to restrict oneself to a narrow, Anglo-centric way of thinking about what knowledge is. More to the point, it is to prioritize an understanding of knowledge that is tied to *verbal attributions*—that is, the use of the verb "know"—over other possible ways of attributing knowledge. In the Buddhist (and broader Indian) tradition(s) of epistemology, by contrast, knowledge is tied not so much to the precise verb used, but rather to a specific *instrumental attribution*—that is, through an appeal to a *pramāṇa* (qua instrument of knowledge).

10.2.2. Intuitions about Instruments of Knowledge

It is crucial to elaborate on the preceding point. As readers have seen throughout this book, the Indian epistemological tradition has historically been wed to a reliance on the *instruments* or *means* by which knowledge is obtained—that is, *pramāṇas*. This is not the place to recapitulate what has been said earlier about Indian theories concerning instruments of knowledge or about Buddhist accounts of knowledge episodes arising from said instruments, but it is important to remind readers that Indian epistemology's emphasis on these instruments of knowledge is quite different from what we find in analytic epistemology. Speaking loosely, we might say that whereas the contemporary analytic tradition of epistemology places at its forefront an investigation of *what knowledge is* or *what conditions are necessary and sufficient for knowledge*, the Indian epistemological tradition aims first and foremost at figuring out *how knowledge is obtained* or *what the sources of knowledge are*. This is not to say that analytic epistemologists are not at all interested in identifying privileged sources of knowledge, nor that Indian epistemologists have no interest in figuring out what knowledge is. Rather, the point is simply that the foci of these two traditions' respective epistemological programs are different.

This is a key point to be attentive to, because when we turn to the epistemological research conducted by contemporary experimental philosophers, the sorts of questions that those investigations have focused on—questions such as "Does Bob really know that Jill drives an American car, or does he only believe it?"—are almost universally expressed and framed in a way that accords with the analytic tradition's focus on identifying *what knowledge is*. Of course, this shouldn't surprise us, given that nearly all of these experimental philosophers are squarely rooted in the analytic tradition of philosophical discourse. But these issues might have been approached quite differently were they pursued from the perspective of the Buddhist tradition of epistemology.

Given the Indian epistemological tradition's emphasis on instruments of knowledge, philosophers in the Buddhist tradition of epistemology are less concerned with the question of what knowledge is and are more concerned with *etiological* questions surrounding knowledge—such as how episodes of knowledge are causally generated. Given this, we can speculate that, were a classical Buddhist epistemologist to conduct an empirical study of folk intuitions about knowledge, the questions asked would very likely *not* be ones along the lines of (1). Instead, the relevant questions to be asked would be ones that focus on people's "intuitions" about how a belief or cognition was generated. For example, the relevant surveys might ask (after describing some scenario),

(3) Has Bob's belief that Jill drives an American car been generated through proper reasoning?

or

(4) Has Bill's visual experience of the moon been produced through an appropriate causal process?

The wording of these two questions moves the focus away from seeking out *what knowledge is*—after all, neither the word "knowledge" nor the verb "know" appears in these sentences—and turns the focus instead toward figuring out whether the means by which the belief/experience was formed was legitimate.

Again, the central point that I am trying to make is that the standard way in which experimental philosophers currently present their survey questions about knowledge reflects just *a single, culturally specific* way in which people might think about and talk about knowledge. It reflects, in particular, a parochial understanding of propositional knowledge that is associated with the analytic tradition of epistemology. Exposure to other traditions of epistemology, such as the classical Buddhist tradition of epistemology in India and Tibet, would facilitate the recognition that there are other ways to probe people's intuitions about knowledge. The studies that are carried out by experimental philosophers would be well served to consider implementing questionnaires that make use of various question wordings, including (3) and (4). To do so would help to deliver more robust data on folk attributions of knowledge.

10.2.3. Shared Intuitions about Knowledge

Attention to the Buddhist tradition of epistemology can reveal more than just the parochial nature of investigations of knowledge carried out by scholars in the Anglo-American tradition of philosophy. A close examination of how Buddhist epistemological thought developed in India and Tibet can potentially serve to bolster some of the intuitions that contemporary philosophers have about knowledge. If, for example, shared epistemological puzzles gave rise to strikingly similar responses within these two different traditions of philosophy, this would provide at least some inductive support for the plausibility of these responses.

One respect in which classical Buddhist epistemology proceeds similarly to contemporary analytic epistemology is in those two traditions' emphasis on a kind of epistemic particularism. Just as we find in contemporary epistemology, Buddhist epistemologists make use of a wide variety of examples—examples of both the presence of knowledge and the absence of knowledge—so as to support their theories. My point, of course, is not merely that examples are used in their writings, but more pertinently that a wide range of examples—examples on which clear intuitions can be formed—are used in order to develop a workable theory of knowledge. We saw this reliance on such intuitive examples at various places in this book, but most prominently in chapters 2, 6, and 8. Those were the chapters that related most closely to determining the *boundaries* of knowledge. The use of vivid examples for which intuitive judgments can easily be formed plays an important role in establishing the scope and boundaries of knowledge.

The most prominent display of this phenomenon is in the examples that Buddhist epistemologists use to show that knowledge requires more than just (accidentally) true cognition. As discussed in chapter 8, the eighth-century philosophy Dharmottara made prominent use of sample scenarios where a person forms a correct judgment but where, intuitively, readers ought to recognize that there is a lack of knowledge. As a reminder, one such example Dharmottara employs is that of a person who mistakenly takes there to be a funnel of smoke in the distance, and thus deduces that there is a fire in that location. In reality, there is no smoke, just a swarm of bugs circling above meat that is cooking atop a fire. The person's judgment that there is fire in that location is, as presented in the example, correct, but there is a strong intuition that this judgment should not qualify as an instance of knowledge.[11]

I argued in chapter 8 that the use of these sorts of examples is indicative of a recognition on the part of Buddhist philosophers (at least from the eighth century onward) that in order to have an episode of knowledge one's cognitions must be *nonaccidentally true*. This recognition that knowledge requires nonaccidental true belief is not very remarkable in its own right, but it is still worth noting the similarities between how examples like Dharmottara's were used by Buddhist epistemologists to reach a clearer understanding of knowledge and how Gettier cases have been used by contemporary epistemologists to sharpen their understandings of the conditions necessary for knowledge.

The point of Dharmottara's examples is not merely to show that accidentally correct cognitions are insufficient for knowledge. Examples of that sort can additionally play a part in guiding philosophers' *positive* accounts of the conditions necessary for knowledge. Though Dharmottara's own explanations fall short of satisfactorily illuminating why accidentally correct cognitions fail to be instances of knowledge, later Tibetan epistemologists do provide more explicit detail of what is needed, and they do so by appealing to the very same examples that Dharmottara provided. What is necessary for knowledge, on these Tibetan accounts, is a cognition that is *sensitive* to the truth in the sense that 'if the state of affairs had been false, the cognition of that state of affairs would not have occurred.' In other words, these Tibetan philosophers contend that knowledge of an object or state of affairs requires there to be an invariable dependence (*avinābhāva*) between the cognition, C(*p*), and the object/state of affairs, *p*.

There are many striking similarities between the Tibetan Buddhist response to examples of accidentally correct cognitions and responses to the Gettier problem in twentieth-century analytic epistemology. The clearest parallel is that between Tibetan responses to Dharmottara's examples (of accidentally correct cognitions) and Robert Nozick's invocation of a sensitivity requirement on knowledge as a way of responding to the Gettier problem. In both cases, it is agreed that knowledge requires something along the lines of a *law-like connection* between a person's belief/cognition and that which is believed/cognized. In both cases this law-like connection is secured by requiring one's belief/cognition to be sensitive to the truth—where this sensitivity is manifested in an appeal to certain counterfactual conditionals.

These similarities do not, of course, serve to prove that knowledge requires a law-like connection between a person's belief and the truth of what is believed. As the last fifty years have shown, there are numerous other ways in which to respond to Gettier cases, many of which fall short of requiring such a law-like connection. Nevertheless, the fact that the early Tibetan response to Dharmottara's examples of accidentally correct cognitions is so similar to the responses that twentieth-century philosophers like Robert Nozick and D. M. Armstrong give to the Gettier problem is significant. Aside from reflecting a shared intuition that accidental truth is insufficient for knowledge, it additionally reflects a common intuition about what it means for a belief/cognition to be nonaccidentally correct. Several other examples could be cited of intuitions about knowledge shared in common between contemporary analytic epistemologists and classical Buddhist epistemologists, but what has been described earlier should suffice for the purposes of this chapter.

10.3. The Value of Buddhist Epistemology

Let us move on to the broader matter of what sort of value there is in having contemporary philosophers learn about and grapple with the arguments found in the Buddhist tradition of epistemology. Epistemology, as currently taught in colleges and universities in Europe, the United States, and elsewhere, is widely agreed to be central to contemporary philosophy.[12] It is, moreover, an active field of research in philosophy, and an area with numerous thriving branches of contemporary scholarship. Insofar as this is the case, it may be difficult to see how the views of classical Buddhist epistemologists—some of whom were writing about knowledge nearly fifteen hundred years ago—can be of benefit to contemporary epistemologists. It would be a stretch to argue that there is some present void in contemporary analytic epistemology that can only be filled once philosophers gain a deeper understanding of classical Buddhist epistemology. (This is not to say that there are no voids in contemporary epistemology. It is just to acknowledge that raising philosophers' understandings of Buddhist epistemology will do rather little to fill whatever voids presently exist in epistemology.)

Yet there are multiple ways in which contemporary philosophers can benefit from learning about the claims and arguments put forward by epistemologists in the Buddhist tradition of philosophy. The value that derives from learning about Buddhist epistemology falls, I believe, into two categories: Buddhist-specific value and diversity-general value. By Buddhist-specific value, I am referring to any measure of value that derives from learning *that Buddhist philosophers* supported these-and-those epistemological positions and did so by such-and-such arguments. For example, there may be some value in learning that classical Buddhist epistemologists (by and large) adopted something along the lines of a *sense-datum* theory of perceptual experience, and that they supported the view that perception, properly speaking, is devoid of conceptual activity. Likewise, there may be some value in learning that classical Buddhist epistemologists were (by and large) proponents of a *reductive* account of testimonial knowledge and that their theory of inferential reasoning supports the *counterclosure* of knowledge. Yet I can imagine that for many contemporary analytic epistemologists, these Buddhist-specific values would be considered less relevant than the diversity-general value associated with learning about Buddhist epistemology.

The diversity-general value that derives from learning about Buddhist epistemology is, in many ways, easier to articulate. The Buddhist tradition of epistemology that was built upon the Indian treatises of knowledge composed by Dignāga and Dharmakīrti in sixth and seventh centuries is a clear example of an epistemological tradition that developed largely independent of the historical trajectory of theories of knowledge in the European tradition. As such, exposure to the claims and arguments made by philosophers in the Buddhist epistemological tradition can help contemporary philosophers reflect on their own assumptions about how the nature of knowledge is to be understood and how claims of knowledge are to be investigated. It allows them to see, in short, that there are other, very different, ways to think about the core problems of epistemology.

At an even broader level, learning about Buddhist epistemology can help contemporary philosophers to see that epistemology, as a core area of philosophy, arose in India well before the so-called epistemological turn in European philosophy. While ancient Greek philosophers certainly grappled with questions of knowledge, the idea of epistemology as a distinct field of philosophy is a relatively recent one. The actual English term "epistemology" did not come into usage until 1847, and it is only sometime thereafter that epistemology was thought of as a full-blown field of philosophical study. In the Buddhist tradition of philosophy, however, there was a much earlier recognition of epistemology as a distinct and fundamental area of study.

In the preceding paragraphs, I have spoken of Buddhist epistemology as though it is a set of theses and arguments whose present value lies in exposing contemporary analytic epistemologists to another historical tradition of epistemology. I would now like to suggest, however, that there is a different way of thinking about the value of Buddhist epistemology—one in which this value comes from *reorienting* how philosophers think of the domain of epistemology. While analytic epistemologists often portray their musings on knowledge as having a universal scope, one thing that the recent work on experimental epistemology shows us is that any and all investigations of the theory of knowledge are, by necessity, tied to the specific linguistic and conceptual frameworks in which philosophers speak and think about knowledge. This is certainly not to say that there are no universal truths about the nature of knowledge. It is, instead, simply to acknowledge that one's historical, linguistic, and philosophical background plays a role in shaping the ways in which thinkers make sense of philosophical questions about knowledge. Insofar as this is the case, epistemologists would be well served (a) to appreciate the existence of these alternative epistemological frameworks, (b) to explore the differences between these frameworks, and in so doing (c) to engage in cross-cultural epistemology. In the remainder of this chapter, I will discuss what I see as some of the most important benefits of pursuing cross-cultural epistemology.

10.3.1. Reconsidering Epistemological Assumptions

Over the course of the preceding nine chapters, I have had reason to mention, time and again, a number of key differences between classical Buddhist theories of knowledge and contemporary analytic accounts. Some of these differences are just on matters of detail, but other differences are much more fundamental. Awareness of and reflection on some of these more fundamental dissimilarities can play a pivotal role in reorienting how contemporary epistemologists think of their own theories. It can do so by showing that many of the basic building blocks of contemporary analytic epistemology—some of the most widely accepted principles in the field—may not be essential at all and could be supplanted with different starting points.

One clear example of this is contemporary epistemology's emphasis on a theory of knowledge in which the relevant mental component is *belief*—where belief is understood to be a persisting, dispositional state of an individual. It is simply not necessary for one's theory of knowledge to be built upon such dispositional states, as evidenced by the fact that the Buddhist (and broader Indian) tradition of epistemology constructs its theories, instead, upon momentary mental events—cognitive episodes. The idea that belief is a persisting mental state, and thus that knowledge, too, is a state that persists over time, has a long history in the European tradition of philosophy. But it is by no means the only way in which to make sense of what it means to know something. In fact, etiological accounts of knowledge—including the causal theory of knowledge that was proposed by Alvin Goldman in the 1960s—may be more easily explained and defended within the framework of an episodic theory of knowledge than they are within a "stative theory." Causal theories of knowledge are, for example, well equipped to account for the causal generation of beliefs. When beliefs are treated as dispositional states, however, causal theories that focus on the processes that produce a belief appear to provide an insufficient characterization of what is required for knowledge. On an episodic theory like that adopted by Buddhist epistemologists, by contrast, the process that generates one's cognition can more sufficiently determine what cognitive episodes will qualify as episodes of knowledge.

In addition to holding a causal and episodic theory of knowledge, Buddhist epistemologists maintain that this causal account of knowledge is to be explicated by way of an appeal to various *instruments* of knowledge. While it is true that Dignāga and his followers conceive of *pramāṇas* not merely as instruments of knowledge but also as the cognitions that result from the use of such instruments, there is little question that Buddhist epistemologists proceed under a conceptual framework in which knowledge is to be understood in relation to *cognition-forming processes* that depend on the exercise of epistemic instruments. This appeal to instruments of knowledge bears a close resemblance to recent virtue-theoretic accounts of knowledge that make use of belief-forming *faculties*, such as are adopted by Ernest Sosa and John Greco. The accounts supported by Sosa and Greco can, in fact, be bundled together with those of classical Buddhist (and other Indian) epistemologists and characterized as what we might call *faculty-productive* theories of knowledge. Proponents of faculty-productive theories contend that whether a person does or does not have knowledge depends on whether an appropriate faculty (or instrument) was or was not employed for the formation of one's belief/cognition.

Given the similarities between Buddhist accounts of knowledge and the accounts adopted by thinkers like Sosa and Greco, and given that Sosa and Greco are also, quite appropriately, identified as reliabilists, it is not so surprising that some recent scholars of Buddhist philosophy have described Buddhist epistemologists as likewise supporting epistemic reliabilism. Yet, despite the fact that these accounts hold in common a core belief in the importance of epistemic faculties and can thus be characterized as being proponents of faculty-productive theories of knowledge, the Buddhist account is—as I have argued in chapter 2—*not* a version of epistemic reliabilism. This is, once again, because reliabilist theories of knowledge generally accept fallibilism with respect to belief-forming processes, whereas the Buddhist account of knowledge requires a kind of infallibilism.

Various further examples could be given of similarities between the views of classical Buddhist epistemologists and contemporary analytic epistemology. Whatever intrinsic value there is in discovering that positions and theses similar to those upheld by contemporary epistemologists are also adopted by epistemologists in the Buddhist tradition, exposure to these Buddhist accounts can help contemporary epistemologists to see more clearly—and perhaps think differently about—the philosophical positions that they themselves accept. In some cases this may lead philosophers to reconsider the legitimacy of assumptions that they hold about the nature of knowledge and belief, and in other cases it may lead them to better contextualize and argumentatively defend the views they hold on matters that were formerly merely presumed to be true.

10.3.2. Seeing Yourself from Seeing Others

In addition to calling attention to a number of underlying assumptions made by contemporary analytic epistemologists, cross-cultural epistemology can help to change the way in which philosophers characterize their own views. It can help to expose fundamental distinctions that might otherwise be entirely ignored or assumed to be of minimal importance. In this way, cultivating a deeper understanding of Buddhist epistemology can help contemporary analytic epistemologists reframe how they think of their own philosophical theories.

This benefit can be better appreciated by reflecting on a somewhat recent example of precisely this sort of conceptual change in analytic epistemology that was brought on, at least in part, by exposure to the Indian tradition of epistemology. As was mentioned in chapter 5, Buddhist epistemologists following Dharmakīrti are reductionists about testimonial knowledge. They contend that testimony is not a separate *pramāṇa* but is instead reducible to a version of inferential reasoning. The (non-Buddhist) Nyāya School of Indian philosophy, however, contends that testimony is an independent *pramāṇa*—that it is an irreducible source of knowledge. This contrast between reductive and nonreductive accounts of testimonial knowledge is now quite familiar within contemporary analytic epistemology. But explicit talk of this dichotomy is, in fact, a relatively recent addition to analytic philosophy. Though in his 1992 book, *Testimony: A Philosophical Study*, the philosopher C. A. J. Coady makes repeated references to the "reductive" view of testimony—which he associates with the Scottish philosopher David Hume—the distinction between reductive and nonreductive theories of testimonial knowledge did not become popularized until after the publication of the 1994 book *Knowing from Words: Western and Indian Philosophical Analysis of Understanding and Testimony*. That book collected together writings on the epistemology of testimony by a handful of prominent Anglo-American analytic epistemologists—including Keith Lehrer, Ernest Sosa, and C. A. J. Coady—and various philosophers specializing in the Indian tradition of philosophy—such as B. K. Matilal, J. N. Mohanty, and Arindam Chakrabarti. The essays in that book and the discussions about knowledge and testimony that took place between the contributors to the volume played a prominent role in popularizing the distinction between reductive and nonreductive accounts of testimony. In this way, exposure to the Indian epistemological tradition, and its emphasis on fundamental sources of knowledge, was instrumental in helping contemporary analytic epistemologists reframe the ways in which they thought about testimonial knowledge.

It is possible that there are a number of ways (yet to be identified) in which a deeper understanding of Buddhist epistemology could lead to the introduction of new conceptual distinctions within contemporary analytic epistemology—conceptual distinctions that would serve to reframe, and facilitate the rethinking of, various debates within epistemology. What sorts of distinctions present in the Buddhist tradition of epistemology should or could be appropriated by analytic epistemologists is not something that can be determined here. There is, it seems, little predictability about which particular themes and terminological distinctions in twentieth and twenty-first-century analytic epistemology will catch fire and which will languish in obscurity. Nevertheless, increased exposure to the Buddhist tradition of epistemology can only serve to increase the possibility that contemporary philosophers will identify valuable ways in which to reframe their epistemological views in the light of the Buddhist tradition.

10.3.3. Bennett's Developmental Model

The earlier comments have focused largely on the benefits that accrue to contemporary epistemologists from cultivating an understanding of the Buddhist tradition of epistemology. But it would be wrong, or at best misleading, to think that these benefits will be realized automatically from exposure to the themes and arguments in Buddhist epistemology of the sort that have been described in this book. Awareness of other historical traditions of epistemological theorizing, including the Buddhist tradition of epistemology, is a good thing, but it is only a first step. Cross-cultural epistemology, when fully realized, must go well beyond a simple awareness of other traditions of epistemological theorizing. In fact, as I see it, fostering awareness is only the first stage in a long, developmental process. I shall conclude this book by describing a *developmental portrait* of cross-cultural epistemology.

The developmental portrait of cross-cultural epistemology that I have in mind is modeled after Milton Bennett's developmental model of intercultural sensitivity.[13] On Bennett's account, intercultural understanding proceeds through a series of developmental stages. Briefly, Bennett's developmental stages are as follows:

1. Denial
2. Defense
3. Minimization
4. Acceptance
5. Adaptation
6. Integration

In the first stage of intercultural development, *Denial*, there is a failure to recognize cultural difference. Though called "denial" by Bennett and others, this stage is more accurately viewed as a kind of sweeping cultural ignorance.

In the second stage, *Defense*, there is a recognition of some forms of cultural difference, but that recognition is accompanied by an "us versus them" polarization that can lead to a belief in the superiority of one's own cultural tradition over the other. In the stage of *Minimization*, a person recognizes cultural difference but responds to that recognition by (over)emphasizing the commonality between one's own culture and the other culture. As such, similarities between cultural traditions are highlighted at the expense of a deep appreciation of cultural differences. In the fourth stage, *Acceptance*, there is a deeper recognition of and attentiveness toward differences between cultures, and there is a recognition of the need for culturally specific frameworks of interpretation. In the fifth and sixth stages, *Adaptation* and *Integration*, a person's understanding of cultural difference is developed to such an extent that one can navigate cultural differences effectively by shifting perspectives and adapting one's behaviors to different cultural contexts.

In terms of how this applies to contemporary philosophy's engagement with Buddhist epistemology, a number of observations can be made. First, it is important to note that, in general, movement from lower to higher developmental stages is far from easy. A person cannot simply leap from a Defense mindset to an Adaptation mindset on a whim. Intercultural development takes a lot of time and hard work. The same is true of philosophers' interactions with and appreciations of other philosophical traditions, including the Buddhist epistemological tradition. Simply reading a book, such as this one, on Buddhist epistemology will have modestly little impact on how one frames and interprets questions of epistemology. With that said, this book is designed to play just one small piece in the project of cultivating a philosophical mindset that is more open to learning from different traditions of epistemology, including Buddhist epistemology.

There is little question that different philosophers will fall into different developmental stages with respect to their interaction with Buddhist epistemology. As is likely, many contemporary Anglo-American epistemologists are still entirely, or almost entirely, ignorant of the existence of Buddhist epistemology (and of Indian epistemology more generally). Yet, due in part to the pioneering work of philosophers like B. K. Matilal in the second half of the twentieth century—and in part due to recent developments in experimental philosophy, some of which have included explorations of cultural similarities/differences in philosophical intuitions—a growing number of philosophers in the Anglo-American tradition do now have a limited awareness of certain features of Indian and Buddhist theories of knowledge. It may be fair to say, therefore, that contemporary analytic epistemologists fall, collectively, somewhere around Bennett's stage of Defense with respect to their interaction with Buddhist epistemology. For philosophers with this as their primary orientation, there may be some recognition of the existence of Buddhist theories of knowledge, but this recognition is often accompanied by a belief in the superior rigor and insightfulness of contemporary analytic epistemology.

Given that the primary orientation of many philosophers is one of Defense, it would be natural to pitch the themes in this book at the level Minimization. That is, the material in this book could be used to show people who are trained in the analytic tradition of epistemology the plentiful points of overlap and commonality that exist between analytic epistemology and the Indian and Tibetan Buddhist traditions of epistemology. As a matter of fact, it may be that many readers understood such a minimization of epistemological differences to be the central project of this book.

That is not actually what I have endeavored to do here, however. As is mentioned in the preface of this book, I do not believe that it should be necessary to *prove* to philosophers that classical Buddhist epistemologists engaged in epistemological theorizing just as rigorous and argumentative as is found in the Western tradition of philosophy. To be sure, throughout the course of this book I have identified a large number of similarities between the Buddhist and Anglo-American traditions of epistemology. My true goal, however, has been to help readers see that, in addition to these numerous similarities, there are a number of important respects in which Buddhist epistemological theorizing is distinct from that found in contemporary epistemology. In this way, I have tried to encourage a movement not so much from Defense to Minimization, but rather from Minimization to Acceptance. I have aimed to show readers that there is value in being aware of and sensitive to how another philosophical tradition—the Buddhist tradition of epistemology—grappled, in their own distinctive ways, with a range of familiar epistemological themes.

Examining the views and arguments adopted by thinkers in the Buddhist tradition of epistemology, and seeking to extract value from that tradition of epistemology, may seem like a daunting task. Relatively few of the historical works in the Buddhist tradition are linguistically accessible to Western-trained philosophers and students of philosophy; and even in cases where primary or secondary literature from the Buddhist epistemological tradition *is* linguistically accessible to Western-trained students and scholars, that primary and secondary literature often times takes up themes that are so remote from those themes that are central to contemporary epistemology as to be effectively worthless in the minds of these Western-trained readers. What I have been trying to show in this book, however, is that many of the most important themes in contemporary epistemology are also central to the historical Buddhist tradition of epistemology that developed in India and later moved into Tibet. Yet, though the core topics and epistemological puzzles addressed in these traditions are largely the same, and while the proposed solutions to some of these puzzles are the same as well, there are, in most cases, important conceptual differences in how these philosophical traditions go about framing and interpreting these epistemological puzzles. The greatest value in learning about the Buddhist tradition of epistemology comes not from identifying novel answers to longstanding epistemological puzzles, but from seeing those same puzzles and topics from a different conceptual framework.

Further Reading

For a straightforward example of experimental epistemology as it relates to the Gettier problem and cross-cultural intuitions about knowledge, see Machery, E. et al. (2017). Gettier across cultures. *Nous*, *51*(3), 645–664.

For an interesting take on Indian philosophy's relevance to broader engagements in "public philosophy," see Vaidya, A. (2015). Public philosophy: Cross-cultural and multi-disciplinary. *Comparative Philosophy*, *6*(2), 35–57.

For a much more extensive discussion of Buddhist thought in relation to the larger field of philosophy, see Garfield, J. (2015). *Engaging Buddhism: Why it matters to philosophy.* Oxford: Oxford University Press.

Notes

Preface

1. Frege (1884/1980), p. 1.
2. Matilal (1986b), p. 4.
3. As an example of this approach, see Tillemans (2011), wherein his twelve-page "introduction to Buddhist epistemology" is composed of four topics: Epistemology and Ontology, Concepts and Language, Logic and Philosophy of Logic, and Religion.
4. For an excellent introduction to the variety of philosophical concerns relating to the Buddhist theory of exclusion, see Siderits et al. (2011).

Chapter 1

1. Except when noted otherwise, all terms provided in parentheses are the Sanskrit equivalents for the preceding English terms.
2. For a much more detailed discussion of these and related points, see Burton (2016).
3. Plato's *Meno*, 98a, as translated in Plato (2002).
4. Throughout this book I will speak frequently of the "Anglo-American" philosophical tradition, as well as of the "European" and "contemporary analytic" traditions of philosophy/epistemology. By "Anglo-American" philosophy, I am referring to the tradition of philosophical discourse that has flourished over the past three hundred years both in the United Kingdom and (somewhat later) in North America and other parts of the English-speaking world (such as Australia and New Zealand).
5. This notion of an "ascending scale" of analysis is first developed in Dreyfus (1997). It is additionally featured prominently in, for example, Dreyfus and McClintock (2003) and Dunne (2004). McClintock prefers the locution of a "sliding scale of analysis." This view that Dharmakīrti adopts such an ascending scale of analysis has been called into question by, for example, Dan Arnold (2008). See Prueitt (2016), pp. 41–49, for a comprehensive discussion of this dispute.
6. For a detailed account of this period of early Tibetan epistemology, see van der Kuijp (1983).
7. See Herzberger (1986).
8. For a recent look at the broad impact of Gettier's article, see Borges et al. (2017).
9. BonJour (1985), p. 5.
10. The notions of warrant and reliability will be discussed more fully in chapter 2 as well as in chapter 9.
11. Ganeri (2018), p. 15.

12. Throughout this book, I shall speak of "attaining knowledge," "obtaining knowledge," etc. This manner of speech is meant to be informal on my part. In the Western tradition of epistemology, it is common to portray knowledge as a kind of bank or reservoir of information; a person acquires or accumulates knowledge. Though I will use this language myself throughout this book, in the Indian and Buddhist traditions of epistemology, what is at issue are *episodes* of knowledge—fleeting moments of awareness. Thus, strictly speaking, these episodes of knowledge are not literally acquired and held in some reservoir of known information. Nonetheless, for the broader purposes of this book, it is still convenient to speak of a person attaining knowledge, etc.
13. Wittgenstein's "standard metre" reference is made in Wittgenstein (1953/1958), §50. The philosophical literature coming in response to Wittgenstein's claim is large, and those responses (such as in Kripke [1982]) involve much more than just the epistemological question of how to measure a measurement tool. For more on this, see, for example, Salmon (1987–8).
14. Chisholm (1966), p. 57. Steup (2018), in his summary article on epistemology, adds a fifth item to his list of knowledge sources: testimony.
15. See, in particular, Matilal (1986b, 2002).
16. Even though Buddhist epistemologists commonly provide examples of perceptions that involve compound, spatiotemporally extended objects—such as the moon, a pot, or a conch shell—the claim that perception can provide knowledge of such compound objects is not wholly uncontroversial. In particular, many Buddhist philosophers are inclined toward a form of metaphysical atomism and thus deny that these sorts of compound objects are real entities capable of being perceived. For more on this, see Dunne (2004), pp. 98–113.
17. There are a fairly large number of scholarly works dedicated to explicating the Buddhist understanding of a person of authority. Important contributions include Steinkellner (1983), Tillemans (1993), Seyfort Ruegg (1994, 1995), Krasser (2001), and Silk (2002).
18. For much more on the episodic nature of cognition/knowledge in the Indian tradition of philosophy, see Matilal (1986b) ch. 4, and Potter (1984).

Chapter 2

1. Even though there is a widespread acceptance of Dharmakīrti's definitions of knowledge, this is not to say that there are no Buddhist philosophers who hold accounts of knowledge very different from Dharmakīrti. But the philosophers holding these alternative accounts, such as Candrakīrti, are generally not members of—or active participants in—the classical Buddhist epistemological tradition.
2. For more on Buddhist (and early Tibetan) theories of definition, see Hugon (2009).
3. This view is supported in Franco (1997). For the opposite perspective on this same philological dispute, see Krasser (2001).
4. This proposal is suggested in Taber (2003).
5. PV II, 5c.

6. This leaves unresolved what precisely is meant by a "true object" or "true state of affairs." As is explained more fully in later sections of this chapter, truth is not a separate, explicit component of *pramāṇa* for Indian Buddhist epistemologists. As such, there is no explicit articulation of any full account of truth within their discussions of knowledge. In an important sense, truth's metaphysical status is something that need not be answered by Dharmakīrti qua epistemologist. Rather, his definition(s) should be compatible with various different metaphysical accounts of truth. How we are to understand this 'truth constraint' on knowledge is the central topic of section 2.4.2.
7. This explicit appeal to truth is found in, for example, Śaṅkaranandana's definition of *pramāṇa* that is put forward in the tenth or eleventh century, and which is relied upon by many later Tibetan epistemologists.
8. PV II, 1a.
9. PVP, 2a.
10. Though being an episode of knowledge requires engaging *objects* that are capable of performing functions, it must also be emphasized that Dignāga and his followers defend the position that episodes of cognition themselves are real, particular entities. As real entities, all cognitions have the capacity to perform functions. But this functional capacity (of cognitions) does not serve to distinguish episodes of knowledge from other instances of cognition. Rather, it is the cognitive episodes' objects having the capacity to perform functions that is what is necessary for knowledge.
11. PVP, 6b.
12. This position is adopted in Katsura (1984) and is accepted also by Dreyfus (1997).
13. This is the translation given in Katsura (1984).
14. Dreyfus (1997), p. 293. Dreyfus uses the term "normative truth" in a rather idiosyncratic way. Here is what Dreyfus says about normative truth (p. 293): "here truth does not mean just factuality, but something stronger, what we could call *normative truth*; that is, truth in accordance with the proper standards of evaluation."

    Dreyfus contends that it is Dharmakīrti's second definition of *pramāṇa* that supports a commitment to normative truth, whereas the first definition, which appeals to nondeceptiveness, only makes the case for a weaker, pragmatic connection to truth. I am more inclined to support the view (as adopted by Dharmottara) that Dharmakīrti's two characterizations of *pramāṇa* are to be seen as equivalent. As such, I believe both definitions of *pramāṇa* should be understood as grounding the idea that in episodes of knowledge one's cognition invariably tracks the truth.
15. Krasser (2001).
16. See Hugon and Stoltz (2019), pp. 29–31.
17. For more on those forms of cognition that fall short of knowledge, and their defining conditions, see Hugon and Stoltz (2019), ch. IV.
18. Russell (1912/1959), ch. 5.
19. Gettier (1963), p. 121.
20. For an earlier treatment of the relationship between Indian theories of knowledge and the "justified true belief" account of knowledge, see Potter (1984). Readers should note that Potter (1984) covers a great many topics—some of which are only tangentially related to the "justified true belief" account of knowledge—and that the article

is concerned with the Indian epistemological tradition broadly construed, and not specifically with the Indian Buddhist account of knowledge.

21. *Sum* I, Q. 16, Art. 2, agr. 2. Thomas Aquinas attributes this definition to Isaac Israeli ben Solomon (c. 832–932).
22. For more on the *Sautrāntika* system of thought, see the articles contained in *26*(2) of the *Journal of the International Association of Buddhist Studies*, which is dedicated to that topic. In particular, note Honjō (2003) and Kritzer (2003).

    It is additional necessary to point out that the *Sautrāntika* system of thought is not the only external realist account within the Buddhist tradition of philosophy. In particular, it differs in subtle but important ways from the *Vaibāṣika* system. Of note is that the *Sautrāntika* system endorses a reductive, or atomistic, account of external reality in which it is denied that there are macro-level external objects, but are instead only aggregates of atoms. For a clear presentation of this sort of account see Dunne (2004), pp. 98–113.
23. Given that Dharmakīrti and other Buddhist epistemologists adopt these shifting perspectives, it is now somewhat common to refer to these epistemologists as proponents of the *Yogācāra-Sautrāntika* tradition of philosophy. This terminology is endorsed, for example, by Mark Siderits in his (2007), ch. 10.
24. PVinṬ, 125a.2–b.1.
25. These two features of justification—called here *justification fallibilism* and *deductive closure of justification*—are introduced in Gettier (1963), p. 121.
26. This assumption that justified beliefs are consistent with those beliefs being false cannot hold universally, of course, for any necessary truth about which I hold a justified belief—such as the belief that 2 + 2 = 4—is not one that could possibly be false. Nevertheless, Gettier's point is that a belief's being justified is logically independent of its being true or false, at least for contingent propositions.
27. See Gettier (1963).
28. Not all philosophers agree that warrant and reliability are fallible. See, for example, Merricks (1995). Merricks proclaims that "Pollock, Lehrer, Nozick, Dretske, Goldman, and Tomberlin, among others, provide accounts of warrant that entail truth" (p. 841). In point of fact, this claim is not well supported by the details of these named philosophers' accounts, and Merricks central argument for the conclusion that warrant entails truth is not persuasive.
29. Zagzebski (2017), p. 181. Zagzebski's initial discussion of this point is in Zagzebski (1994).
30. Cowherds (2011).
31. Coseru (2012).
32. See Garfield (2015), p. 222 (n. 7) and p. 331.
33. Goldman and Beddor (2016).
34. Goldman (1979), p. 11.
35. Armstrong (1973), p. 166.
36. Armstrong (1973), p. 187.
37. Williamson (2000), p. 47.
38. Armstrong (1973), p. 189.

Chapter 3

1. Meinong's view is most famously referenced in Russell (1905), but it is derived from Meinong (1904).
2. PS 3c. For these references to Dignāga's views in his *Compendium of Knowledge*, readers should consult the important book by Hattori (1968).
3. PS 3d.
4. See, for example, Hayes (1988).
5. Hayes (1988).
6. These three conditions are the *ālambana pratyaya* (object condition), the *adhipati pratyaya* (empowering condition), and the *samanantara pratyaya* (predecessor condition). Also considered necessary is the *hetu pratyaya* (causal condition), which is a general term for whatever remaining causal factors are necessary for perception.
7. Such a naïve realist account of perception is adopted by the twelfth-century Tibetan epistemologist Chaba Chokyi Senge (Tib: phya pa chos kyi seng ge) and his followers. See Hugon and Stoltz (2019), especially ch. I.1.
8. For two very different accounts of the phenomenology of perception and the role(s) played by phenomenal forms (*ākāras*) in Buddhist theories of perception, see Dreyfus (1996) and Coseru (2009). See also the collection of essays contained in Garfield (2019) relating to Sellars's "Myth of the Given" in the context of Buddhism.
9. It must again be noted—as it was in chapter 1, note 16—that many Buddhist philosophers adopt a form of ontological atomism in which it is denied that macroscopic, composite objects have a real existence. This thus complicates the Buddhist epistemologist's account of the causal process in perception.
10. The role of accuracy conditions is discussed at some length in Siewert (1998) and Siegel (2011), as well as in the much shorter Siegel (2009).
11. PV III, 300cd (emphasis added).
12. For more on Dharmakīrti's proofs of idealism, see Kellner (2017).
13. For more on Candrakīrti's relation to Dignāga's views of perception, see Arnold (2005), pp. 175–183.
14. See, for example, Devendrabuddhi's claims on this point, PVP 4a.1–2—a translation of which can be found in Dunne (2004), pp. 265–266—as well as Dunne's (2004, pp. 298–309) detailed discussion of this topic.
15. There are a variety of scholarly discussions on the question of whether Dignāga and Dharmakīrti shared a common understanding of the different types of perception. The matter is taken up, for example, in Franco (1993) and Yao (2004), with the latter article receiving a brief response by Eli Franco (2005).
16. For more on mental perception and its relation to reflexive perception, see Kobayashi (2010).
17. PVin I, 28. For Dharmakīrti's explicit claims about yogic perception, readers should consult the translations contained in (the appendix of) Dunne (2006).
18. For particularly clear discussions of yogic perception, see Woo (2003) and Dunne (2006).
19. The most famous example of appeals to clairvoyance, and skepticism concerning its epistemic status, is found in BonJour (1980).

20. See Dunne (2006) for a helpful discussion of the differences between yogic perception and hallucination.
21. This nomenclature of a "constitutive understanding of self-awareness" is discussed at length in Arnold (2010). For more on the view that self-awareness can be understood in two different ways, see Williams (1998).
22. Arnold (2010), passim.
23. Coseru (2012), pp. 244–249.
24. For more on Charles Bonnet syndrome, see Jan and del Castillo (2012).
25. Whether jaundice *actually* gives rise to yellow experiences of the sort standardly supposed by Indian epistemologists is not so much the point here. Even if the example of jaundice is not fully accurate, the reader can understand the broader possibility of visual error tied to the misoperation of one's sense organs.
26. This connection is discussed in Prueitt (2017), with much more care and attention than is provided here.
27. For more on the theory of disjunctivism in relation to illusion and/or hallucination, see Brewer (2008) and Fish (2009).
28. This is not how the disjunctivist position is typically understood by contemporary philosophers of mind. It is frequently argued that while perception and hallucination can give rise to indistinguishable *experiences*, there is no *object* at all that is experienced in cases of hallucination.
29. This disjunctivist understanding of perceptual experience, within early Tibetan Buddhist epistemology, is discussed at greater length in Hugon and Stoltz (2019), ch. I.1.

Chapter 4

1. A brief account of "Buddhist argumentation" can be found in Tillemans (2008), which is an introductory essay for a journal volume devoted to explicating various features of the Buddhist account of argumentation and inference.
2. This is discussed by Dharmottara at the very beginning of NBṬ II. For more on this, see ch. 3 of Prasad (2002), which is devoted to Dharmottara's views on this topic.
3. This contrast between the logic of inference and the epistemology of inference is addressed (in a manner slightly different from my own presentation) in Tanaka (2013).
4. See Frege (1884/1980), Introduction (pp. i–xi). Note also B. K. Matilal's obsession with the depsychologization of logic in (especially) ch. 4 of Matilal (1998).
5. PS 3d. In Hattori (1968), p. 25, this is translated as "the association of name, genus, etc."
6. PVin 252b.4.
7. Dreyfus (1997), p. 320.
8. This issue is discussed more fully in Hugon and Stoltz (2019), ch. IV.4.
9. See Dreyfus (1997), ch. 18, for a particularly detailed discussion of this conundrum. Dreyfus's presentation focuses largely on later, Tibetan, responses of how to resolve this difficulty.

10. For more detailed accounts of the three characteristics, see Hayes (1988), pp. 145–154, or Matilal (1986a).
11. A clear account of the notions of *sapakṣa* and *vipakṣa* can be found in Tillemans (1990).
12. See Ganeri (2001), ch. 1. The claim that Dignāga's theory of inference involves, at its root, *inductive* considerations has been long supported by other scholars—most notably, Richard Hayes (see Hayes 1986, 1988).
13. It has long been common in writings on Indian logic to speak of this universal entailment (*vyāpti*) as a "pervasion." The idea is that the property to be proven "pervades" the evidence, in the sense that everything having the evidential property also has the property to be proven. Or, expressed in terms of classes or sets, the class of items having the evidential property is *subsumed under* the class of items having the property to be proven. While there is nothing fundamentally wrong with translating the Sanskrit term *vyāpti* as "pervasion," it is not a term that has any relevant logical (or philosophical, or mathematical) import in Anglo-American contexts. As such, I have consistently preferred to express this relationship as one of "entailment."
14. For a helpful—indeed, insightful—translation of and commentary on Dharmakīrti's theory of inference, see Hayes and Gillon (1991).
15. For an excellent, albeit somewhat brief, account of these three forms of evidence, see Gillon (1986). For a much more detailed account of Dharmakīrti's theory of inference and evidence, see Prasad (2002).
16. Here, the relationship of "ontological dependence" refers to the following: the property x ontologically depends on the property y just in case, for any object o, x is instantiated in o only if y is instantiated in o.
17. For a more detailed account of Dharmakīrti's theory of causal inference, see Gillon and Hayes (2008).
18. Matilal (1998), p. 111.
19. For basic formulations of the principle of deductive closure, see Stine (1976).
20. To my knowledge, the term "counter-closure" originates with Luzzi (2010). The term has thus only recently been popularized. For more on this, see Fitelson (2017).
21. To be more precise, in claiming that q is derived via an inference from $p_1, p_2, \ldots p_n$, what are at issue are just those premises that are *essential* to the inference. The claim is thus that all those premises essential for reaching the conclusion must be known to be true.
22. Warfield (2005), p. 407–408.

Chapter 5

1. NyS 1.1.7.
2. Phillips (2011), p. 83.
3. The translation "credible witness" for *āpta* is used by Ganeri (1999).
4. For fuller discussions of these conditions, see Ganeri (1999), pp. 73–81 and Phillips (2011), pp. 90–95.

5. For much more on the distinction between knowledge and the certification of knowledge, see Phillips (2011), chs. 1 and 2.
6. Fricker (1994), p. 126.
7. The expression "radically inaccessible" is the terminology adopted in Tillemans (1999).
8. PVSV ad PV I, 318. As translated in Tillemans (1999, p. 43): "It is not so that because [someone] is unmistaken about some things he will be so in all, for deviance is observed (*vyabhicāradarśanāt*) and it is not established that there is any pervasion (*vyāpti*) between his [verbal] activity and being non-belying. Now, we accept this defining character of scripture for lack of any [other] way. There is no certainty from this [scripture]. Thus it was said that scripture is not a *pramāṇa*."
9. PV I, 216 as translated in Dunne (2004), p. 364.
10. Franco (1997), p. 29.
11. PVSV ad PV I, 218, as translated in Dunne (2004), p. 367.
12. As an aside, it is important to distinguish *reduction* from *dependence*. It is unquestionably the case that testimonial knowledge depends, in certain respects, on perception (and quite possibly on inference as well). All testimonial knowledge requires some form of perception: either *hearing* the speech of another person or *seeing* the written words of another. In this sense, testimonial knowledge is clearly dependent on perception. It does not follow from this, however, that testimony is thereby reducible to perception (or even perception supplemented by inferential reasoning). It may still be the case that knowledge by testimony requires some additional element beyond that found in perception and inference.
13. Strawson (1994), p. 23.
14. For more on Hume and Reid as exemplars of reductionism and nonreductionism, respectively, see Lackey (2008), ch. 5.
15. Lackey (2008), pp. 176–177.
16. Audi (1997), p. 409. There are, of course, many explicit proponents of the transmission theory of testimony. Other defenders include Hardwig (1985), Burge (1993), Williamson (1996), Adler (2006), and Owens (2006).
17. See, in particular, Lackey (1999, 2006), as well as Lackey (2008), ch. 2.
18. PVSV ad PV I, 217 as translated in Dunne (2004), p. 366.
19. Tillemans (1999), pp. 37–41.
20. As already noted in chapter 1, readers should consult, for example, Steinkellner (1983), Tillemans (1993), Seyfort Ruegg (1995), or Krasser (2001), for more on the notion of Buddha as a person of authority.
21. Franco (1997), p. 19.

Chapter 6

1. It can be argued that there are goals of belief formation other than knowledge. In particular, people may form beliefs for pragmatic reasons, such as for reasons of emotional security. A wife may believe that her husband will recover from stage 4 lung cancer—despite possessing much medical evidence to the contrary—precisely

because that belief will promote her emotional wellbeing. In this case, the wife's belief is not aimed at knowledge.

2. For more on Ngog Lotsawa Loden Sherab (Tib: *rngog lo tsA ba blo ldan shes rab*; 1059–1109), see Hugon (2014).
3. Aside from Ngog Lotsawa, the most important contributions during this period were made by Chaba Chokyi Senge (Tib: *phya pa chos kyi seng ge*; 1109–1169). For a quick introduction to Chaba's role in the larger context of Tibetan Buddhist epistemology, see van der Kuijp (1978).
4. As will be detailed in section 6.2 of this chapter, though these eleventh- and twelfth-century Tibetan epistemologists believe that there are two forms of knowledge—perceptual knowledge and inferential knowledge—they generally draw a distinction between 'perception' (in general) and 'perceptual knowledge' (proper). These Tibetans explicitly deny that all perceptual cognitions are instances of knowledge. For more on the account of perception that is adopted by the twelfth-century Tibetan scholar Chaba Chokyi Senge, see Hugon (2011).
5. In Tibetan, these three categories are, respectively, (1) *log shes*, (2) *snang la ma nges pa*, and (3) *yid dpyod*. More detailed historical overviews of these three forms of cognition, in addition to discussions of various possible English translations for these terms, are provided in Hugon and Stoltz (2019), ch. IV.
6. Among Indian philosophers, one can identify both proponents of "aspectarianism" and proponents of "nonaspectarianism"—that is, persons who contend that perceptual experiences have phenomenal aspects and those who deny that they do. While Indian Buddhist epistemologists generally endorse a form of aspectarianism, readers will see later in this section that some Tibetan Buddhists adopt a version of nonaspectarianism.
7. This case is discussed briefly in Franco (2006) and in Stoltz (2013).
8. For much more on the Buddhist exclusion (*apoha*) theory, see the collection of essays contained in Siderits et al. (2011).
9. For Chaba's account, see Hugon and Stoltz (2019), ch. II, 112.111.2.
10. For much more on the history of the term "nonascertaining perception" (*snang la ma nges pa*), see Hugon and Stoltz (2019), ch. IV.1.
11. This formulation can be found in various places within Chaba's most important text, *Epistemology: The Dispeller of the Mind's Darkness* (Tib: *tshad ma yid kyi mun sel*). See Hugon and Stoltz (2019), ch. I.2.
12. In connection with this, it should be noted that the relevant Tibetan term for nonascertaining perception—*snang la ma nges pa*—appears to be a Tibetan creation. As such, it is not entirely clear what the Sanskrit equivalent of the term "ascertaining" would be. Possible interpretations include both *avasāya* and *niścaya*.
13. For more on the history of the category of "nonascertaining perception," including its relation to the claims of Dharmottara, see Hugon and Stoltz (2019), ch. IV.1. Though eleventh- and twelfth-century Tibetans based their accounts of nonascertaining perception on claims coming from Dharmottara in his NBṬ, there are also some claims made by the earlier Indian Buddhist thinker Śākyabuddhi (c. 660–720) that could have spurred on the question of whether perceptual cognitions always lead to the ascertainment or determination of their objects.

14. In Tibetan, this form of cognition is called *yid dpyod*—literally, “mental evaluation.” For more on the nature (and history) of this term see Hugon and Stoltz (2019), ch. IV.3.
15. Episodes of factive assessment not only do not rely on adequate evidence; they also do not depend on “experience.” This nondependence on experience is important as it serves to distinguish factive assessment from conceptual postknowledge cognitions like those described in section 6.3.1 earlier.
16. Here, the informally expressed claim that ‘S knows *e*’ corresponds to the formal requirement (from chapter 4) that the cognizer ascertains (PD) that the evidence is a property of the subject/locus of the inferences, and ‘S knows that *e* entails *p*’ corresponds to the formal requirement that the cognizer ascertains (V) that the evidence entails the property to be proven. See chapter 4, section 4.3.2.
17. Sakya Paṇḍita’s objections are found in his *Rigs gter*, ch. II. For more on these objections, see Stoltz (2007), §IV.
18. Recently recovered Tibetan manuscripts attribute this alternative definition to Chaba’s teacher, Gya Marpa (Tib: *rGya dmar pa Byang chub grags*). For more on this, see Hugon and Stoltz (2019), ch. IV.3.

Chapter 7

1. Though the use of skeptical scenarios in European philosophy has a long history, there is an overabundant appeal to such scenarios in contemporary analytic philosophy. The use of skeptical scenarios is so common in contemporary epistemology that it is difficult to catalog the most notable examples of works making use of these scenarios. Readers could consult Nozick (1981), part 3.II; Stroud (1984), ch. 1; and Sosa (1989).
2. This example, from Candrakīrti, is described in a variety of contemporary sources, including Lopez (2006), p. 49; Larsson (2012), p. 6; and Stoltz (2015).
3. For more on this text, see Garfield (1995) and Westerhoff (2009).
4. There are now a number of different English translations of various portions of Nāgārjuna’s *Dispeller*. Westerhoff (2010) translates the entire text. The verses dedicated to examining instruments of knowledge have previously been translated in Bhattacharya (1971) and in Siderits (1980, 1981).
5. VV 31, as translated in Westerhoff (2010), p. 69.
6. For more on the epistemic regress problem, see BonJour (1978).
7. This view, ($E_{\sim}$), is developed in VV 43–48.
8. This view, (E_{o}), is discussed in VV 32.
9. This view, (E_{s}), is discussed beginning in VV 33 and continues in earnest up to VV 38. Arguments on related matters continue through VV 41.
10. The idea that foundational beliefs may be self-justifying in much the same way as the “prime mover” can move both other objects and itself was popularized by Roderick Chisholm. See Chisholm (1966), p. 30.
11. For more on this, see Westerhoff (2010), pp. 73–74. For more on the relation between Nāgārjuna’s arguments about self-establishment and the Nyāya tradition, see Bhattacharya (1977) and Bronkhorst (1985).

12. VV 33, as translated in Westerhoff (2010), p. 72.
13. See Siderits (1980), p. 315 and Westerhoff (2010), pp. 81–82 for a different perspective on this argument.
14. See Priest (2002), ch. 2 for more on the problems concerning infinity in (pre-Kantian) Western philosophy.
15. Among Klein's numerous articles on infinitism, readers should consult Klein (1999, 2007).
16. See Greco (2009).
17. On this interpretation, Nāgārjuna's texts languished in obscurity, at least within Buddhist epistemological circles. An opposing view is adopted in Franco (1986), wherein it is maintained that Dignāga's epistemological project does, in significant ways, take into account the skeptical arguments of Nāgārjuna. Franco is clear to point out, however, that his claims involve much speculation and are "nothing but a supposition" (p. 87).

Chapter 8

1. Among the most important contributions on epistemic luck are those by Duncan Pritchard, including Pritchard (2005, 2008). Additional helpful readings include Yamada (2011) and Turri (2015).
2. There are at least two different ways in which we might say that a belief is accidentally true. In one sense, an accidentally true belief is one where the proposition believed is true, but that proposition's truth has or had a low objective probability. For example, suppose I purchase a single lottery ticket, and a day later when the winning numbers are revealed, I come to see that my ticket was a winner. There is a sense in which my belief that I won the lottery is an accidentally true belief. But that is not the sense of being "accidentally true" that is relevant here. Rather, in the relevant epistemic context, an accidentally true belief is one that has a low *subjective* probability of being true. On this interpretation, it is the *belief* that has a low likelihood of being correct, not the objective status of the proposition believed.
3. This example is found in his PVinṬ 5b. It should also be pointed out that Dharmottara likely has additional goals in mind, besides identifying the scope of knowledge episodes, when he considers examples like that of the person who correctly believes, without evidence, that there is water in a nearby well.
4. On Nozick's original (1981) account, a belief tracks the truth, or is sensitive to the truth, provided that *two* counterfactual conditionals are satisfied:

   (a) If p had been false, S wouldn't have believed p.
   (b) If p had been true, S would have believed p.

   On that account, a smoke detector is sensitive to the truth provided that it beeps *when and only when* there is smoke. In the years since Nozick's book was originally published, however, it has become standard to understand the thesis of sensitivity as merely including the first conditional, (a). As such, throughout this book, it will be maintained that a sensitive belief is one that simply satisfies that first counterfactual.
5. PVin I, 3.

6. PVin I, 3.
7. At least a few Tibetan authors, including the c. late twelfth- to early thirteenth-century scholar Dorje Özer (Tib: *gtsang drug pa rdo rje 'od zer*), explicitly reference the earlier-mentioned passage from Dharmakīrti's *Ascertainment of Knowledge* (PVin I, 3) when discussing the definition of *pramāṇa* and its extension to episodes of perception. See *gSal byed* 23b.9.
8. It is not just David Lewis's (1973/2001) account of counterfactual conditionals that considers only relevantly similar counterfactual situations. A similar feature holds within Robert Stalnaker's (1968) account of conditionals as well.
9. Goldman (1976), p. 773.
10. For more on the historical background of "countering the capacity to produce superimpositions," see Introduction 2 in Hugon and Stoltz (2019)—and, more specifically, I.2 §3.1—where the matter is discussed in much greater detail. Additional historical background information on eliminating/excluding superimpositions is contained in §4 of that same introduction.

Chapter 9

1. These two conditions are (PD) and (V), which are presented in chapter 4, section 4.3.2.
2. Here, I am referring to the form of externalism about mental content that has been proposed, most famously, in Putnam (1973) and Burge (1979).
3. This sort of view is most notably held by Matthias Steup. See Steup (1999).
4. Plantinga's account of warrant is introduced in his (1993b) and is explicated further in his (1993a).
5. For the sake of simplicity, this chapter sets aside the Buddhist epistemologist's 'novelty constraint' on knowledge episodes.
6. The claim that Plantinga's own account of warrant is one that entails truth is defended in Merricks (1995). Much more standard, however, is the opposite view, represented in, for example, Zagzebski (1994). I take Zagzebski's positions to capture the standard position on this issue.
7. See chapter 3, section 3.4.
8. This point is not always appreciated by scholars of Buddhism as well as it should be. To repeat, the Buddhist account of reflexive perception provides no grounds for concluding that they adopt an internalist account of warrant nor that they endorse the KK thesis. As Dreyfus (1997) notes on this point (p. 340): "[Reflexive perception] does not necessarily, however, validate these states. For example, we seem to be seeing water without knowing whether our seeing is factual or not. In this case, we know that we have an experience, but we do not know that we know."
9. Just as it is common to translate the term *pramāṇa* as "valid cognition" (at least in the Buddhist context), so, too, the term *prāmāṇya* is now regularly translated as "validity." I wish to avoid both of these terms, and thus translate *pramāṇa* as "episode of knowledge" and *prāmāṇya* as "knowledge-hood."
10. The views of Kumārila and his followers are carefully discussed in Taber (1992), as well as in Arnold (2005), chs. 3 and 4.

11. Matilal (2002), p. 156.
12. As an example of an account that is formulated very differently from what is found in Matilal (2002), see Mohanty (2000), pp. 36–38. Chakrabarti (1984) criticizes (earlier versions of) Mohanty's account, but Chakrabarti's understanding of the topic departs also from that of Matilal in many respects.
13. Although Kumārila's discussions of intrinsic knowledge-hood appear to postdate Dharmakīrti, Steinkellner (1992) points out that there are two brief claims within Dharmakīrti's works that some later Buddhists saw as addressing the issue of the determination of knowledge.
14. See Steinkellner (1992), p. 259, as well as the more detailed account of Śāntarakṣita's views that are contained in Hattori (1997).
15. For details on these later accounts, see Krasser (2003).
16. This is from Sakya Paṇḍita's *Rigs gter* (*rang 'grel*) ch. VIII, as contained in Sa skya (1989), p. 220.
17. A relevantly similar claim is made in Dasti and Phillips (2010). They are speaking primarily of the non-Buddhist tradition of Indian philosophy, but the claim holds true even more credibly for the Buddhist epistemological tradition in India. Dasti and Phillips's account is contested by Ganeri (2010). This disagreement between these scholars pertains to the (Navya Nyāya) account held by Gaṅgeśa, and it does not directly address the views of Buddhist epistemologists. Yet, to the extent that the same issues can be mapped onto the Buddhist tradition, my understanding is much closer to that of Dasti and Phillips than it is to Ganeri.
18. This distinction between internalism and externalism with respect to cognitive episodes is not the same as, but operates in a sense parallel to, the distinction between internalism and externalism with respect to mental content. The account presented here is essentially the same as what Timothy Williamson characterizes as internalism and externalism with respect to "mental states," where he states that "internalists hold that one's mental states are determined by one's internal physical states; the mind is in the head" (Williamson 2000, p. 49).
19. A somewhat different, and more detailed, version of this same argument as it plays out in twelfth-century Tibetan Buddhist epistemology is provided in Stoltz (2013), pp. 414–416.

Chapter 10

1. Williamson (2007), p. 179.
2. Though it has become standard in discussions of experimental philosophy to speak of philosophical "intuitions," there is little question that many of those beliefs classified as philosophical intuitions are not the result of any sort of intuitional faculty, but are, rather, the result of rational judgments—rational judgments that are influenced by prior experiences, as well as by one's culture and philosophical training.
3. BonJour (1980).
4. Examples of excellent discussions of the link between philosophical intuitions and experimental methods in philosophy include Machery (2011) and Nagel (2012), as well as the very accessible accounts in Sosa (2007a; 2007b, ch. 3).

5. Weinberg et al. (2001), p. 444.
6. This is not the place to detail the various experimental studies that have been conducted on philosophical intuitions about knowledge and cross-cultural attributions of knowledge. For more on this topic, see, in particular, Machery et al. (2017). Another valuable overview is provided in Turri (2013), as well as in the back-and-forth debate found in Starmans and Friedman (2012, 2013) and Nagel et al. (2013a. 2013b).
7. Gettier (1963), 121.
8. Weinberg et al. (2001), p. 443.
9. One online source (https://hindiforlearners.wordpress.com/2013/01/23/20-most-common-verbs-in-hindi/) claims that *jānnā* is the sixth most common verb in Hindi.
10. For example, Matilal (1986b), p. 105, states: "We may recognize that the verb 'to know' in ordinary speech (similarly the root *jñā* in Sanskrit) often means nothing more than 'is aware' or 'rightly believes'. Sanskrit philosophers, however, use a different term, one not related directly to *jñā*, to denote a concept that comes closer to the philosophical notion of knowledge: prama consisting of the prefix *pra* indicating excellence, perfection, and the root *mā*, 'to measure', 'to know'."
11. This example is described more fully, and its logical structure is examined, in Stoltz (2007).
12. The centrality of epistemology within contemporary philosophy departments can be measured in a number of different ways. It is perhaps noteworthy that a (nonscientific) poll of readers of the blog site Leiter Reports ranked epistemology at the top of the list of areas of study most important for a strong PhD program in philosophy (https://leiterreports.typepad.com/blog/2012/07/what-areas-are-most-important-for-a-strong-phd-program.html).
13. See Bennett (1986, 1993).

Bibliography

Abbreviations for Classical Texts

Meno *The Meno* of Plato
MMK *Mūlamadhyamakakārikā* of Nāgārjuna
NB *Nyāyabindu* of Dharmakirti
NBṬ *Nyāyabinduṭīkā* of Dharmottara
NyS *Nyāyasūtra* of Gautama
PS *Pramāṇasamuccaya* of Dignāga
PSV *Pramāṇasamuccayavṛtti* of Dignāga
PV *Pramāṇavārttika* of Dharmakīrti
PVin *Pramāṇaviniścaya* of Dharmakīrti
PVinṬ *Pramāṇaviniścayaṭīkā* of Dharmottara
PVP *Pramāṇavārttikapañjikā* of Devendrabuddhi
PVSV *Pramāṇavārttikasvavṛtti* of Dharmakīrti
Rigs gter Tshad ma rigs pa' i gter gyi rang gi 'grel pa of Sa skya Paṇḍita
gSal byed Yang dag rigs pa'i gsal byed sgron ma of gTsang drug pa rDo rje 'od zer
Sum Summa Theologiæ of Thomas Aquinas
VV *Vigrahavyāvartanī* of Nāgārjuna

Modern Sources

Adler, J. (2006). Transmitting knowledge. *Nous*, *30*, 99–111.

Armstrong, D. M. (1973). *Belief, truth and knowledge*. London: Cambridge University Press.

Arnold, D. (2005). *Buddhists, Brahmins, and belief: Epistemology in South Asian philosophy of religion*. New York: Columbia University Press.

Arnold, D. (2008). Buddhist idealism, epistemic and otherwise: Thoughts on the alternating perspectives of Dharmakīrti. *Sophia*, *47*(1), 3–28.

Arnold, D. (2010). Self-awareness (*svasaṃvitti*) and related doctrines of Buddhists following Dignāga: Philosophical characterizations of some of the main issues. *Journal of Indian Philosophy*, *38*, 323–378.

Audi, R. (1997). The place of testimony in the fabric of knowledge and justification. *American Philosophical Quarterly*, *34*, 405–422.

Bennett, M. (1986). Toward ethnorelativism: A developmental approach to training for intercultural sensitivity. *International Journal of Intercultural Relations*, *10*(2), 179–196.

Bennett, M. (1993). Toward ethnorelativism: A developmental model of intercultural sensitivity. In R. M. Paige (Ed.), *Education for the intercultural experience* (2nd ed., pp. 21–71). Yarmouth, ME: Intercultural Press.

Bhattacharya, K. (1971). The dialectical method of Nāgārjuna. *Journal of Indian Philosophy, 1*, 217–261.

Bhattacharya, K. (1977). On the relationship between the *Vigrahavyāvartanī* and the *Nyāyasūtras*. *Journal of Indo-European Studies, 5*, 265–273.

BonJour, L. (1978). Can empirical knowledge have a foundation? *American Philosophical Quarterly, 15*(1), 1–13.

BonJour, L. (1980). Externalist theories of empirical knowledge. In P. French, T. Uehling Jr., & H. Wettstein (Eds.), *Midwest studies in philosophy, vol. 5* (pp. 53–73). Minneapolis: University of Minnesota Press.

BonJour, L. (1985). *The structure of empirical knowledge*. Cambridge, MA: Harvard University Press.

Borges, R., de Almeida C., & Klein, P. (Eds.). (2017). *Explaining knowledge: New essays on the Gettier problem*. Oxford: Oxford University Press.

Brewer, B. (2008). How to account for illusion. In A. Haddock & F. Macpherson (Eds.), *Disjunctivism: Perception, action, knowledge* (pp. 168–180). Oxford: Oxford University Press.

Bronkhorst, J. (1985). Nāgārjuna and the Naiyāyikas. *Journal of Indian Philosophy, 13*, 107–132.

Burge, T. (1979). Individualism and the mental. *Midwest Studies in Philosophy, 4*, 73–121.

Burge, T. (1993). Content preservation. *The Philosophical Review, 102*, 457–488.

Burton, D. (2016). *Buddhism, knowledge and liberation*. New York: Routledge.

Chakrabarti, K. (1984). Some remarks on Indian theories of truth. *Journal of Indian Philosophy, 12*(4), 339–355.

Chisholm, R. (1966). *Theory of knowledge*. Englewood Cliffs, NJ: Prentice-Hall.

Coseru, C. (2009). Buddhist 'foundationalism' and the phenomenology of perception. *Philosophy East and West, 59*(4), 409–439.

Coseru, C. (2012). *Perceiving reality: Consciousness, intentionality, and cognition in Buddhist philosophy*. Oxford: Oxford University Press.

Cowherds. (2011). *Moonshadows: Conventional truth in Buddhist philosophy*. Oxford: Oxford University Press.

Das, N. (2018). Śrīharṣa. In E. Zalta (Ed.), *The Stanford encyclopedia of philosophy* (Winter 2018 edition), https://plato.stanford.edu/archives/spr2018/entries/sriharsa/.

Dasti, M., & Phillips, S. (2010). Pramāṇa are factive—A response to Jonardon Ganeri. *Philosophy East and West, 60*(4), 535–540.

Dreyfus, G. (1991). Dharmakīrti's definition of *pramāṇa* and its interpreters. In E. Steinkellner (Ed.), *Studies in the Buddhist epistemological tradition: Proceedings of the second international Dharmakīrti conference, Vienna, June 11–16, 1989* (pp. 19–38). Vienna: Austrian Academy of Sciences Press.

Dreyfus, G. (1996). Can the fool lead the blind? Perception and the given in Dharmakīrti's thought. *Journal of Indian Philosophy, 24*, 209–229.

Dreyfus, G. (1997). *Recognizing reality: Dharmakīrti's philosophy and its Tibetan interpretations*. Albany: State University of New York Press.

Dreyfus, G., & McClintock, S. (Eds.). (2003). *The svatāntrika-prāsaṅgika distinction: What difference does a difference make?* Boston: Wisdom Publications.

Dunne, J. (2004). *Foundations of Dharmakīrti's philosophy*. Boston: Wisdom Publications.

Dunne, J. (2006). Realizing the unreal: Dharmakīrti's theory of yogic perception. *Journal of Indian Philosophy, 34*, 497–519.

Fish, W. (2009). *Perception, hallucination, and illusion*. Oxford: Oxford University Press.

Fitelson, B. (2017). Closure, counter-closure, and inferential knowledge. In R. Borges, C. de Almeida, & P. Klein (Eds.), *Explaining knowledge: New essays on the Gettier problem* (pp. 312–324). Oxford: Oxford University Press.

Franco, E. (1986). Once again on Dharmakīrti's deviation from Dignāga on *pratyakṣâbhāsa*. *Journal of Indian Philosophy, 14*, 79–97.

Franco, E. (1993). Did Dignāga accept four types of perception? *Journal of Indian Philosophy, 21*, 295–299.

Franco, E. (1997). *Dharmakīrti on compassion and rebirth*. Vienna: Arbeitskreis für Tibetische und Buddhistische Studien.

Franco, E. (2005). On *Pramāṇasamuccayavṛtti* 6ab again. *Journal of Indian Philosophy, 33*, 631–633.

Franco, E. (2006). A new era in the study of Buddhist philosophy. *Journal of Indian Philosophy, 24*, 221–227.

Frege, G. (1980). *The foundations of arithmetic: A logico-mathematical enquiry into the concept of number*. Evanston, IL: Northwestern University Press. (Original German work published 1884).

Fricker, E. (1994). Against gullibility. In B. K. Matilal & A. Chakrabarti (Eds.), *Knowing from words* (pp. 125–161). Dordrecht: Kluwer Academic.

Ganeri, J. (1999). *Semantic powers: Meaning and the means of knowing in classical Indian philosophy*. Oxford: Clarendon Press.

Ganeri, J. (2001). *Philosophy in classical India: The proper work of reason*. London: Routledge.

Ganeri, J. (2010). The study of Indian epistemology: Questions of method—a reply to Matthew Dasti and Stephen H. Phillips. *Philosophy East and West, 60*(4), 541–550.

Ganeri, J. (2018). Epistemology from a Sanskritic point of view. In S. Stich, M. Mizumoto, & E. McCready (Eds.), *Epistemology for the rest of the world* (pp. 12–21). New York: Oxford University Press.

Garfield, J. (1995). *The fundamental wisdom of the middle way*. Oxford: Oxford University Press.

Garfield, J. (2015). *Engaging Buddhism: Why it matters to philosophy*. Oxford: Oxford University Press.

Garfield, J. (Ed.). (2019). *Wilfrid Sellars and Buddhist philosophy: Freedom from foundations*. New York: Routledge.

Gettier, E. (1963). Is justified true belief knowledge? *Analysis, 23*(6), 121–123.

Gillon, B. (1986). Dharmakīrti and his theory of inference. In B. K. Matilal & R. Evans (Eds.), *Buddhist logic and epistemology* (pp. 77–87). Dordrecht: D. Reidel.

Gillon, B., & Hayes, R. (2008). Dharmakīrti on the role of causation in inference as presented in *pramāṇavārttika svopajñavṛtti* 11–38. *Journal of Indian Philosophy 36*(3), 335–404.

Goldman, A. (1967). A Causal Theory of Knowing. *The Journal of Philosophy, 64*, 357–372.

Goldman, A. (1975). Innate knowledge. In S. Stich (Ed.), *Innate ideas* (pp. 111–120). Berkeley: University of California Press.

Goldman, A. (1976). Discrimination and perceptual knowledge. *The Journal of Philosophy, 73*, 771–791.

Goldman, A. (1979). What is justified belief? In G. Pappas (Ed.), *Justification and knowledge* (pp. 1–25). Dordrecht: Reidel.

Goldman, A., & Beddor, B. (2016). Reliabilist epistemology. In E. Zalta (Ed.), *The Stanford encyclopedia of philosophy* (Winter 2016 edition), https://plato.stanford.edu/archives/win2016/entries/reliabilism/.

Greco, J. (2009). Religious knowledge in the context of conflicting testimony. *Proceedings of the American Catholic Philosophical Association, 83*, 61–76.

Hardwig, J. (1985). Epistemic dependence. *The Journal of Philosophy, 82*, 335–349.

Hattori, M. (1968). *Dignāga, on perception*. Cambridge, MA: Harvard University Press.

Hattori, M. (1997). The Buddhist theory concerning the truth and falsity of cognition. In P. Bilimoria & J. N. Mohanty (Eds.), *Relativism, suffering and beyond: Essays in memory of Bimal K. Matilal* (pp. 361–371). Delhi: Oxford University Press.

Hayes, R. (1986). An interpretation of *anyāpoha* in Diṅnāga's general theory of inference. In B. K. Matilal & R. Evans (Eds.), *Buddhist logic and epistemology* (pp. 31–57). Dordrecht: D. Reidel.

Hayes, R. (1988). *Dignaga on the interpretation of signs*. Dordrecht: Kluwer Academic.

Hayes, R. & Gillon, B. (1991). Introduction to Dharmakīrti's theory of inference as presented in *pramāṇavārttika svopajñāvṛtti* 1–10. *Journal of Indian Philosophy, 19*, 1–73.

Herzberger, R. (1986). *Bhartṛhari and the Buddhists: An essay in the development of fifth and sixth century Indian thought*. Dordrecht: Reidel.

Honjō, Y. (2003). The word sautrāntika. *Journal of the International Association of Buddhist Studies, 26*(2), 321–330.

Hugon, P. (2009). The origin of the theory of definition and its place in Phya pa Chos kyi seṅ ge's philosophical system. *Journal of the International Association of Buddhist Studies, 32*, 319–368.

Hugon, P. (2011). Phya pa Chos kyi seng ge's views on perception. In H. Krasser, H. Lasic, E. Franco, & B. Kellner (Eds.), *Religion and logic in Buddhist philosophical analysis: Proceedings of the fourth international Dharmakīrti conference* (pp. 159–176). Vienna: Verlag der Österreichischen Akademie der Wissenschaften.

Hugon, P. (2014). Tracing the early developments of Tibetan epistemological categories in Rngog Blo ldan shes rab's (1059–1109) Concise Guide to the *Nyāyabinduṭīkā*. *Journal of Tibetology, 9*, 194–234.

Hugon, P., & Stoltz, J. (2019). *The roar of a Tibetan lion: Phya pa Chos kyi seng ge's theory of mind in philosophical and historical perspective*. Vienna: Austrian Academy of Sciences Press.

Jan, T., & del Castillo, J. (2012). Visual hallucinations: Charles Bonnet syndrome. *Western Journal of Emergency Medicine, 13*(6), 544–547.

Katsura, S. (1984). Dharmakīrti's theory of truth. *Journal of Indian Philosophy, 12*(3), 215–235.

Kellner, B. (2017). Proving idealism Dharmakīrti. In J. Ganeri (Ed.), *The Oxford handbook of Indian philosophy* (pp. 307–326). New York: Oxford University Press.

Klein, P. (1999). Human knowledge and the infinite regress of reasons. *Philosophical Perspectives, 13*, 297–325.

Klein, P. (2007). Human knowledge and the infinite progress of reasoning. *Philosophical Studies, 134*(1), 1–17.

Kobayashi, H. (2010). Self-awareness and mental perception. *Journal of Indian Philosophy, 38*, 233–245.

Krasser, H. (2001). On Dharmakīrti's understanding of pramāṇabhūta and his definition of pramāṇa. *Vienna Journal of South Asian Studies, 45*, 173–199.

Krasser, H. (2003). On the ascertainment of validity in the Buddhist epistemological tradition. *Journal of Indian Philosophy, 31*, 161–184.

Kripke, S. (1982). *Wittgenstein on rules and private language: An elementary exposition.* Cambridge, MA: Harvard University Press.

Kritzer, R. (2003). Sautrāntika in the Abhidharmakośabhāṣya. *Journal of the International Association of Buddhist Studies, 26*(2), 331–384.

Lackey, J. (1999). Testimonial knowledge and transmission. *The Philosophical Quarterly, 49*, 471–490.

Lackey, J. (2006). Knowing from testimony. *Philosophy Compass, 1*, 432–448.

Lackey, J. (2008). *Learning from words: Testimony as a source of knowledge.* Oxford: Oxford University Press.

Larsson, S. (2012). *Crazy for wisdom: The making of a mad yogin in fifteenth-century Tibet.* Leiden: Brill.

Lewis, D. (2001). *Counterfactuals.* Malden, MA: Blackwell. (Original work published 1973).

Lopez, D. (2006). *The madman's middle way: Reflections on reality of the Tibetan monk Gendun Chopel.* Chicago: University of Chicago Press.

Luzzi, F. (2010). Counter-closure. *Australasian Journal of Philosophy, 88*(4), 673–683.

Machery, E. (2011). Thought experiments and philosophical knowledge. *Metaphilosophy, 42*, 191–214.

Machery, E., Edouard Machery, Stephen Stich, David Rose, Amita Chatterjee, Kaori Karasawa, Noel Struchiner, Smita Sirker, Naoki Usui & Takaaki Hashimoto. (2017). Gettier across cultures. *Nous, 51*(3), 645–664.

Matilal, B. K. (1986a). Buddhist logic and epistemology. In B. K. Matilal & R. Evans (Eds.), *Buddhist logic and epistemology* (pp. 1–29). Dordrecht: D. Reidel.

Matilal, B. K. (1986b). *Perception: An essay on classical Indian theories of knowledge.* Oxford: Clarendon Press.

Matilal, B. K. (1998). *The character of logic in India.* Albany: State University of New York Press.

Matilal, B. K. (2002). Knowledge, truth and pramātva. In J. Ganeri (Ed.), *Mind, language and world: The collected essays of Bimal Krishna Matilal* (pp. 149–161). New Delhi: Oxford University Press.

Matilal, B. K., & Chakrabarti, A. (Eds.). (1994). *Knowing from words: Western and Indian philosophical analysis of understanding and testimony.* Dordrecht: Springer Science+Business Media.

Meinong, A. (1904). *Untersuchungen zur Gegenstandstheorie und Psychologie.* Leipzig: Verlag von Johann Ambrosius Barth.

Merricks, T. (1995). Warrant entails truth. *Philosophy and Phenomenological Research, 55*(4), 841–855.

Mohanty, J. N. (2000). *Classical Indian philosophy.* Lanham, MD: Rowman & Littlefield.

Nagel, J. (2012). Intuitions and experiments: A defense of the case method in epistemology. *Philosophy and Phenomenological Research, 85*, 495–527.

Nagel, J., Juan, V. S., & Mar, R. A. (2013a). Lay denial of knowledge for justified true beliefs. *Cognition, 129*, 652–61.

Nagel, J., Mar, R., & San Juan, V. (2013b). Authentic Gettier cases: A reply to Starmans and Friedman. *Cognition, 129*, 666–669.

Nozick, R. (1981). *Philosophical explanations.* Oxford: Oxford University Press.

Owens, D. (2006). Testimony and assertion. *Philosophical Studies, 130*, 105–129.

Phillips, S. (2011). *Epistemology in classical India: The knowledge sources of the Nyāya school.* New York: Routledge.

Plantinga, A. (1993a). *Warrant and proper function*. New York: Oxford University Press.

Plantinga, A. (1993b). *Warrant: The current debate*. New York: Oxford University Press.

Plato. (2002). *Five dialogues* (2nd ed.) (G. M. A. Grube, Trans.; J. M. Cooper, Revised). Indianapolis: Hackett.

Potter, K. (1984). Does Indian epistemology concern justified true belief? *Journal of Indian Philosophy, 12*, 307–327.

Prasad, R. (2002). *Dharmakīrti's theory of inference: Revaluation and reconstruction*. New Delhi: Oxford University Press.

Priest, G. (2002). *Beyond the limits of thought*. Oxford: Clarendon Press.

Pritchard, D. (2005). *Epistemic luck*. Oxford: Oxford University Press.

Pritchard, D. (2008). Sensitivity, safety, and anti-luck epistemology. In J. Greco (Ed.), *The Oxford handbook of skepticism* (pp. 437–455). Oxford: Oxford University Press.

Prueitt, C. (2016). *Carving out conventional worlds: The work of apoha in early Dharmakīrtian Buddhism and Pratyabhijñā Śaivism* (Unpublished doctoral dissertation). Emory University, Atlanta.

Prueitt, C. (2017). Shifting concepts: The realignment of Dharmakīrti on concepts and the error of subject/object duality in Pratyabhijñā Śaiva thought. *Journal of Indian Philosophy, 45*, 21–47.

Putnam, H. (1973). Meaning and reference. *The Journal of Philosophy, 70*, 699–711.

Russell, B. (1905). On denoting. *Mind, 14*, 479–493.

Russell, B. (1959). *The problems of philosophy*. Oxford: Oxford University Press. (Original work published 1912).

Sa skya paṇḍita. (1989). *Tshad ma rigs pa'i gter gyi rtsa ba dang 'grel pa*. Tibetan People's Press.

Salmon, N. (1987-8). How to measure the standard metre. *Proceedings of the Aristotelian Society, 88*, 193–217.

Seyfort Ruegg, D. (1994). *Pramāṇabhūta, *pramāṇa (bhūta)-puruṣa, pratyakṣadharman* and *sākṣātkṛtadharman* as epithets of the *ṛṣi, ācārya* and *tathāgata* in grammatical, epistemological and Madhyamaka texts. *Bulletin of the School of Oriental and African Studies, 57*(2), 303–320.

Seyfort Ruegg, D. (1995). Validity and authority or cognitive rightness and pragmatic efficacy? On the concepts of *pramāṇa, pramāṇabhūta* and *pramāṇa(bhūta)puruṣa*. *Asiatische studien/Études asiatiques, 49*(4), 817–827.

Siderits, M. (1980). The Madhyamaka critique of epistemology I. *Journal of Indian Philosophy, 8*, 307–335.

Siderits, M. (1981). The Madhyamaka critique of epistemology II. *Journal of Indian Philosophy, 9*, 121–160.

Siderits, M. (2007). *Buddhism as philosophy: An introduction*. Indianapolis: Hackett.

Siderits, M., Tillemans, T., & Chakrabarti, A. (Eds.). (2011). *Apoha: Buddhist nominalism and human cognition*. New York: Columbia University Press.

Siegel, S. (2009). The visual experience of causation. *The Philosophical Quarterly, 59*, 519–540.

Siegel, S. (2011). *The contents of visual experience*. Oxford: Oxford University Press.

Siewert, C. (1998). *The significance of consciousness*. Princeton, NJ: Princeton University Press.

Silk, J. (2002). Possible Indian sources for the term *tshad ma'i skyes bu* as *pramāṇapuruṣa*. *Journal of Indian Philosophy, 30*, 111–160.

Sosa, E. (1989). The skeptic's appeal. In M. Clay & K. Lehrer (Eds.), *Knowledge and skepticism* (pp. 51–68). Boulder, CO: Westview Press.

Sosa, E. (2007a). Experimental philosophy and philosophical intuition. *Philosophical Studies, 132*, 99–107.

Sosa, E. (2007b). *A virtue epistemology: Apt belief and reflective knowledge, vol. 1.* Oxford: Oxford University Press.

Stalnaker, R. (1968). A theory of conditionals. In N. Rescher (Ed.), *Studies in logical theory* (pp. 98–112). Oxford: Blackwell.

Starmans, C., & Friedman, O. (2012). The folk conception of knowledge. *Cognition, 124*, 272–283.

Starmans, C., & Friedman, O. (2013). Taking "know" for an answer: A reply to Nagel, San Juan, and Mar. *Cognition, 129*, 662–665.

Steinkellner, E. (1983). *Tshad ma'i skyes bu*: Meaning and historical significance of the term. In E. Steinkellner & H. Tauscher (Eds.), *Contributions on Tibetan religion and philosophy: Proceedings of the Csoma de Koros symposium held at Velm-Vienna, Austria, 13–19 September 1981* (pp. 275–284). Vienna: Arbeitskreis für Tibetische und Buddhistische Studien.

Steinkellner, E. (1992). Early Tibetan ideas on the ascertainment of validity (*nges byed kyi tshad ma*). In S. Ihara & Z. Yamaguchi (Eds.), *Tibetan studies: Proceedings of the 5th seminar of the International Association for Tibetan Studies, Narita 1989* (pp. 257–273). Narita: Naritasah Shinshoji.

Steup, M. (1999). A defense of internalism. In L. Pojman (Ed.), *The theory of knowledge: Classical and contemporary readings* (2nd ed.) (pp. 373–384). Belmont, CA: Wadsworth.

Steup, M. (2018). Epistemology. In E. Zalta (Ed.), *The Stanford encyclopedia of philosophy* (Winter 2018 edition), https://plato.stanford.edu/archives/win2018/entries/ epistemology/.

Stine, G. (1976). Skepticism, relevant alternatives, and deductive closure. *Philosophical Studies, 29*(1), 249–261.

Stoltz, J. (2007). Gettier and factivity in Indo-Tibetan epistemology. *The Philosophical Quarterly, 57*, 394–415.

Stoltz, J. (2013). Cognition, phenomenal character, and intentionality in Tibetan Buddhism. In S. Emmanuel (Ed.), *A companion to Buddhist philosophy* (pp. 405–418). Malden, MA: Wiley-Blackwell.

Stoltz, J. (2015). Gendun Chöpel on the status of Madhyamaka. *Journal of Buddhist Philosophy, 1*, 39–57.

Strawson, P. (1994). Knowing from words. In B .K. Matilal & A. Chakrabarti (Eds.), *Knowing from words* (pp. 23–27). Dordrecht: Kluwer Academic.

Stroud, B. (1984). *The significance of philosophical skepticism.* Oxford: Oxford University Press.

Taber, J. (1992). What did Kumārila Bhaṭṭa mean by svataḥ prāmāṇya? *Journal of the American Oriental Society, 112*(2), 204–221.

Taber, J. (2003). Dharmakīrti against physicalism. *Journal of Indian Philosophy, 31*, 479–502.

Tanaka, K. (2013). Buddhist philosophy of logic. In S. Emmanuel (Ed.) *A companion to Buddhist philosophy* (pp. 320–330). Malden, MA: Wiley-Blackwell.

Tillemans, T. (1990). On sapakṣa. *Journal of Indian Philosophy, 18*, 53–79.

Tillemans, T. (1993). *Persons of authority: The* sTon pa tshad ma'i skyes bur sgrub pa'i gtam *of A lag sha Ngag dbang bstan dar, a Tibetan work on the central religious questions in Buddhist epistemology*. Stuttgart, Germany: Franz Steiner Verlag.

Tillemans, T. (1999). *Scripture, logic, language: Essays on Dharmakīrti and his Tibetan successors*. Boston: Wisdom Publications.

Tillemans, T. (2008). Introduction: Buddhist argumentation. *Argumentation, 22*, 1–14.

Tillemans, T. (2011). Buddhist epistemology (*pramāṇavāda*). In J. Garfield & W. Edelglass (Eds.), *The Oxford handbook of world philosophy* (pp. 233–244). Oxford: Oxford University Press.

Turri, J. (2013). A conspicuous art: Putting Gettier to the test. *Philosophers' Imprint, 13*, 1–16.

Turri, J. (2015). Unreliable knowledge. *Philosophy and Phenomenological Research, 90*, 529–545.

Vaidya, A. (2015). Public philosophy: Cross-cultural and multi-disciplinary. *Comparative Philosophy, 6*(2), 35–57.

van der Kuijp, L. (1978). Phya-pa Chos-kyi Seng-ge's impact on Tibetan epistemological theory. *Journal of Indian Philosophy, 5*, 355–369.

van der Kuijp, L. (1983). *Contributions to the development of Tibetan Buddhist epistemology: From the eleventh to the thirteenth century*. Wiesbaden, Germany: Franz Steiner.

Warfield, T. (2005). Knowledge from falsehood. *Philosophical Perspectives, 19*, 405–416.

Weinberg, J., Nichols, S., & Stich, S. (2001). Normativity and epistemic intuitions. *Philosophical Topics, 29*, 429–460.

Westerhoff, J. (2009). *Nāgārjuna's Madhyamaka: A philosophical introduction*. Oxford: Oxford University Press.

Westerhoff, J. (2010). *The dispeller of disputes: Nāgārjuna's Vigrahavyāvartanī*. Oxford: Oxford University Press.

Williams, P. (1998). *The reflexive nature of awareness: A Tibetan Madhyamaka defence*. Richmond, VA: Curzon Press.

Williamson, T. (1996). Knowing and asserting. *The Philosophical Review, 105*, 489–523.

Williamson, T. (2000). *Knowledge and its limits*. Oxford: Oxford University Press.

Williamson, T. (2007). *The philosophy of philosophy*. Malden, MA: Blackwell.

Wittgenstein, L. (1958). *Philosophical investigations*. (G. E. M. Anscombe, Trans.). Englewood Cliffs, NJ: Prentice-Hall. (Original English work published 1953)

Woo, J. (2003). Dharmakīrti and his commentators on yogipratyakṣa. *Journal of Indian Philosophy, 31*, 439–448.

Yamada, M. (2011). Getting it right by accident. *Philosophy and Phenomenological Research, 83*, 72–105.

Yao, Z. (2004). Dignāga and four types of perception. *Journal of Indian Philosophy, 32*, 57–79.

Zagzebski, L. (1994). The inescapability of Gettier problems. *The Philosophical Quarterly, 44*(174), 65–73.

Zagzebski, L. (2017). The lesson of Gettier. In R. Borges, C. de Almeida, & P. Klein (Eds.), *Explaining knowledge: New essays on the Gettier problem* (pp. 179–190). Oxford: Oxford University Press.

Index

For the benefit of digital users, indexed terms that span two pages (e.g., 52–53) may, on occasion, appear on only one of those pages.

Tables are indicated by *t* following the page number

Printed in the USA
CPSIA information can be obtained
at www.ICGtesting.com
CBHW050123141223
2640CB00004B/25

9 780190 907549